Governance and Management of Education in India

Governance and Management of Education in India

A Comparative Analysis of Structures, Processes and Systems

K. Sujatha • R. S. Tyagi

NIEPA

SHIPRA

Rs. 800; US$ 32

ISBN: 978-81-938382-1-1

First Published in India, 2019

Governance and Management of Education in India: A Comparative Analysis of Structures, Processes and Systems

Published by:
SHIPRA PUBLICATIONS
LG 18-19, Pankaj Central Market,
I.P. Ext., Patparganj, Delhi-110092, India
Tel.: +91 11 2223 5152/6152, 9650028065
E-mail: info@shiprapublication.com
www.shiprapublication.com

Foreword

INDIA has one of the largest networks of schools in the world. School education in India, especially at the compulsory levels of education, is mostly funded by the government. The enrolment ratios have increased and are close to the universal levels at the primary stage of education. The Right to Education (RTE) Act has given urgency and the needed priority to expand education. The concern now is increasingly shifting to the quality of provisions and enhancement of the quality of teaching-learning processes in the classroom settings.

The Eighty Sixth Constitutional Amendment Act of 2002 envisaged the provision of free and compulsory education for all children in the age group of six to fourteen years as a Fundamental Right. This led to the Right to Education Act, 2009. The national and state governments have been implementing several programmes to achieve the goal of universalisation at the elementary level and to expand the base of education at the secondary level. The centrally sponsored programmes such as the District Primary Education Programme (DPEP), Sarva Shiksha Abhiyan (SSA) and the Rashtriya Madhyamik Shiksha Abhiyan (RMSA) are examples of the efforts to expand the base of education and improve the quality of school education.

The system of educational planning and administration plays a vital role in designing the programmes and implementing them effectively. The administrative structures and management practices at the school level vary substantially between institutions and between states. The Central and State Governments, in recent decades, have adopted important reforms and changes in their governance structures, administrative processes and institutional operations to make the delivery of educational programmes and services effective.

In view of the importance of educational administration and reforms adopted from time to time, the National Institute of Educational Planning and Administration (NIEPA) has been carrying out national surveys on educational administration in all the states and union territories in India. The present survey is the third in the series carried out by NIEPA. The Third All India Survey on Educational Administration was conducted thorough the active participation of all the state education departments. The survey outcome comprises 23 state reports and national synthesis report.

The empirical evidence generated through the survey indicates that most states have tried to integrate school education as one administrative unit. Between the second and third surveys, one notices the creation of administrative and academic structures at the block level for academic monitoring for improving the teacher support system. At present, most states have full-fledged block education offices headed by class two gazetted officers and also the needed academic support provided by block resource centres. Another important change noticed is the evidence based decision making taking place at the state, district and sub-district levels. The effects of the role played by DISE data in the use of educational administration of educational programmes was, at the sub-national levels, indeed a major development. In fact, the availability of data in electronic form was helpful in introducing transparency in the monitoring of educational programmes and in teacher recruitment, posting and transfers.

The surveys also pointed to the issues related to low accountability, delays in implementation of programmes, and lack of coordination among different departments, especially between the elementary and secondary levels of education. In fact, many states are flooded with inundated litigations, which is a major concern for many educational administrators.

The present book is an outcome of comparative research in the form of 23 state studies on administration of school education in India. I hope this publication will serve the needs of educational planners, administrators and policy makers as well as students, teachers and researchers. On behalf of the Institute, I would like to express my sincere thanks to Prof. K. Sujatha (Former Head, Department of Educational Administration, NIEPA) and Dr. R. S. Tyagi (Former Associate Professor, Department of Educational Administration, NIEPA) for designing and successfully implementing the third All India Survey of Educational Administration, for preparing the national synthesis report and for preparing this manuscript for publication.

N. V. Varghese
Vice-Chancellor
National Institute of Educational
Planning and Administration

New Delhi
April 05, 2019

Preface

The National Institute of Educational Planning and Administration has initiated series of national level studies on Administration of School Education including governance structure, management process and procedures in different States and Union Territories in India. The first such pioneering effort was initiated in 1973 which aimed at examining the state of art of the educational administration in the country through all India survey of administration of school education followed by the second survey conducted during 1991-2001. The second survey focussed not only on governance, structure and functions of school education but also captured the emerging changes due to the implementation of National Policy on Education (1986) and Programme of Action (1992). The second survey also presented the experiments and innovations being adopted by different states in administration of school education for achieving universalisation of elementary education. The major initiative in administration of school education was adoption of decentralisation and introduction of local level participatory decision-making. All the state reports along with a comparative analytical national report of second survey were published by NIEPA. Consequent to recommendations of second survey, several states have adopted reforms in governance and management of school education for effective implementation of educational programmes of elementary and secondary education.

In view of several changes that took place in administration of school education in different states, NIEPA has conducted the Third Survey on administration of school education during 2014-2016. The Third Survey focussed on status of governance and management of school education. The survey also aims to identify the changes that have taken place in the administration of school education during the last two decades and to examine new intervention strategies including use of information technology that have been introduced in the system. The most visible effect on administration was the implementation of District Primary Education Programme (DPEP), Sarva Shiksha Abhiyan (SSA), Rashtriya Madhyamika Shiksha Abhiyan (RMSA) and Right to Education Act in the country. The major focus of the programme management was on performance, accountability, use of information technology, changes in teacher management and the transparency of education officers at all levels of administration, right from school to State level. Separate management structures were also created at State, district, block and cluster levels to perform the targeted activities of educational management. The continuous emphasis was on quality improvement by laying emphasis on processes of school management and teachers' eligibility conditions for recruitment, transfer and training. School Management Committees were made accountable for preparation and implementation of school development plan along with the other management activities of schools. A major transformation of educational administration has been witnessed in implementation of e-governance which has made the educational management programmes more effective and efficient. E-governance in administration has given impetus to the process of teacher management-recruitment and selection, posting and transfers of teachers which has become online while making the system transparent and accountable. It has also helped in data management from school to directorate and secretariat levels.

Comparative analysis of educational administration in the present publication not only presents the changes that have taken place in the educational management but it has also sought to understand the major issues that are still confronting educational administration. The major change that has emerged during the last two decades in educational administration is that it has transformed itself from maintenance-based to development-oriented, based on tasks and targets wherein performance accountability and transparency have become the mainstay of educational management.

This national-level study is an outcome of the inferences drawn from 23 State survey reports. We are extremely thankful to all the 23 State Education Secretaries for providing support in conducting the survey in their respective States. We also owe our thanks to all the Nodal Officers of the survey for their help and cooperation in completing the study of their States. We extend our grateful thanks to the members of National Level Advisory Committee, as also the Project Management Advisory Committee for providing guidance and help in conducting the Third Survey.

We are highly grateful to Prof. R. Govinda, (Former Vice-Chancellor, NUEPA), for his keen interest and cooperation to undertake the Third Survey on Administration of School Education. We are thankful to Prof. Jandhyala B. G. Tilak for his cooperation in completion of National Synthesis Report. We are extremely grateful to Prof. N. V. Varghese, Vice-Chancellor, NIEPA for his cooperation and encouragement in finalising the National Report for publication as Comparative study on Governance and Administration of School Education in India. We also thank Prof. Kumar Suresh, Head, Department of Educational Administration for his cooperation. We appreciate and acknowledge with thanks three expert reviewers for their valuable suggestions and observations on the study. We thank sincerely Mr. Pramod Rawat and Mr. Amit Singhal of Publication Unit, NIEPA for their constant cooperation in bringing out this publication. We thank all those who provided help in conducting the Third All India Survey of Educational Administration.

K. Sujatha

April 05, 2019 **R.S. Tyagi**

Contents

List of Tables and Figures

TABLES

FIGURES

Abbreviations

ABL	Activity Based Learning
ALIMCO	Artificial Limbs Manufacturing Corporation
AWP&B	Annual Work Plan and Budget
B.Ed.	Bachelor of Education
B.El.Ed.	Bachelor of Elementary Education
BRC	Block Resource Centre
BRCC	Block Resource Centre Coordinator
CCE	Continuous and Comprehensive Evaluation
CEO	Chief Executive Officer
CIET	Central Institute of Educational Technology
CRC	Cluster Resource Centre
CRCC	Cluster Resource Centre Coordinator
CTE	College of Teacher Education
CWSN	Children With Special Needs
D.Ed.	Diploma in Education
D.El. Ed.	Diploma in Elementary Education
DDO	Drawing and Disbursing Officer
DIET	District Institute for Education and Training
DPEO	District Primary Education Officer
DPEP	District Primary Education Programme
DRG	District Resource Group
ECCE	Early Childhood Care and Education
EFA	Education For All
EGS	Education Guarantee Scheme
ELTI	English Language Teaching Institute
GER	Gross Enrolment Ratio
GOI	Government of India
IASE	Institute of Advance Studies in Education
ICT	Information and Communication Technology
JRM	Joint Review Mission
M.Ed.	Master of Education
MDG	Millennium Development Goals

MDM	Mid-Day Meal
MHRD	Ministry of Human Resource Development
MOOCs	Massive Open Online Courses
MoU	Memorandum of Understanding
MPSSAM	Madhya Pradesh Sarva Shiksha Abhiyan Mission
NCC	National Cadet Corps
NCERT	National Council of Educational Research and Training
NCTE	National Council for Teacher Education
NER	Net Enrolment Ratio
NGO	Non-government Organization
NIEPA	National Institute of Educational Planning and Administration
NPE	National Policy on Education
NSDC	National Skill Development Council
NUEPA	National University of Educational Planning and Administration
OOSC	Out Of School Children
PPP	Public Private Partnership
PRI	Panchayati Raj Institution (Local Self-Government)
PTR	Pupil Teacher Ratio
RIE	Regional Institute of Education
RMSA	Rashtriya Madhyamik Shiksha Abhiyan
RTE	Right of the Children to Free and Compulsory Education Act
SBI	State Bank of India
SCERT	State Council of Educational Research and Training
SIEMAT	State Institute of Educational Management and Administration Training
SDMC	School Development and Management Committee
SMC	School Management Committee
SOS	State Open School
SRG	State Resource Group
SSA	Sarva Shiksha Abhiyan
TEIs	Teacher Education Institutions
TET	Teacher Eligibility Test
TLM	Teaching Learning Material
UEE	Universalisation of Elementary Education
UNICEF	United Nations International Children Emergency Fund
ZSK	Zila Shiksha Kendra

1
Introduction

Developments in Educational Governance

Governance of school education in India has undergone tremendous changes over the years due to the education policy reforms, expansion of education system, focus on delivery mechanism, quality improvement and enhancement of responsibilities of educational administrators. However, the educational governance system varies among different States due to diverse political, economic and educational contexts. There has been phenomenal transformation in the management strategies of educational programmes, with the main emphasis being on structural changes so as to make administration more responsive to the educational needs of the people at the grassroot level and also make the delivery of educational programmes more effective. Participatory and decentralised decision-making at the district, block and school level provided more impetus for implementation of educational programmes. Since there has been a paradigm shift in the fast-changing learning strategies and the educational management practices, changes in communication and information technology added new dimensions in the management and implementation of educational programmes.

Governance encompasses structures and processes that are designed to ensure accountability, transparency and responsiveness of the education system along with the rule of law, stability, equity and inclusiveness, empowerment, and broad-based participation. Developments in the education system witnessed the greater impact of the policy and programmes formulated and coordinated by the Central Government after education came under the Concurrent List of the Constitution, making it a joint responsibility of Centre and State. Educational policy reforms led to a major shift in the management of educational development strategies, resulting in a downward swing in the command and control in educational management from Central and State level to district level, from district level to block level and from block level to village/habitation level. These changes were primarily directed to make the educational system, in general, and its administration, in particular, more responsive to the needs of the people at the grassroots. As a result, the administration now takes a holistic view of education in which the latter is perceived as an instrument of social change. The emergence of educational development programmes like District Primary Education Programme and the Sarva Shiksha Abhiyan have brought a much needed shift in the delivery mechanism, increased investment in basic education, in expenditure pattern specifically from staff salary oriented budget to infrastructure development oriented budget, with financial aid from international agencies. There is also a shift from supply-oriented paradigm to demand-oriented paradigm in so far as the educational needs at the local level are concerned.

Under the changed management strategies, the major thrust areas of the governance of education, as such, were emphasis on education of focus groups, including Scheduled Castes (SC), Scheduled Tribes (ST), and Other Backward Communities (OBCs), minority, girls, children with special needs, decentralised educational planning and management at district, block, cluster and village levels; coordination in the management of education with local bodies; developments in Educational Management Information System (EMIS); developments in the new curricula and teaching-learning processes; formation of strategies and development plans; holistic and systematic approach with convergence of different departments; IT/ICT in education for transparency, information, quality and outreach; accountability to targets; and involvement of community, school management by self-governing bodies (municipalities in urban areas and panchayati raj institutions in rural areas) in educational planning and management.

The Third Survey

The National Institute of Educational Planning and Administration (NIEPA) had conducted two Educational Administration Survey (First in 1973 and second in 1990s) covering all the States and Union Territories. The basic purpose of the survey was to examine the status of educational administration and its responsiveness to the changing demands of the system. However, several educational policies and programmes have been initiated during the last two decades in different States, resulting in reforms and changes in the administrative structures and functioning at different levels i.e. State, region, district, sub-district and institutional levels. The initiatives and interventions have added new dimensions to educational governance. To examine the status of educational administration at different levels and to map out changes in educational governance, NIEPA conducted the 3rd All India Survey of Educational Administration (2014-16) alongwith a number of thematic studies covering different aspects of educational administration and governance. It not only helped in identifying the contemporary issues and problems of educational administration but it also provided the necessary roadmap for the future policy and concrete strategy for governance and administration of school education. Furthermore, it has also been the endeavour of NIEPA to periodically update the available information on the scenario of educational planning and administration.

The third survey covers the present status of educational administration in respect of structure, processes and changes that have taken place in the governance of school education during last two decades. It covers the organizational set-up, role, functions and activities of the education department at the secretariat, directorate, district, block, cluster and institutional levels, including parallel management structures under SSA and RMSA. It explores the role and functions of the departments other than the education department in educational management. Themes like administrative structures and functions, educational management by local bodies, NGOs and community participation, education of disadvantaged groups, personnel management, with focus on teacher management, academic management, inspection and supervision and institutional management have also been studied. The survey is primarily restricted to and focused towards administration of school education.

It has covered the secondary and primary data and information. Primary data pertains to the year 2013-14. Research framework was designed to collect the sample for the survey. In each of the States, three districts, one educationally advanced, one middle and one backward district were selected for the survey. Three sample blocks, having the same criteria, were included in each of the selected districts. From each of the blocks, eight schools were identified comprising two primary, two upper primary, two secondary and two senior secondary schools. Five regional workshops in the country were organised to discuss the methodology, modalities and four types of questionnaires.

To collect the data from the identified sample, a State-Level Workshop was organised in each State by its education department. State-level questionnaire sought information on organisational structure, processes and functions at the secretariat and directorate levels, management by local bodies, personnel management, coordination with other departments (management educational program), academic management, examination board, text book management and inspection and supervision. Similarly, district-level questionnaire sought information on district-level education structure, teacher management, recruitment of education administrators, inspection, grievance redressal, litigation cases as well as difficulties and suggestions. Block-level format also included questions probing similar areas with a difference of their functional level. Institution-level formats included basic questions for information on powers and functions of heads of schools, decision-making, office management, teaching-learning process, teacher arrangement, infrastructural facilities alongwith provision of institutional planning and problems relating to school administration.

The present publication comprises eight chapters. All the chapters give comparative scenario of the different aspects of educational administration. The different structures and functions of administration of school education have been comparatively and critically analysed in detail. The critical analysis of educational management indicates that several efforts have been made to decentralise planning and management of school education to the local level so as to make the delivery of educational programmes more effective. However, the present publication reveals that administration of school education in the past encountered enormous challenges and is still suffering from several weaknesses and dysfunctions.

The National Report

The second chapter on Administration of School Education in India—Structure and Functions' highlights the changing scenario of structure and functions of educational administration at national, State, area, district, block, cluster and school levels. It also covered the programme management structure like SSA and RMSA and convergence of education department with these programmes. It also highlights the linkages of education department with the management of school education under local bodies and with the different departments. It reveals that at the national level, for giving emphasis on school education and for better coordination and effective implementation of educational programmes, the school education has been made as one unit (Classes I-XII) instead of the earlier structure wherein elementary education was a separate unit and secondary education was attached with the higher education. Since then, there has been major focus on educational programmes like SSA, RTE, and particularly RMSA and KGBV. This trend has also been followed in some of the States where not only at secretariat and directorate level, but also at district and block level, the structure and functions of school education has been made one unit of educational governance alongwith the responsibility of managing SSA and RMSA. The district-level management of primary and secondary education has been particularly strengthened for effective coordination, implementation and monitoring of educational programmes.

Chapter three deals with 'E-governance in Educational Administration'. E-governance in educational management is one of the major landmarks which has made administrative processes and procedures easier and effective, reducing time gap in information management. In several states like Kerala, Karnataka, Gujarat, Punjab, Uttarakhand, Maharashtra and Sikkim, information regarding administrative, academic and financial matters in the form of Government Orders, circulars, and other documents are directly sent by the directorates at regional, district, block, cluster and school levels. Recruitment and posting of teachers, admission of students have also been made online in several States. It shows that there has been ample use of e-governance in different aspects of educational administration in all the States. It has brought in administration the transparency and effectiveness in implementation of educational programmes. The better use of e-governance in preparation of educational plans, coordination and monitoring of educational programmes, maintaining service conditions of teachers and non-teaching staff, and in communicating of information from secretariat to directorate, district, block and at school levels. Several States have used it in teacher recruitment, and postings and transfers. Applications from eligible candidates for teachers' recruitment and selection are received online; on this basis, a merit list is prepared and if there is no interview, the list of selected teachers is published online. Teachers are requested to opt for their place of posting on the basis of their native place and as per the recruitment rules. The best use of e-governance has also been done in the implementation of programmes for disadvantaged groups like, for example, the scholarship amount is directly sent to the children's bank account, and on-line publication of other information regarding the availability of educational programmes and incentives and scholarships.

Chapter four deals with 'Teacher Management'. The teacher is the hub of all educational activities. Tremendous changes have taken place in the teacher management system in all the States. The process of recruitment and selection has changed from being confined to regular teachers to recruitment of teachers on short vacancies or additional teachers on contract basis on a consolidated salary. Almost in all the States, teachers in primary schools are recruited on probation in the first stage and, thereafter, they are regularised. In some States, their pay scales differ from that of regular teachers, particularly where school education is under local bodies. Financial responsibility lies with the local bodies. Teachers' qualifications have also been changed in view of the emphasis on recruiting quality teachers. Alongwith the academic and professional qualifications, Teacher Eligibility Test has been made compulsory in all the States and UTs, particularly since RTE has been implemented from April 2010. For quality improvement of elementary education, the emphasis has been laid on in-service teacher training since the implementation of SSA with the RTE Act too emphasising on quality improvement of education. Reforms in postings and transfers have also been carried out in almost all the States and UTs. Teachers in primary schools are posted within the block. Several States have stopped the transfer of teachers, and only mutual transfers are done as per the rules of the State government.

The system of 'Inspection and Supervision' in schools has been discussed in a comparative perspective in chapter five. Different States have established their inspection and supervision system in school as per their administrative structures at various levels. Almost all the States have assigned the responsibility of inspection and supervision of schools to district and block-level administrative functionaries. The block resource centre in SSA also works in consultation with Block Education Officer. Some States have assigned the integrated responsibility of SSA alongwith the regular streams administration to the block education officer. Almost in all the States, block education offices have been established and given the responsibility of monitoring, inspection and supervision. As regards the process of inspection, some States form inspection teams and, almost in all the States, senior officers also visit the schools from time to time. District education officers and block education officers are mainly responsible for inspection and supervision. In some States, grades are awarded to schools after inspection. Inspection is mainly conducted in respect of administrative, physical and financial matters while supervision is conducted for academic matters to determine the gap between competencies and performance of teachers. This forms the basis for providing suggestions to teachers for improving the teaching-learning process. Inspection norms are also different from State to State. However, several constraints occur in the inspection system and this is related to quality improvement of schools.

Chapter six discusses the information on 'Institutional Management'. It deals with the types of institutions that existed under different managements in the States. Different types of norms are adopted by different States for establishing and upgrading educational institutions. It was observed that powers of heads of institutions also differ not only from State to State but with the level of institutions, e.g. primary and upper primary, secondary and senior secondary as also the types of management of schools. The numbers of days for which the schools function also vary, not only in different States but also within a particular

State as per the location of schools. The variability also persists according to climate of the region. Decision-making is an important function at school level. In government schools, SMC in primary and upper primary schools and SDMC in secondary and senior secondary schools play an important role in the decision-making process. Besides, the block education officer and district education officer impact the decision-making process in government schools. Keeping records is an important function of schools. The RTE Act makes it necessary to keep the school records upto date.

The practice of preparing school development plan in primary and upper primary schools and also in secondary schools has been started in almost all the States. The school development plan, which is prepared with the help of School Management Committee in primary and upper primary schools and the School Development and Management Committee in secondary schools, provides an opportunity to schools for setting targets of educational activities for the development of schooling facilities. Almost in all the States, awareness and sensitisation programmes relating to managing disasters and safety in schools have been conducted at school level together with distribution of printed materials and installation of equipment like fire extinguishers in schools.

Chapter seven deals with the 'Changes in Administration of School Education in India During last Two Decades'. There have been phenomenal changes that have taken place in the administrative structure and functions along with the management and implementation of educational programmes for elementary and secondary education. It seems that in order to make the delivery of educational programmes more effective, maintenance-based administration has been transformed in the direction of decentralisation and participatory decision-making at the local level with effective monitoring of educational programmes. Creation of Block Resource Centres and Cluster Resource Centres, alongwith the convergence and coordination with the block education officer for providing academic and administrative resource support to schools, has become a major step towards changes in educational administration. Educational administrators at directorate, district and block levels now have the tasks and the targets to achieve them instead of just maintaining the system and utilising resources. This has made the education system transparent and the functionaries accountable for the assigned tasks.

Due to development programmes like SSA and RMSA, more funds are available for infrastructure development and implementation of programmes. Local level participation in school management is more persistent now than before in activities like micro planning and school mapping with the help of the community and, specifically, the school management committee. Since April 2010, RTE has given these developments a new direction towards quality improvement in education. More focus has now been laid on effective implementation of educational programmes for disadvantaged groups and, especially, for Children With Special Needs.

Major issues of educational administration that emerged from the Third Survey have been discussed in chapter eight. Several issues have come up during the study, right from school level to secretariat level. One of the major issues is related to the establishment of parallel management structures. In several States, SSA and RMSA have separate management structures other than the regular department of educational administration, and, as a result, the problems of coordination and convergence in implementation of educational programmes and related activities occur occasionally. Lack of coordination hampers the effective implementation and monitoring of programmes. RTE implementation strategy recommends that programme management structures be subsumed by the regular education department. In several States like Madhya Pradesh, Gujarat, Uttarakhand, Bihar and Odisha, the responsibility of SSA and RMSA have been entrusted to the district education officers, while at the block level, the block education officer is also in charge of BRC and CRCs as s/he is responsible for elementary education. The National Policies on Education, 1986 and Programme of Action, 1992 and other Committees recommended that school education from Class I-XII should be one unit for better coordination and convergence. However, barring a few States, this model of administrative structure has not been followed.

Problem with the recruitment and selection of teachers, transfers and postings, their service conditions, frequent transfers of senior-level officers like Education Secretary and Director of Education are the main issues being faced by the educational administration today. Inadequate inspection and supervision of schools, in spite of having BRCs and CRCs, adversely affects the teaching-learning process and, ultimately, the quality of education in schools. Suggestions for improvement in the functioning of educational administration on these aspects have also been discussed.

2

Administration of School Education in India

Structures and Functions

Administration and Management

The functions of administration, as elaborated by a number of administrative theories, are based on contextuality but the common tasks of administration involve planning, organising, leading, controlling and monitoring. In particular, planning has been defined as setting goals and developing blueprints and strategies for their implementation; organising involves bringing together humans, financial and physical resources; leading refers to as guiding, motivating and supervising subordinates while controlling involves performance. The emphasis of administration is on receiving inputs and utilisation of resources. The term administration as discussed by several researchers is different from management. While administration is defined more as process-oriented which involves framing of rules, management consists of rational assessment of a situation and systematic selection of goals and purposes. Management is task-based and target-oriented.

Sapre (2001) defined that administration is generally input-oriented and considers inputs as an indicator of progress while management is output-oriented; it is concerned with the results. Administration is accountable for control and maintenance, management is accountable for growth. While administration has a boundary role and is based on rules, regulations, codes, acts and statutes, management tends to be flexible. The reward system is yet another element that distinguishes the two models. Seniority is the basis of promotion in the administration whereas performance is the measure of output in the management. Administration tends to be reactive. Many decisions reflect a short term, some times even fragmented view of a complex situation arising from its urgency and the need for immediate action. Management is proactive; the system approach has become a way of thinking for dealing with problematic situations. However, there is controversy as to which is the main, is it management or administration? Some management scientists say that management is a sub-set of the administration. The concern of administration, in this context, is administering the rules, regulations, statutes, acts et al – i.e. the formally established legal basis of educational governance, and secondly, the administrative structure at various hierarchical levels of the system.

Practices of educational administration comprise rules governing issues like grant-in-aid, recognition and upgradation of schools, personnel recruitment, promotions and transfers, financial matters and disciplinary actions, codes of ethics and, ultimately, maintenance of the system and procedures. The second element is administrative structures. For example, while most of the States in India started with a unified administrative structure of the education department at the state level, over a period of time the administrative machinery has diversified and become multifaceted. There are, for example, several ministers and secretaries of education in the same State, looking after mass education, school education and higher education. Administration of technical education in many of the States is separate from the education department. Professional education like Medicine, Agriculture etc. are under the control of other departments.

Educational Administration in India

The Constitution of India lays down the major goals for education and provides a foundation for the sharing of legislative authority between the Union and its constituent States and UTs. The 42nd Amendment of the Constitution placed education in the Concurrent List, making it a joint responsibility of the Centre and the States. The system of educational administration, thus, follows two levels of control, namely Central government and the State government. States have to accept full responsibility for the school education as a whole though in some of the States, local bodies are sharing this responsibility of managing schools at the district, block, town and village levels. In other words, school education is predominantly a local state partnership. Besides, non-government institutions also manage primary, upper primary, secondary and senior secondary schools. Education management in India, therefore, is not only confined to government and local bodies but also to a large number of non-government organisations. Figure 2.1 shows the whole educational enterprise in India.

Fig. 2.1: Educational Management in India

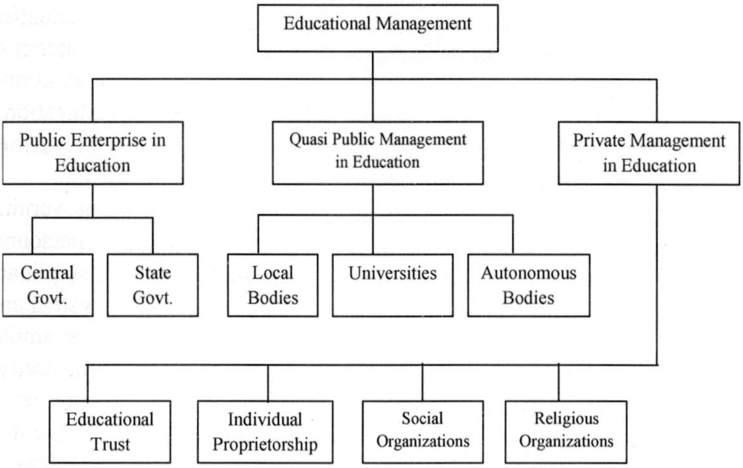

The States and Union Territories govern education in their own respective ways. There are differences in the process of their policy formulation, planning, administration, and management. Administration has the legal basis which comprises education Acts, Codes, rules and regulations. It includes governing issues like Grant-in-aid, recognition and opening and upgradation of schools, personnel recruitment, promotion and transfers, financial matters and disciplinary actions, codes of ethics and conduct.The major element in administration is the administrative structures and functions, right from institutional level to secretariat level.

Educational Administration at National Level

The Central government discharges its functions and responsibilities in education within the framework and broad principles enshrined in the Constitution and the specific Acts passed by the Parliament, through the Ministry of Human Resource Development and the education and training divisions of various other ministries. The Ministry of Human Resource Development is under the overall charge of the Human Resource Development Minister who is assisted by two Ministers of State, one each from two departments, namely the Department of School Education and Literacy and the Department of Higher Education. Each department is headed by a Secretary to the Government of India. The Secretary, Department of Higher Education is assisted by an Additional Secretary, five Joint Secretaries, one Economic Advisor and one Deputy Director General (Statistics). The Secretary, Department of School Education & Literacy is assisted by six Joint Secretaries and one Economic Advisor.

The departments are organized into Bureaux, Divisions, Branches, Desks, Sections and Units. Each Bureau is under the charge of a Joint Secretary, assisted by Divisional Heads at the level of Director/Deputy Secretary/ Deputy Educational Advisors.

In order to discharge some of its Constitutional, advisory and other functions in the field of education, the Union Government has set-up a number of organizations at the national level. There is Central Advisory Board of Education (CABE), the members of which include the Ministers of Education in the States and by the Board's various Committees. There are few other advisory and expert consultative bodies like the National Council of Educational Research and Training (NCERT), National Institute of Educational Planning and Administration (NIEPA), National Council for Teacher Education (NCTE) etc. which help the Ministry of Human Resource Development.

While the Department of School Education and Literacy is responsible for development of school education and literacy in the country, the Department of Higher Education takes care of what is one of the largest Higher Education systems of the world, just after the United States and China. The Department of School Education and Literacy has its eyes set on the "universalisation of education" and making better citizens out of our young brigade. For this, various new schemes and initiatives are taken up regularly, and recently, those schemes and initiatives have also started paying dividends in the form of growing enrolment in schools. The Department of Higher Education, on the other hand, is engaged in bringing world class opportunities of higher education and research to the country so that Indian students are not found lacking when facing an international platform. For this, the Government has launched joint ventures and signed MoUs to help the Indian student benefit from the world opinion.

The main objectives of the Ministry are:

1. Formulating the National Policy on Education and to ensure that it is implemented in letter and spirit;
2. Planned development, including expanding access and improving quality of the educational institutions throughout the country, including the regions where people do not have easy access to education;
3. Paying special attention to disadvantaged groups like tribals, the poor, females and the minorities;
4. Provide financial help in the form of scholarships, loan subsidy, etc. to deserving students from deprived sections of the society; and

5. Encouraging international cooperation in the field of education, including working closely with the UNESCO and foreign governments as well as the universities, to enhance the educational opportunities in the country.

Educational Administration at State Level

Tremendous changes have taken place in the educational administration during the last two decades as a result of the policy reforms in the governance of school education. Education being in the Concurrent List of the Constitution, several development programmes were introduced by the Centre and States which transformed the educational administration from maintenance-based to mission mode of management. Local and global changes in educational administration have also made the administrative structures, functions and processes more responsive towards effective delivery of educational services. There has been a much needed shift not only in the delivery mechanism of educational services, increased investment in elementary and secondary education, but also in expenditure pattern specifically from staff-salary oriented budget to infrastructure development oriented budget.

Education being one of the largest sectors, its administration has a vast and complex set-up. Every State has established its own education department. The education department follows a hierarchical set-up, with Education Minister at the top and school as an institution at the bottom. The three important functions: Policy and Plan formulation, undertaken at secretariat level, while implementation of the programmes have been assigned with the directorates and supervisory and monitoring functions are performed at regional, district, block and cluster levels. The size of department varies from State to State, depending on various factors, such as size of State, demography and political system.

Structure and Function at State Level

At present, administrative machinery in all the States is headed by the Minister in-charge of Education Department who is of cabinet rank. In some of the States like Uttar Pradesh, there is another Minister of State to assist the Cabinet minister. The trends of organisation of educational administration emerged along two lines-unified and diversified education departments. While unified management helps in establishing coordination between different sectors of education, the diversified structure becomes important in focusing on sector-wise educational programmes. In the States with unified system, all the sectors of education, i.e. elementary, secondary, senior secondary and higher education, are managed under one education department. In the States with diversified educational department, there are separate ministers for different sectors of education, viz. higher, secondary and elementary education. The nature of diversification also varies from State to State according to their administrative and political requirements. Sometimes, administrative structure and functions change in the State with changes in the political dispensation.

Unified Education Department

In 12 States—Assam, Mizoram, Manipur, Jharkhand, Jammu & Kashmir, Himachal Pradesh, Punjab, Haryana, Goa, Andhra Pradesh, Bihar and Uttarakhand—the education department is unified and deals with different sectors of education.

Separate Education Department

In nine States viz. Odisha, Nagaland, Uttar Pradesh, West Bengal, Chhattisgarh, Madhya Pradesh, Karnataka, Tamil Nadu and Kerala, there are separate education departments for higher and school education. States like Odisha and Nagaland have two separate departments for school education and higher education. Uttar Pradesh is the only State where separate departments are functioning for elementary (Basic), secondary and higher education, with three separate education ministers of Cabinet rank. There are also State education ministers under each Cabinet minister. However, at present, the charge of the higher education department is with the Chief Minister, with one State Education Minister under him. There are also three State education ministers, at present for elementary education, looking after different branches, under one Cabinet minister. A State like West Bengal has a much diversified structure of education as it has established Departments for School Education, Higher Education, Technical Education and Mass Education & Library, with four education ministers—one for each of the four education sectors. Table 2.1 elaborates the unified and separate administrative structure at the ministry level. Table 2.2 indicates administrative structure at secretariat level.

Administrative Structure and Functions at Secretariat level

Secretariat is the highest administrative unit below the ministry of education in the States. The education secretary of the State government is the administrative head of the educational secretariat. He works as the principal adviser to the minister of education on all policy matters and looks after all the activities relating to administration within the education

Table 2.1: Administrative Structure at State Ministry Level

Status of Ministry	*Unified Education Departments headed by one Education Minister*		*Separate Ministers for School and Higher Education Departments*	
	No. of States	*Name of the State*	*No. of States*	*Name of the State*
	12	Assam, Mizoram, Manipur, Jharkhand, J&K, HP, Punjab, Haryana, Goa, AP, Bihar, Uttarakhand	9	Odisha, Nagaland, Uttar Pradesh, Chhattisgarh, Madhya Pradesh, West Bengal, Karnataka, Tamil Nadu, Kerala

Source: Third All India Survey of Educational Administration.

Table 2.2: Administrative Structure at Secretariat Level

	One Principal Secretary		*Separate Principal Secretary/Secretary*	
Status of Secretariat	12	Assam, Mizoram, Manipur, Jharkhand, J&K, HP, Punjab, Haryana, Goa, AP, Bihar, Uttarakhand	9	Odisha, Nagaland, Uttar Pradesh, Chattisgarh, Madhya Pradesh, West Bengal, Karnataka, Tamil Nadu, Kerala

Note: West Bengal has four Education Ministers for Higher, Technical, School Education, and Mass Education and Literacy.

Source: Third All India Survey of Educational Administration.

department. Education Secretary is a senior IAS officer. Being the head of the Education Department, the Secretary is responsible for matters related to policy and programmes' formulation, preparation of Plan and non-Plan schemes, modification in existing schemes, scrutiny and approval of department budget and estimates, coordination among different directorates of the state and with other departments. In Karnataka, the Principal Secretary of Primary and Secondary Education oversees the work of the Commissioner of Public Instruction, State Project Directors of SSA and RMSA, Directors of Pre-University Education, Mass Education, Public Libraries, Printing & Stationery.

Different States use different nomenclature for the post of Secretary. In States like Gujarat, Odisha, Mizoram, Assam and Andhra Pradesh, Education Secretary is known as Commissioner-cum-Secretary. States like Assam and Gujarat also have Additional Chief Secretary responsible for education. Mizoram has Parliamentary Secretary over Commissioner-cum-Secretary depending on the seniority of the officials. The survey report from different States reflects a remarkable shift in organisation of secretariat level set-up. As observed in the ministry-level structure, the secretariat-level administrative structures are also functioning along unified and diversified lines. A total of 12 States are functioning under unified command of administration at ministry and secretariat level. These States, as shown in Table 1, with unified secretariat are Assam, Mizoram, Manipur, Jharkhand, Jammu & Kashmir, Himachal Pradesh, Punjab, Haryana, Goa, Andhra Pradesh, Bihar and Uttarakhand.

As discussed earlier, a total of nine States viz. Odisha, Haryana, Nagaland, Uttar Pradesh, Chattisgarh, Madhya Pradesh, West Bengal, Karnataka and Tamil Nadu have diversified pattern of education administration at the secretariat level. Among the nine States, Odisha, Haryana and Nagaland have separate secretariat for school and higher education. Assam, Uttar Pradesh and Uttarakhand have separate secretary for elementary and secondary education. West Bengal has maximum number of secretaries with separate secretariat for school education, higher education, technical education, mass education and library. Uttarakhand and Assam are two States where the Ministry set up is under the charge of one minister but the secretariat is diversified with separate secretaries for elementary and secondary education.

The Education Secretary is assisted by a number of subordinate officers, as shown in Table 2.3. It is indicated that Additional Secretaries in Mizoram, Karnataka, Gujarat, Nagaland, Odisha, Jammu and Kashmir, Himachal Pradesh, Tamil Nadu and Bihar are in the second rung after Education Secretary. On the other hand, in the case of Assam, Andhra Pradesh, Punjab and West Bengal, Joint Secretaries are in the second layer. However, Special Secretary in Uttar Pradesh forms the second tier of hierarchy after the Education Secretary. Third layer of education officers also has different designations in different States. For example, Joint Secretary in Mizoram, Karnataka, Gujarat, Nagaland and Tamil Nadu, Special Secretary in Jammu and Kashmir and Bihar, Deputy Secretary in Himachal Pradesh, Uttar Pradesh and Punjab, Assistant Secretary in Andhra Pradesh form the third layer of administrative hierarchy in Secretariat. Deputy Secretary in Tamil Nadu, Mizoram, Karnataka, Gujarat, Nagaland and Jammu and Kashmir, and Assistant Secretary in Bihar and West Bengal are in the fourth tier of administration at secretariat level.

Examples of Unified and Separate Education Department at Secretariat Level

Unified Administrative Structure of Assam

Education Department is headed by the Additional Chief Secretary. Under

Table 2.3: Secretariat Level Structure in the States

S. No	Name of State	Education Minister	Principal Secretary/Chief Secretary	Secretary	Additional Secretary	Special Secretary	Joint Secretary	Deputy Secretary	Assistant Secretary	Under Secretary
1.	Andhra Pradesh	1	1 (CS)+1 (PS)				3		5	
2.	Assam	1	1 (Additional Chief Sect)	1+1+1 (Commissio-ner and Sect.) (EE+SE+HE)			1+1+1	1+1+1		1+1+1
3.	Bihar	1	1	1	1	1	1		1	
4.	Gujarat		1 Addtl. Chief Sec		1		2	3		
5.	Haryana	1	1 (School Ed)+1 (HE)							
6.	Himachal Pradesh	1	1		1			2 (EE+HE)		2+2 (1PE,1UP+1SE, 1College)
7.	Jammu & Kashmir	I Minister+1 Minister of State		1	1	2		1		1
8.	Karnataka	1	1	1	2		1	1		1
9.	Maharashtra	1 Cabinet+ 2 state (Sch Edu+ HE&Tech E)	3 Sec (Sch Edu+HE+Tech Edu)							

(Contd.)

Table 2.3: *Contd.*

S. No	Name of State	Education Minister	Principal Secretary/Chief Secretary	Secretary	Additional Secretary	Special Secretary	Joint Secretary	Deputy Secretary	Assistant Secretary	Under Secretary
10.	Mizoram	1	1 (Parliamentary Sect)	1 (Commissioner and Sect)	1		1	1		2
11.	Nagaland	1+1 (School +Higher Edu)	1 +1 (Comm and Sec)	1+1	1+1		2+1	1+0		2+2
12.	Odisha	1+1 (School+HE)		1+1 (Comm and Sec)						
13.	Punjab	1	1							
14.	Telangana	1	1 Principal Sec				2		2	
15.	TN	1		1	1		2	1		
16.	Uttar Pradesh	1+1+HE independent charge	3	1 (Basic ed)+1 (Sec Ed)		3(Basic ed) + 2(Sec Ed)				
17.	Uttar Pradesh	1+1+1 (BE+SE+HE)	1+1+1			2+2+HE		1+1+ HE level info missing		
18.	West Bengal	4 (Sch Ed+HE+Tech+Mass Edu)	1 (School Education)	4			1 (School Edu)	1 (School Edu)	1 (School Edu)	

Source: Third All India Survey of Educational Administration.

EE = denotes elementary education and **HE** = higher education, **UP** = upper primary and **SE** = secondary education.

BE = basic education

him, there are Commissioners and Secretaries, one each for Elementary Education Department, Secondary Education Department and for Higher Education Department (who are members of the Indian Administrative Service). The Commissioner and Secretary is assisted by Secretary, Joint Secretaries, Deputy Secretaries and Under Secretaries. Sometimes, the Secretariat is headed by a Principal Secretary, and, at times, the Commissioner and Secretary is assisted by officers in the rank of Additional Secretaries also. The number of Secretaries, Joint Secretaries and Deputy Secretaries also varies from time to time. Normally, the Education Department is headed by an IAS officer in the rank of the senior-most Additional Chief Secretary/Principal Secretary, as desired by the Government. The number of Deputy Secretaries and Under Secretaries working in the Education Department also varies from time to time.

Functions and Responsibilities of Education Secretary

The Education Secretary of the Government is the administrative head of one or more departments. He is the principal adviser to the Minister of Education on all policy matters and looks after all the activities relating to administration within his department. He is normally assisted by Joint Secretary/Deputy Secretary, Under Secretary, Superintendent and other Subordinate Staff. A Secretary may sometimes be assisted by a Joint Secretary. The following organogram shows the existing organizational Structure of the Education Department in Assam at the secretariat level.

Fig. 2.2: Secretariat Level Structure of Assam

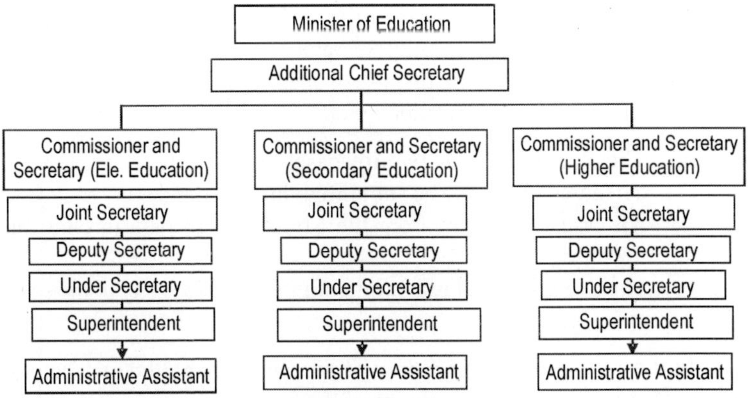

Following are the main functions of the Education Secretary:

1. Matters related to and involving new policy or principle;
2. All matters related to preparation or adoption of new plan and

non-Plan schemes and important modifications in the existing schemes;

3. Progress of the Plan schemes;
4. Matters relating to legislative measures, rules and regulations;
5. Exercise of powers vested in the State Government under Act, Rules and Regulations;
6. Matters to be placed before the Parliament and the Legislative Assembly or their committees;
7. Scrutiny and approval of Departmental Budget and Estimates, Supplementary Grants and Sanction of Re-appropriation by the Resolution;
8. All proposals involving new items of Expenditure;
9. Sanction of Expenditure from the Contingency Fund;
10. General Service conditions of Government servants under the Department;
11. Appointment to the post for which Governor is the Appointing Authority;
12. Disciplinary cases of the officers where Disciplinary Authority is the Governor;
13. Tour of Officers outside the State;
14. Appointment of Commissions and Committees;
15. Matter related to inter-State relation and Foreign Governments; and
16. Any other matters which the Minister may specify by general or special order.

With the approval of the Minister of Education, an Additional Secretary, Joint Secretary, Deputy Secretary or Under Secretary may be authorised by the Secretary to dispose of specific classes of cases without reference to the Secretary provided that:

a. The Secretary may require cases of importance within the delegated classes to be submitted through him;
b. All cases, on return from the Minister, will pass through the Secretary: and
c. The Secretary retains the right of intervention in any of the cases at any stage

In the absence of the Secretary of the Department, the next senior-most officer will perform the duties of the Secretary.

Diversified Administrative Structure in Uttar Pradesh

In regard to the present educational set-up in Uttar Pradesh, it may be pointed out that the Minister of Education (Secondary) and the Minister of Basic Education are overall incharge of their respective sectors of school education. Earlier, the Principal Secretary (Education) was the Chief Executive Officer of the department and was required to oversee the work of Secretary, Basic Education and Secretary, Secondary Education, as per Figure 2.3. Now there are two separate Principal Secretaries for each of Secondary and Basic Education who look after their respective sectors. For each of the two sectors, there are special Secretaries below the rank of the Secretary. These Special Secretaries are assisted by Joint Secretaries, Deputy Secretaries and Under Secretaries for (i) establishment class-1 and above, adult and non-formal education (ii) private high schools and intermediate colleges. Management dispute and personnel matters; (iii) Secondary government high schools and intermediate colleges; (iv) establishment Secretariat Education Branch: (v) co-ordination; and (vi) basic education in private schools and SCERT. There are departmental officers to assist the secretaries. One looks after Basic Shiksha Parishad Schools and Centrally sponsored schemes and another is incharge of libraries. There is a Senior Research Officer Incharge of plan, budget and its monitoring. There is also a State Standing Committee on Education for advising the Ministers of Education, from time to time, on educational matters.

In Uttar Pradesh, there is an Education Minister and a State Minister who look after higher education. Principal Secretary, Higher Education is Chief Executive Officer of the department. The State also has a Director of Higher Education who controls the administrative set-up of its sector.

Structure and Functions at Directorate Level in States

Directorate is the third and most important tier of administration. It is the link between the education secretariat and field-level administrative units. Directorates are the main implementing bodies in respect of educational policies and programmes in the State. Their main functions include enforcement of legal basis, including rules and regulations of education, implementation of educational programmes, personnel management of gazetted and non-gazetted staff of the department and ensure the delivery of educational programmes, besides monitoring and supervision and coordination of all educational activities. Director is the head of directorate concerned in all the States. There are variations in the designations of the heads of the directorate in different States. For example:

- In Karnataka, Commissioner for Public Instruction (CPI) is the in-charge of all the Directors of Public Instructions including DPI, Primary, DPI, Secondary, DPI, KSEEB, DPI, Minority,

Fig. 2.3: Educational Administrative Set-up at Secretariat Level in Uttar Pradesh

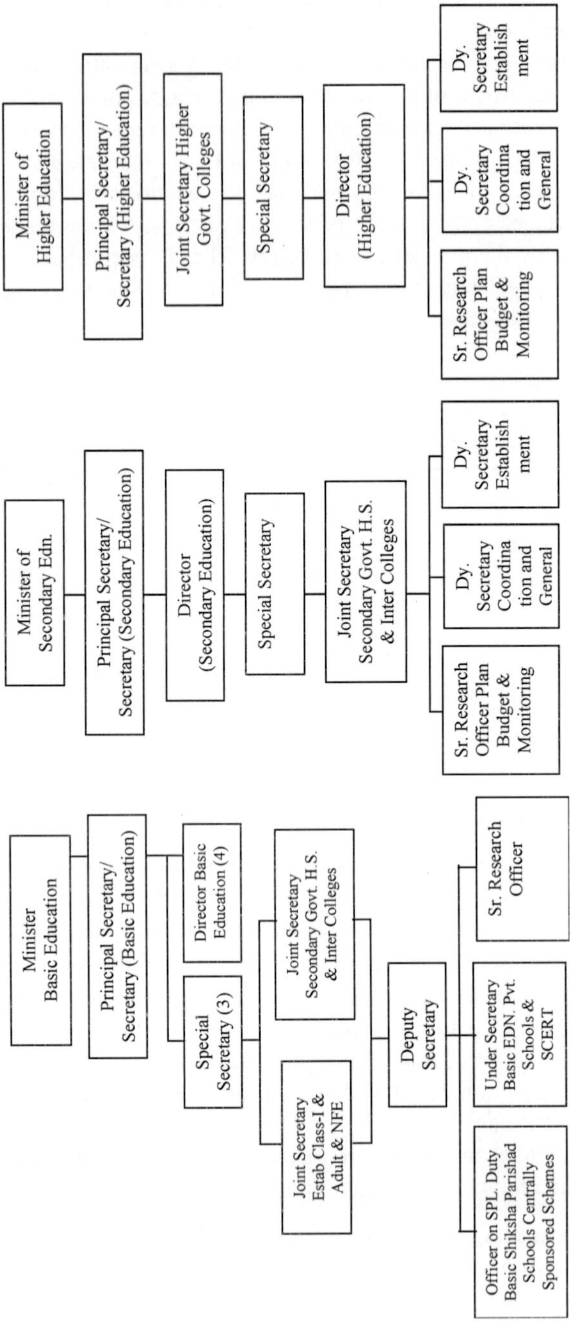

DPI, Exam and DPI, DSERT. In Kerala and Karnataka, Directorate of School Education is known as Directorate of Public Instruction which deals with issues upto secondary schools.

- In Andhra and Telangana, there are Commissionerates of School Education where the Commissioner is the head of the department.
- In Madhya Pradesh, Commissioner, Public Instruction is the in charge of secondary education and has controlling authority over Director of School Education (secondary).
- For elementary education, there is a Rajya Shiksha Kendra (a conglomeration of SCERT, SSA, Adult and Literacy) in Madhya Pradesh which is also headed by the Commissioner and Secretary of Elementary Education.
- Similarly, in Maharashtra, Commissioner of Education is the executive head having controlling authority over all the Directors of Education.
- In Uttarakhand, there is a Director General who is the head of Director, Elementary Education, Director, Secondary Education and Director, Research and Training.

Table 2.4: Cadre of Directors in Different States

Recruitment of Directors in Different States		
Recruitment from IAS Cadre.	*From IAS or State Cadre*	*From Promotion or from State Provincial/Educational Services*
Kerala, Karnataka, Mizoram, Maharashtra, Madhya Pradesh, West Bengal, Delhi	Odisha, Bihar, J&K, Haryana, Punjab Uttrakhand, Nagaland, Assam and J&K	Punjab, Andhra Pradesh, Telangana, Tamil Nadu, Himachal Pradesh Gujarat, Uttar Pradesh.

Source: Third All India Survey of Educational Administration of Respective States.

As indicated in Table 2.4, there are variations in the process of recruitment of directors of education in different States.

- There are States where recruitment of directors is made directly from IAS Cadre. These include Kerala, Mizoram, Maharashtra, Madhya Pradesh, Delhi and West Bengal.
- In the second category, recruitments are made either from IAS Cadre or State Cadre. These States include Odisha, Bihar (In Bihar, Director of Primary Education is IAS and Director,

Secondary Education—State Cadre), Jammu and Kashmir, Haryana, Punjab, Uttarakhand, Nagaland and Assam.

- Third category includes States where directors are appointed either by promotion from teaching posts like in Himachal Pradesh or from State Provincial/Educational Services. In Uttar Pradesh, directors of education in all sectors of education belong to Uttar Pradesh Provincial Service. Other States are Karnataka, Andhra Pradesh and Tamil Nadu.

Type of Administrative Structure at Directorate Level

There are education sector-wise directorates almost in all the States. In order to provide focus on the educational programmes and also with the aim to decentralise the decision-making process, the States have constituted education sector-wise directorate. Majority of the States have established Directorate of Elementary Education (Classes I-VIII) because of the universalising of elementary education and for conducting programmes of elementary education, like SSA and RTE and other related programmes. In view of the focus of the programmes of secondary education like science education and vocational education and, of late, the programme like RMSA, separate directorates were created. However, few States have unified directorate of school education. All the Directors are assisted by a number of other officials such as Additional Directors, Joint Directors, Assistant Directors and Assistant Deputy Directors. The directorate emerged as one of the most diversified administrative units. With the exception of Mizoram, Manipur, Nagaland, Goa, West Bengal and Jammu and Kashmir, all the states have diversified directorates (Table 2.5).

In Himachal Pradesh, Classes IX-XII are attached with the Directorate of Higher Education.

The States with minimum two levels of diversification i.e. with two separate directorates for elementary and secondary education are Assam, Odisha, Himachal Pradesh, Tamil Nadu, Haryana, Maharashtra, Karnataka, Kerala and Uttarakhand. While Directorates in Nagaland are dealing with School Education and Higher Education, the rest of the States in this category have directorates for elementary education and secondary education. Kerala presents a unique scenario where Directorate of Public Instruction manages school education upto Class X while Directorate of Higher Secondary Education deals with Classes XI and XII. In all the States, the Directorate of Higher Education is separate, barring Himachal Pradesh where Classes IX-XII are attached to the Directorate of Higher Education.

Table 2.5: Different Types of Directorates in the States

Directorate of Elementary Education (Classes I-VIII)	*Directorate of Secondary Education (Classes IX-XII)*	*Directorate of School Education (Classes I-X)*	*Directorate of Higher Secondary Education (Classes XI-XII)*	*Directorate of School Education (Classes I-XII)*
Assam, Odisha, Nagaland, Himachal Pradesh, Tamil Nadu, Gujarat, Haryana, Rajasthan, Madhya Pradesh, Maharashtra, Karnataka and Uttarakhand	Assam, Odisha, Nagaland, Himachal Pradesh, Madhya Pradesh, Tamil Nadu, Haryana, Maharashtra, Gujarat, Rajasthan, Karnataka, and Uttarakhand	Kerala	Kerala	Jammu and Kashmir, Mizoram, Manipur, West Bengal, Goa

Source: Third All India Survey of Educational Administration.

Examples of some of the Directorates

Uttarakhand presents a coordinated structure at the directorate level (Fig. 2.4). There is a Director General of School Education and, under him, Director, Secondary, Director, Elementary and Director, Academic Research and Training to coordinate with the education officers of their relevant fields. Secondary schools have only secondary level staff and upper primary teachers, headed by the Headmaster.

Figure 2.4: Administrative Structure at Directorate level in Uttarakhand

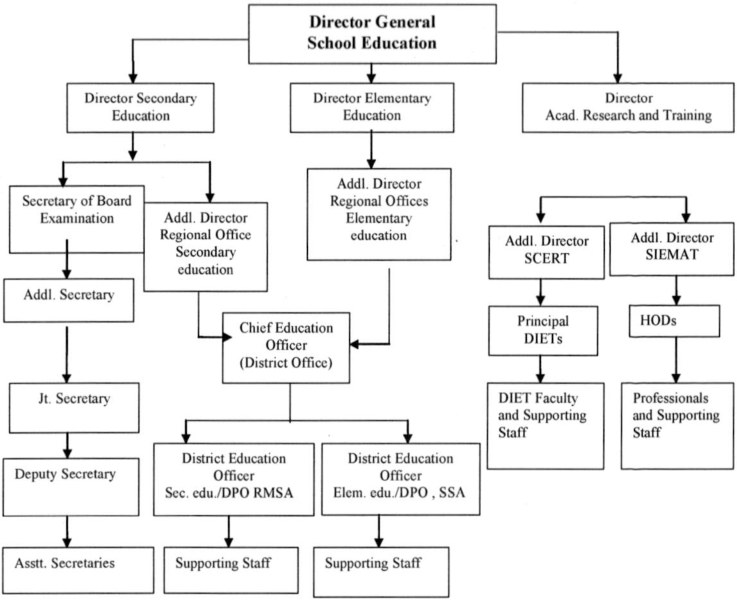

Directorate of Elementary Education in Odisha

The Directorate of Elementary Education, Odisha was established in 1987 to look after the progress of elementary education and to monitor and supervise the functioning of primary schools, upper primary schools and block education offices of the State. The Directorate looks after the establishment of all elementary school teachers of the State. The Director, Elementary Education heads the office (Fig. 2.5). Normally, the Director, Elementary Education is appointed by the Government of Odisha from amongst the officers of the Indian Administrative Service or senior officers of the State Administrative Service. The Director is assisted by three Deputy Directors, one each for planning, primary education and field establishment. The Regional Joint Directors in the three regional directorates and Block Education Officers (BEOs) at block level assist the Director, Elementary Education and oversee the elementary schools.

Fig. 2.5: Directorate of Elementary Education, Odisha

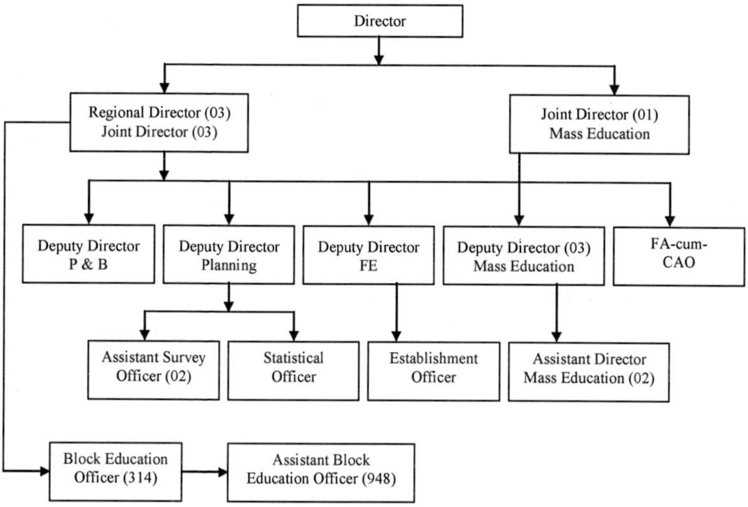

After merger of Directorate of Mass Education with Directorate of Elementary Education in June 2015, the posts in different categories had been continuing in the erstwhile Directorate of Mass Education which has been placed under the control of Director, Elementary Education. One post of Joint Director, three posts of Deputy Directors, one Accounts Officer, two posts of Assistant Director were brought over to the Directorate of Elementary Education. The Saakshar Bharat Programme, under the erstwhile Directorate of Mass Education, is continuing under the administrative control of the Director, Elementary Education. The structure of Directorate of Elementary Education is given in Figure 2.5.

Directorate of Secondary Education, Odisha

The Directorate of Secondary Education was set up in the year 1983 to look after the secondary education in the State (Fig. 2.6). The Director, Secondary Education is the head of the Directorate of Secondary Education. He is assisted by four Deputy Directors, one each for Government schools, Non-government schools, Science Education &Planning, Hindi, Sanskrit, Special Education (including Urdu Education and Education of CWSN) & Sports. There are two Establishment Officers, one Accounts Officer, two Assistant Directors – one for physical education and one for planning. There are also one Special Officer, Art and Craft and one Special Inspecting Officer (Urdu Education).

Fig. 2.6: Directorate of Secondary Education, Odisha

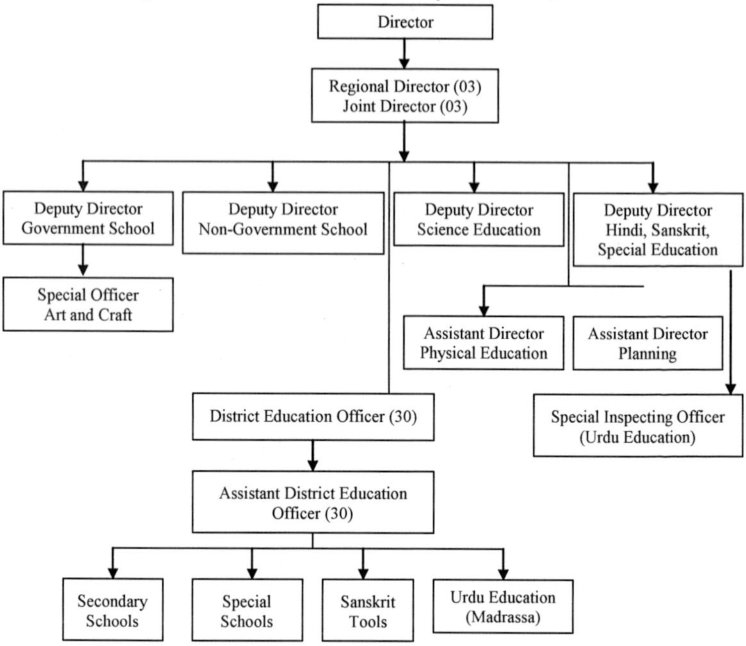

At the field level, there are three Joint Directors in charge of regional Directorates at Bhubaneswar, Sambalpur and Berhampur, supported by 30 District Education Officers (DEO), one each in every revenue district. The structure of the Directorate of Secondary Education is illustrated in Figure 2.6. The Directorate of Secondary Education is responsible for everything associated with secondary schools for Classes IX and X, including human resources, infrastructure, academic activities, and student welfare. The State Government has constituted the Odisha State Board of Madrassa Education for recognition of Madrassas and smooth conduct of different Madrassa examinations vide Resolution No 23931/SME dated 21.08.1971 and reconstituted vide Notification No 1817/SME dated 31.01.2008. The Directorate of Secondary Education also controls the administrative work of 295 Sanskrit Tolls, supported by the Office of Superintendent of Sanskrit Studies located in Puri. Besides, the Directorate is assigned the responsibilities of the scheme of supply of free bicycles to the students of Class X in all government, aided and block grant to high schools.

Other Supporting Directorates and Autonomous Bodies in States

Besides the directorates directly dealing with different levels of school, there are many other directorates, autonomous bodies and State Institutes that are taking care of issues related to school education, as indicated in Table 2.6. State reports show that every State has its own Board of School Education to conduct examinations at different levels of school. These include Uttar Pradesh Board of High School and Intermediate Education, Maharashtra and Karnataka Secondary Education Board (KSEEB) for SSLC Examination and KSEEB for all other examinations. Telangana and Tamil Nadu have Directorate of Government Examinations. Directorate of Mass Education or Directorate of Adult and Non-formal Education are functioning in Assam, Telangana, Maharashtra, Mizoram, Tamil Nadu and Odisha. States like Telangana and Kerala have Directorates dealing with the welfare of Backward Classes, Tribal Welfare and other social welfare issues. There are other Directorates and Institutes for looking after the development of areas such as vocational and technical education, Public Libraries, Distance/Open Education, publishing text books etc.

Linkages of Education Secretariat and Directorate with SSA and RMSA

In most of the States, development programmes like SSA, RMSA have separate State-level offices, with the State Project Director as the head to look after the programme. However, Education Secretary, being the overall in-charge of school education, has direct control over development programmes. Most of the major States have separate registered societies for SSA and RMSA. In Tamil Nadu, Karnataka, Mizoram, Nagaland, Assam, Odisha, Andhra Pradesh, Himachal Pradesh, Haryana, Punjab, West Bengal and Bihar, there are separate registered societies. These States have parallel well-established management structures with advisory bodies, executive bodies and different administrative units in the State Project Director (SPD) office, like planning, MIS, Community Participation, Finance etc. They have direct coordination with mainstream administration, i.e. secretariat and all the directorates.

However, in a few of the smaller States like Mizoram, Sikkim and Uttarakhand, directors of education oversee the SSA and RMSA. In Uttarakhand, the Director General of School Education is State Project Director for SSA and RMSA. In Mizoram and Sikkim, Directors of School Education are the ex-officio State Project Directors of SSA and RMSA. At the national level, there are Registered Education Societies for SSA, RMSA, under MHRD, Government of India, which directly transfers the funds to state education societies wherein funds are directly transferred from state level to district level and then to the school level for conducting the educational programmes.

Table 2.6: Other Directorates and Autonomous Bodies

S.No	*Name of State*	*Other Directorates*	*Autonomous Bodies*	*Any comment*
1.	Assam	- Directorate of Non-Formal and Adult Education, - Directorate of Madrassa Education	- N.C. Hills Autonomous Council. - Bodoland Territorial Council.	
2.	Bihar		- Bihar Board of Open School. - State Council of Educational Research and Training. - Bihar State Textbook Corporation. - Bihar School Examination Board. - Bihar Shaikshanik Adharbhoot Sanrachna Nigam. - State Higher Education Council.	
3.	Karnataka	- Directorate of Urdu and Other Minority Language schools. - Directorate of State Education Research and Training. - Directorate of Mass Education. - Directorate of Vocational Education. - Directorate of Public Library. - Directorate of Pre-University Education. - Directorate of Printing and Stationary,	- Karnataka Text Book Society. - Karnataka Secondary Education Board (KSEEB). SSLC Examination, KSEEB (others). - Regional Institute of English, South India. - State Institute for School Leadership, Educational Planning and Management	

(*Contd.*)

Table 2.6: *Contd.*

S. No.	*Name of State*	*Other Directorates*	*Autonomous Bodies*	*Any comment*
4.	Kerala	- Directorate of Vocational Higher Secondary Education. - Directorate of Scheduled Castes Development Department. - Directorate of Scheduled Tribe Development Department		
5	Maharashtra	- Directorate of Minority and Adult Education. - Directorate of Maharashtra State Council of Educational Research and Training (Vidya Parishad),	- Maharashtra State Secondary and Higher Secondary Education Board. - Maharashtra State Bureau of Text Book Production and Curriculum Research. - Maharashtra State Council of Examination. - State Institute of Educational Technology	
6	Mizoram	- Directorate of State Council of Education Research &Training. - Directorate of Higher and Technical Education. - Directorate of Art and Culture. - Directorate of Hindi Education. - Directorate of Adult Education. - Directorate of Physical Education.		Autonomous District Council

(*Contd.*)

Table 2.6: *Contd.*

S. No.	*Name of State*	*Other Directorates*	*Autonomous Bodies*	*Any comment*
7.	Odisha	- Directorate of Mass Education. - Directorate of Teacher Education and State Council of Education Research & Training. - Directorate of Higher Education.		- English Language Teaching Institute. - State Institute of Open Schooling. - State Resource Center for Adult Education. - State Institute of Educational Technology. - SIEMAT.
9	Tamil Nadu	- Directorate of Matriculation Schools. - Directorate of State Council of Education & Research &Training. - Directorate of Government Examination. - Directorate of Non-formal & Adult education. - Directorate of Public Libraries.	- Directorate of Teacher Recruitment Board. - Directorate of Text Book Corporation.	
10	Telangana	- Directorate of Social Welfare. - Directorate of Backward Class Welfare. - Directorate of Tribal Welfare Education. - Directorate of Teacher Education. - Directorate of Adult and Mass Education. - Directorate of Technical Education.	- Directorate of Government Examination (Independent deptt. under Ministry of Secondary Education).	

(Contd.)

Table 2.6: *Contd.*

S. No.	Name of State	Other Directorates	Autonomous Bodies	Any comment
11	U.P.	- Uttar Pradesh Board of High School and Intermediate Education - State Institute of Education Management And Training. - State Council of Education Research & Training. - Directorate of Urdu and Oriental Languages.		See details in chap. 8

Source: Third All India Survey of Educational Administration.

Structure of SSA and RMSA

Sarva Shiksha Abhiyan (SSA) in Odisha

Sarva Shiksha Abhiyan (SSA) is a national flagship programme, launched in 2001-02, for achieving the goal of universalisation of elementary education. The basic objectives of SSA are; (i) all children (6-14 years) in school, (ii) bridge gender and social category gaps at both primary and upper primary levels, (iii) all children to be retained in the school,(iv) focus on elementary education of satisfactory quality with emphasis on education for life. Odisha Primary Education Programme Authority (OPEPA) was registered as a society under the Societies Registration Act 1860 on 30th January 1996. It is the implementing society for the SSA in the State for Universalisation of Elementary Education. The Chief Minister of Odisha is the President of the Governing Body of OPEPA while the Minister, School and Mass Education Department is the Vice-President of the Governing body. The Chief Secretary, Government of Odisha acts as the Chairman of the Executive Committee of OPEPA while the Commissioner-cum-Secretary, S & ME Department is its Vice-Chairperson. The norms of different staffs and sanctioned strength are decided by the Executive Committee, OPEPA. At the State level, State Project Director is appointed by Government as the Head of the Institution. Additional Directors, Deputy Directors, Assistant Directors, Coordinators, Financial Advisor and Consultants, Research Associates, State Project Engineer are appointed to manage different interventions of OPEPA. Most of these officials are deputed to work at OPEPA from State Administrative Services and State Education Service.

At the district level, the Collector of the district concerned has been declared as Chairman of the District level SSA committee. District Project Coordinator (DPC) has been appointed to act as Head of the District Project Office. One out of two ADEOs has been given the task of DPC at the district level. Senior Technical Consultant, pedagogy coordinator, Planning Coordinator, Girls' education coordinator, Inclusive Education coordinator, Tribal coordinator, Programmer, Financial Consultant have been engaged for different interventions. At the Block level, Block Resource Centre (BRC) and Cluster Resource Centers (CRCs) have been established to implement the SSA activities. The Block Resource Centre Coordinator (BRCC) and the Cluster Resource Centre Coordinator (CRCC) have been engaged to monitor the progress of RTE-SSA activities at Block and Cluster level respectively. Figure 2.7 shows the structure of SSA in Odisha.

Fig. 2.7: Structure of SSA in Odisha

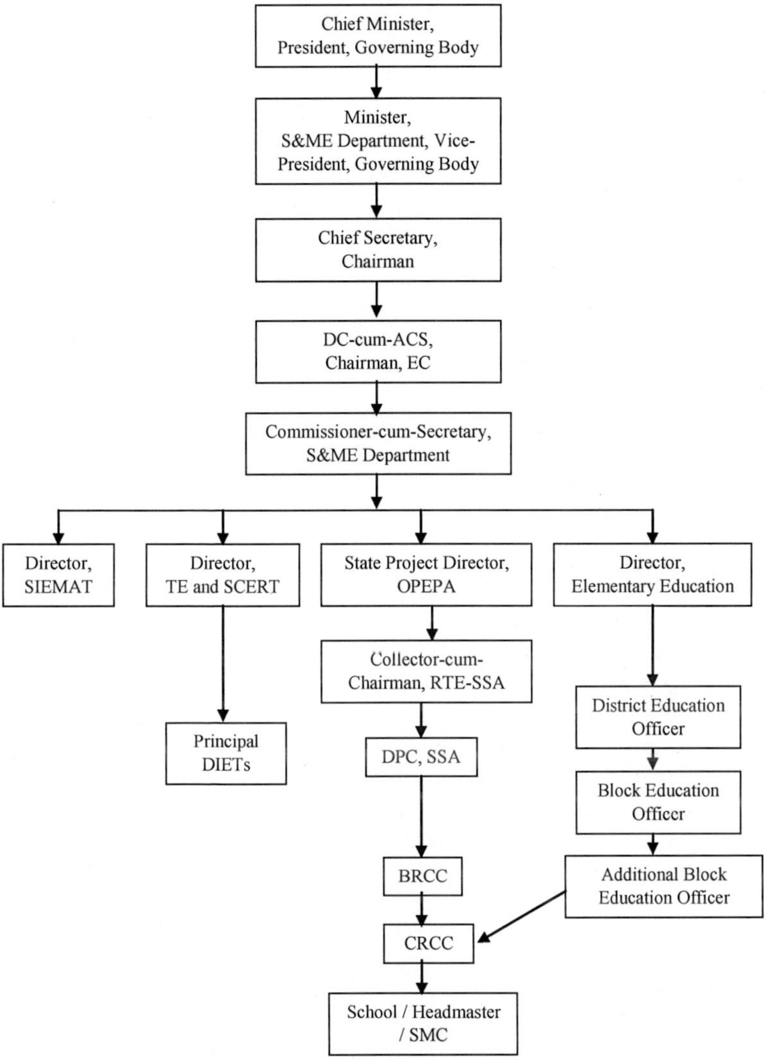

Rashtriya Madhyamika Shiksha Abhiyan (RMSA) in Odisha

Rashtriya Madhyamika Shiksha Abhiyan (RMSA) is a national flagship programme, initiated in 2009-10 to universalise secondary education by making good quality education available, accessible and affordable, with strong focus on gender equity and justice aspects, for all young persons of 14-18 years. The objective of the scheme is to achieve a Gross

Enrolment Ratio (GER) of 75per cent within five years, ensure universal access of secondary education by 2017 and universal retention by 2020. For implementation of RMSA at the State level, the Government has decided to constitute a State Mission Authority, viz. Odisha Madhyamik Shikhsa Mission (OMSM)", under the Societies Registration Act of 1860 (vide Notification No 22549/SME dated 16.12.2010). The Governing Council of the Mission is headed by the Chief Minister of Odisha. The Commissioner-cum-Secretary, School and Mass Education Department is the chairperson of OMSM. As per the Notification No 669/SME dated 07.01.2013 and the decision of the Governing Council of OMSM, at the State level, State Project Director, Additional SPD, Financial Advisor, Deputy Director, State Project Engineer, Assistant Engineer posts have been created and officers from State government are deputed to work in these posts. Besides, posts like Assistant Director (MIS), Assistant Director (Planning), Junior Engineer, Financial Consultant, Planning Coordinator, programmer and other ministerial staffs on contractual basis have been created at State Project Office. Figure 2.8 gives the structure of RMSA in Odisha.

Field-level Set-up of Educational Administration in States

Within a State, there are different levels of administration, depending upon the size and number of institutions, which perform supervisory and monitoring functions. In general, there is also a functional relationship between levels of administration and types of institutions, though the system varies from State to State, as indicated in Table 2.7. At the field level, some of the major States also established regional/divisional level set-up of educational administration where elementary education is managed by Assistant Regional Directors and secondary education by the Regional Joint Directors, as in the case of Uttar Pradesh.

Regional/Divisional Level Administration

In some of the States such as Odisha, Jharkhand, Kerala, U.P, Goa, Uttarakhand, Andhra Pradesh and Bihar, there are regional directorates. This office is generally headed by Regional Deputy/Joint Directors. The Regional Deputy/Joint Directors hold several administrative responsibilities. He/she is the coordinating head and/or liaison officer between the directorate and the whole division with regard to implementation, monitoring and supervision of almost all educational programmes in the respective region. With his/her support and coordination, the Directorate is able to monitor all the districts in the State. S/he is the overall incharge of education within the division, having responsibility for the administration of educational institutions and offices.

Fig. 2.8: Structure of RMSA in Odisha

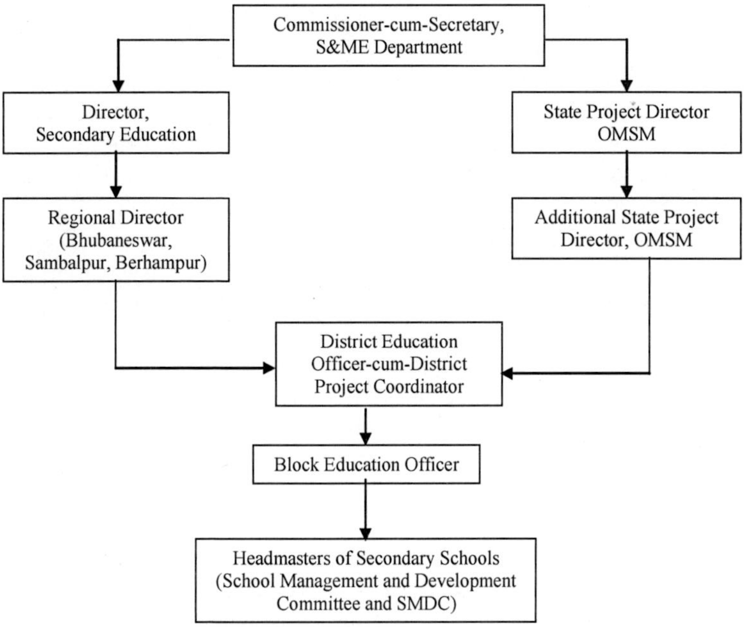

District Level Administration

Each State/Union Territory is divided into a number of districts which are further divided into blocks/mandals, with the district remains the most important unit of educational administration in every State. In some States, there may be educational districts within the revenue districts. The District Education Officer (DEO) in some States is the overall incharge of

Table 2.7: Functional Relationship between Levels of Educational Administration and Types of Institutions

Types of Institutions		*Lowest Level of Administration/ Supervision*
i)	Primary Schools	Block/Taluk/Tehsil
ii)	Middle Schools	Sub-division, Circle/Zone i.e. level between Block and District
iii)	High Schools	District
iv)	Higher Secondary Schools	District/Division/Region i.e. a level between State and District
v)	College/Technical Institutions	State

elementary as well as secondary education, while in some States, there are a number of District Education Officers for each sector of education, like primary, secondary and adult education. The DEO is assisted by a number of officers who deal directly with secondary education in the district. At the block level, a Block Education Officer is incharge of primary education and non-formal education programmes. For administrative purposes, the Block Education Officers function under the overall guidance and directives of the District Education Officer.

Under the renewed emphasis on decentralised administration, District has emerged as an important unit of educational governance. The role and responsibility of DEO mainly includes inspection and supervision, monitoring of teacher recruitment, their promotion, career development, implementing policies and programmes, strengthening local initiative and local controls, co-ordinating with different units of educational governance and supervising the issue of teacher management etc. Wherever regional directorates are established, the DEOs have to report to regional deputy directors in the matters of all correspondence, sanctions etc. relating to educational administration.

As the trend of district-level educational administration emerged, the major States had two separate district education officers—District Education Officer, Secondary and District Elementary Education Officer for looking after the governance of secondary and elementary education respectively in the district.

- The States with unified governance at the district level are Mizoram, Odisha, Bihar, J&K, Karnataka, Nagaland, Andhra Pradesh and Delhi.
- The States having separate district-level education officers for secondary and elementary are Gujarat, Madhya Pradesh, Assam, Jharkhand, Himachal Pradesh, Uttar Pradesh, Punjab, Haryana, West Bengal, Tamil Nadu and Uttarakhand.
- In Kerala, the DEO oversees the administration of high schools, while the post of Assistant Education Officer has been created to look after the management of primary and upper primary schools.
- In Nagaland, the District Education Officer (DEO) is the head of the district level. S/he is responsible for elementary education and is assisted by Deputy District Education Officer (DDEO) who looks after matters related to higher secondary schools. DDEO is further assisted by one Junior Education officer (JEO) for higher secondary and by one JEO for primary sections.

Table 2.8 indicates the educational administration at field level.

Table 2.8: Education Administration at Field Level

S. No.	State	Regional	District	Sub-Regional/Divisional/Zone	Block	Cluster/Circle
1.	Andhra Pradesh	Regional Joint directors	DEO	Dy.E.O (High Sch)+Parishad Education Off. (ZP High Sch)	Mandal Edu. Off. (MEO)+ DIs (Dy Insp. Sch) for Urban (Both E.E.)	
2.	Assam		DEEO for EE + Inspector of School and AIS (Assistant Inspector of School) for Secondary Education	Deputy Inspector for EE in Urban areas (What abt rural areas)	BEEO for EE+No official or structure mentioned for SE	Sub Inspector for Elementary education.
3.	Bihar	Regional Deputy Directors of Education (total no.8)	DEO (Supported by 5 DPOs specialised in EE, SE, MDM, Planning and Establishment)		BEO (for EE and SE)	CRC
4.	Delhi	Regional Directors of Education	Dy. Directors of Education in 11 districts.	Zonal Education Officer in MCD)	Dy. Education Officer	CRC
5.	Goa		Dy. Director of Education	Assistant Director of Education	Deputy Education Officer and Assistant District Education Officer.	
6.	Gujarat		DEO (SE+HSE), D EO, Primary (EE)		BEO/Education Inspector	
7.	Haryana		DEEO (Elementary)+DEO (Secondary)		BEEO (Elementary)+BEO (Secondary)	CRC(SSA)+ assisted by ABRC
8.	Himachal Pradesh		Deputy Director of Educn. (11 for EE+ 12 for Higher Education)		BPEO (Elementary) (No structure for Sec Edu)	

(*Contd.*)

Table 2.8: *Contd.*

S. No.	*State*	*Regional*	*District*	*Sub-Regional/Divisional/Zone*	*Block*	*Cluster/Circle*
9.	J&K		CEO (Chief Education Officer) assisted by DCEO/DEPO		Zonal Education Officer	
10.	Jharkhand	6 Regional. Dy. Director of Education	District Superintendent of Education (EE)+DEO(SE)	Regional Education Officer (EE)+Sub-DEO (SE)	BEEO	
11.	Karnataka		Deputy Director of Public Instruction (at education district)		BEO (for both EE and SE)	
12.	Kerala	Dy Director of Education at revenue districts (14)	District Edu Officer at education district (38) (High Schools)		Assistant Edu Officer (at sub-district or block) (EE)	
13.	Mizoram		DEO (SE) Assistant Education Officer for Elementary Education.		Sub-Deputy Education Officer (for EE) (also use Block for Sub div)	Circle Edu officer (for EE)
14.	Madhya Pradesh	Regional Joint Directors	DEO (Secondary), District Programme Coordinator at Zila Shiksha Kendra		BEO (secondary), Block Resource Centre Coordinator	
15.	Nagaland		DEO Elementary, (assisted by DDEO for Higher Sec Edu, DDEO assisted by JEO), 1 JEO for Prim Edu and 1 for UP		Sub-Deputy Education Officer (for EE) (Sub Division is also called Block)+ No separate structure for secondary	
16.	Odisha	3 Regional Directorate	1 DEO+ 2 ADEO (for all levels)		1BEO+ 3ABEO (all levels)	

(Contd.)

Table 2.8: *Contd.*

S. No.	State	Regional	District	Sub-Regional/Divisional/Zone	Block	Cluster/Circle
17.	Punjab		DEO (SE) assisted by Dy. EO+ DEO(EE)		Block Primary Education Officer	
18.	Tamil Nadu	CEO (at revenue dist. for H Sec Schl.)	DEO (High Schl.)+ DEEO (Ele.Schl.) +Inspector of Matriculation school+ Inspector of Anglo Indian High Schl.)		AEEO+ Addl AEEO+AEEO nursery+AEEO Science (Only for EE)	
19.	Uttar Pradesh	Regional Asst. Director (Basic)+Regional Jt Director+Regional Dy Director (last two for SE)	DEO(Basic)+District Inspector of School (DIOS) (SE)	ADIOS(SE)	BEO (EE)	
20.	Uttarakhand	REO (Regional Education Officers)	Chief Education Officer- DEO (EE)+DEO(SE)		BEO(SE)+Dy Edu Officer (EE)	

EE = Elementary Education; SE = Secondary Education; HSE = Higher Secondary Education AEEO = Assistant Elementary Education Officer; MDM = Mid-day Meal; CRC = Cluster Resource Coordinator.

Source: Third All India Survey of Educational Administration.

Block-level Administration

The block-level educational administration is the main vehicle for implementing policies and programmes related to educational development. Therefore, it is continuously emphasised to have an appropriate structure of educational administration, with well-defined and coordinated functional responsibilities at the block level. The Block Education Officer is the nodal officer in the block. S/he has to supervise all the educational activities of schools. BEOs functions include inspection and supervision of schools, distribution of books, scholarships, uniforms, furnishing of all information required by the DEOs, forming School Management Committees, survey of out-of-school and differently-abled children, collection of data, passing on government instructions to schools and organising regular meeting of the head teachers, attending meetings called by DEO/DPO in the district education office and coordinating with BDO (Block Development Officer). In most of the States, s/he works as the Drawing and Disbursing Officer for the entire staff of schools. In the case of Odisha, s/he is the Additional Executive Officer of the Panchayat Samitis in respect of education and Additional DPC, SSA for RTE-SSA. BEO functions as the main authority for implementing the RTE at the primary level.

In the context of the level of diversification of administration, Haryana, Karnataka and Uttarakhand are the only States where a BEO is also responsible for managing secondary education. In Haryana, the Block Elementary Education Officer and Block Education Officer look after the elementary and secondary schools respectively. In Uttarakhand, Block Education Officer and Deputy Education Officer manage secondary and elementary education respectively. In Karnataka, a BEO also manages secondary schools. In Mizoram, Assam, Nagaland, Odisha, Jharkhand, Jammu and Kashmir, Himachal Pradesh, Kerala, Uttar Pradesh, Punjab and Andhra Pradesh, BEO/MEO looks after the management of elementary education. Most of the States have not decentralised the educational administration of secondary schools at the block level. After the implementation of Right to Education (RTE), the position of BEO in Bihar has changed. The BEO, who was earlier incharge of only the elementary level of education, was made incharge of all the levels of education from primary to senior secondary level.

Cluster-level Structure

Cluster is a group of schools located in a particular geographical area, formed under each taluk or block. The number of clusters in a block varies in proportion to the geographical area and total number of schools in the block. There are approximately eight to 12 schools in each cluster. Clusters are formed for the effective implementation of the educational schemes and programmes, in general, and SSA programmes, in particular. Cluster Resource Centres are meant for the delivery of resource support to the teachers. A Cluster Resource Person (CRP) heads each CRC, CRP is under the control of block level BRC. A CRP spends most of the time on monitoring the schools in the cluster pertaining to academic issues, visits all the schools in the cluster and facilitates the teachers in academic issues. Besides, the CRP also helps senior officials perform academic supervision and school inspections in the cluster.

Linkages with Local Bodies

The local bodies at different levels of administration are expected to converge and coordinate with mainstream educational administration. As per their level of convergence, the States can be divided broadly into two categories—firstly, States wherein the Local Self-Governing (LSG) bodies are directly taking care of school education, and secondly, the States where these bodies are participating indirectly, primarily because of common membership of their members in school committees or they have a standing committee of PRI to deal with educational issues. The case of LSG bodies in Kerala can be a noteworthy example in this category. After enactment of The Kerala Panchayat Raj Act, maintenance and development activities of government in lower primary, upper primary, secondary and higher secondary schools have become the direct responsibility of local bodies. Under the three-tier system of local administration, i.e. district, block and village, high schools and higher secondary schools come under the control of the District Panchayat, upper primary schools under Block Panchayat and lower primary schools under Gram Panchayat. In Municipal and Corporation areas, government schools, at all levels, are controlled by the local body concerned. The important aspect of this devolution is the control over funds. For maintenance and construction etc., the required funds are routed through the local bodies by the government.

Nagaland goes one step ahead in the successful implementation of decentralisation. The policy of decentralisation was put in place much earlier than the Panchayati Raj regime, through the Village Council and Area Council Act of 1978, whereby the village council was empowered to formulate Village Development Schemes and implement development works in the village. The village council, thus, has special powers to supervise and monitor various governmental policies implemented in the village, including educational policies. The council plays a pivotal role in the provision of land for school construction, school playground, teachers' accommodation, electricity and water supply etc. In order to create a sense of ownership of public institutions and to facilitate better management of resources, under the Nagaland Communitisation of Public Institutions and Services Act, 2002, certain responsibilities like management of financial resources and administrative powers of communitised schools have been transferred to village communities through the Village Education Committees (VECs). One of the unique features of the Nagaland LSG scenario is that the VEC is empowered to control teachers in a variety of ways, including the powers to withhold salaries of irregular and absentee teachers and staff. This power is made possible because the salary amount for government employees in the schools is deposited in advance into the VEC account, with the VEC delegated with the power to disburse the salary.

Similarly, in Maharashtra, the responsibility of providing primary education to children in the age group 6-14 years lies with the Zila Parishads. Education Committees have been set up in the local bodies at district level with education officers, appointed by the State government, as their member secretaries and executive head of the Zila Parishads.

There are other States where PRIs have indirectly made their presence felt in educational administration. Either their involvement is visible because of the common membership in school-level management bodies or they have been given control over certain areas of educational management which they access by constituting a standing committee. For example, in Bihar, after the Bihar Panchayat Raj Act 2006, the Zila Parishad, Panchayat Samiti, Gram Panchyat in the rural areas and Nagar Panchayat, Municipal Councils and Municipal Corporations in the urban areas are given the task of consolidating the plans for the development of education through the District Planning Committee. All powers related to recruitment, promotion, deployment, disciplinary actions etc. are delegated to PRIs and Nagar Palikas. For effective functioning, various Standing Committees are made in each tier of PRIs. However, pointing to the ground reality, the State reports indicate that only 'soft powers' are given to the panchayats. Major decisions and powers regarding recruitment rules still vest with the Department of Education while Panchayats are only the implementing agency.

Convergence and Coordination with SSA and RMSA at District Level and with other Departments

In so far as development programmes like SSA and RMSA are concerned, in some of the States, the District Education Officers are in charge of these programmes. However, there are parallel management structures for SSA and RMSA under District Programme Coordinators. In such a situation, regular district education officers have to converge with these programmes.

In the context of SSA, the following trends have emerged:

- The States wherein the responsibility of SSA has been entrusted to the regular district education officers are Maharashtra, Bihar, Uttarakhand, Karnataka, Uttar Pradesh, Himachal Pradesh, Jammu and Kashmir, Punjab, Gujarat and Nagaland. In these States, the existing education officers are designated as DPC (nodal officer at district level) and are responsible for implementation of SSA programme.
- Kerala, Mizoram, Tamil Nadu are the States that have created parallel administration structure for SSA. Most of the States have created a District Project Committee where the District Project Coordinator is the incharge. The DPC is appointed from the education department and works as head of the district office.

The management of RMSA can be noticed on the following line:

- Maharashtra, Uttarakhand, Karnataka, Mizoram, Uttar Pradesh, Assam, Odisha, J&K, Punjab, MP, Andhra Pradesh and Nagaland have not established any separate management structure for functioning of RMSA. In these States, the district education officers are entrusted the charge of DPC, RMSA. They are responsible for all activities relating to planning, management, implementation and monitoring of all components. In other States, parallel management structures have been created for RMSA.

The School education department is vast and most of the schemes cannot be implemented without the proper support of other associated departments. In order to make available effective services to the clientele group, it is very essential that there is coordination and convergence among these departments. Almost all the States coordinate and converge with the following departments at secretariat, directorate, area, district, block, cluster and school levels for management of their school education:

1. Tribal Development Department.
2. Department of Scheduled Castes.
3. Panchayat and Rural Development.
4. Social Justice Department.
5. Women and Child Development Department.
6. Panchayat and Social Welfare Department.
7. Higher Education Department.

8. Backward Classes and Minorities Welfare Department.
9. Planning Department.
10. IT Department.
11. Public Health Department/Public Works Department.
12. Non-government Organisations.

Decision-Making Process

As head of the Education Department, the Education Minister approves all the policies and programmes to be implemented by the State Department of Education. The Education Minister also obtains the approval of the Cabinet in those cases that are beyond the purview of the Education Minister. The Principal Secretary/Secretary, Education is the Chief Executive Officer to execute all the decisions on education policies and programmes taken at the Ministry level. He is assisted by the Commissioner and Secretary, Joint Secretaries and Deputy Secretaries of the Department at the secretariat level. The policies and programmes are implemented through the directorate level subsequent to the district and sub-district level. The transfer and posting of the administrative officers are done by the Education Secretary, with the approval of Minister of Education, though it differs from State to State where decisions are taken by the directorate and then approved by the secretariat. The power of retention and creation of posts lies with the Administrative Department in almost all the States. They obtain necessary approval for the purpose from the departments concerned, whenever required. The Director, as the head at the directorate, takes all decisions relating to the execution of the policies and programmes adopted at the Secretariat level, as per guidelines of the government and the existing rules and procedures in practice. The director exercises the powers vested in him/her and functions accordingly. S/he issues necessary instructions and directions to the district-level functionaries for implementation. The transfer and posting of non-gazetted personnel are generally done at the directorate level.

At the initial stage, DEEO deals with the various issues of teachers such as transfers, GPF, appointment and recruitment, service matters, disciplinary action, as per the instructions and in accordance with the prescribed policy. He prepares action plans for various activities to be carried out at the school level. He has the power to appoint and transfer teachers from time to time, with the approval of director and other senior level officers, as per guidelines provided by the State Government. He creates action plans for quality enhancement of the schools in the district. In some States, he also performs his duty as District Project Co-ordinator, SSA. He finds out the requirements regarding the school building and campus. He provides guidance to the BRC and CRC to carry out academic and non-academic activities and programmes to be conducted at block and school level. He works with SSA and SCERT, DIETs for teachers' training programme to be conducted in the district.

Except in the case of release of salary, the BEEOs at the block level mostly forward all the proposals like transfers, postings, rationalisation of teachers as well as budget requirement, etc. to the DEEO and the DEEO, in turn, forwards the proposals received from BEEOs to the Director, Elementary Education for approval. The DEEO cannot take any decision without approval of the director and the Government. The same happens in the case of secondary education where there is no block-level functionary. The Inspector of Schools/DEO, Secondary releases salaries to the secondary schools. They forward all the proposals like transfers, postings, rationalisation of teachers as well as budget requirement, etc. to the Directorate of Secondary Education. However, at school level, SMC, in primary and upper primary stages, and SDMC, at secondary and senior secondary levels, are involved in the decision-making process.

Stay Period of Education Secretaries

Education Secretaries are responsible for policy and programme formulation, besides implementation and monitoring of programmes. However, during the Third Survey, it was found, on the basis of data received from 10 States, that Education Secretaries are frequently transferred from their posts, thereby adversely affecting the educational policy formulation and implementation of the educational programmes in the State and its educational development as a whole. It was also observed that the State Project Directors are transferred more frequently than the Education Secretaries and this also hampers the smooth implementation of programmes of SSA and RMSA. During personal discussions, the States indicated the urgent need for having an Indian Education Service so that skilled personnel in educational planning and management are available for these posts. Table 2.9 provides the data in this regard.

Major Issues

Several major issues have come up during the Third Survey in respect of structures and functions. One of the issues that has emerged is that several States have created parallel management structures for programme management in the case of SSA and RMSA, instead of these programmes being managed by a regular department of educational administration. Serious lack of coordination between these two management structures have occurred even though a few States have merged the management of

Table 2.9: Stay Period of Education Secretaries during Last Five Years

Sr. No.	*Name of the State*	*Number of Education Secretaries Transferred during last five years 2009 to 2015*
1.	Andhra Pradesh	6
2.	Gujarat	5
3.	Karnataka	5
4.	Madhya Pradesh	4
5.	Maharashtra	6
6.	Goa	7
7.	Himachal Pradesh	7
8.	Odisha	3
9.	Punjab	6
10.	Tamil Nadu	5

Source: Third All India Survey Educational Administration.

these educational programmes with the regular department, thereby managing and implementing these programmes more effectively. Lack of coordination also persists within the education department among different directorates and also at the district level between primary and secondary education when there are two district education officers for primary and secondary. Some States have unified directorate of school education (Class I-XII) like Kerala. The state has created directorate of higher secondary education, has further creating problem of coordination.

Different departments like that of SC, ST, Minority, Tribal and Social Welfare conduct their own education programmes but these departments do not have any convergence either at the directorate level or district level with the education department. It is found that there are plenty of educational programmes conducted by the different departments for education, but because of lack of coordination, these programmes have lost their focus and effectiveness. Inadequate administrative machinery, especially at district level, is also a cause of concern. The education system has increased tremendously in respect of number of schools, students, and teachers, and, with it, the responsibility of educational programmes too has grown in the last two decades, but the size of the administrative machinery has not increased proportionately. This has resulted in a heavy workload on educational administration, hampering their efficiency and performance.

3
E-Governance in Educational Administration

Introduction

Information and Communication Technology (ICT) has become one of the basic building blocks of modern society. ICT has the capacity to enhance the learning process and facilitate communication within education institutions and between educators and learners. Information Technology in education has redefined the terms of teaching and learning. The easy availability of online study and teaching materials has greatly helped both the students and teachers. Using technology effectively in the classroom transforms the classroom, teaching and learning process.

E-governance is a set of technology-mediated processes that are changing both the delivery of public services and the broader interactions between citizens and the government. E-governance may be understood as the performance of the governance via the electronic medium in order to facilitate an efficient, speedy and transparent process of disseminating information to the public, and other agencies, and for performing government administrative activities. The purpose of implementing e-governance is to enhance good governance. Good governance is generally characterised by participation, transparency and accountability. The recent advances in communication technologies and the internet provide opportunities to transform the relationship between governments and citizens in a new way, thus contributing to the achievement of good governance goals.

The use of information technology can increase the broad involvement of citizens in the process of governance at all levels by providing the possibility of online discussion and by enhancing the rapid development and effectiveness of pressure groups. Advantages for the government entail that the government may provide better service in terms of time, making governance more efficient and effective. In addition, the transaction costs can be lowered and government services become more accessible. This chapter highlights the process of e-governance in educational administration in different States.

In educational administration, e-governance is one of the major landmarks that has made administrative processes and procedures easier and more effective, without any time gap in the information management. In several States, as the discussion reflects in the subsequent pages, decisions in respect of administrative, academic and financial matters, including government orders, circulars and documents, are directly sent by the directorate at regional, district, block, cluster and school levels. Recruitment and posting of teachers, admissions of students have also become online in several States. The following are the State-wise highlights:

Recruitment, Selection, Posting and Transfers

In several States, recruitment and posting and transfers are done through e-governance, making the administrative procedures easy and facilitating timely completion of the task. The following States are engaged in the practice of e-governance in educational administration:

Kerala

One of the major developments in the administration is the introduction of e-governance. The two-way communication from the General Education Department and the Directorate of Public Instruction to the Deputy Directors at Revenue District Level, District Education Officers at the educational district level, Assistant Education Officers at the sub-district/block level and to each and every government and aided school from primary to higher secondary is now done through e-governance. Director of Public Instruction can view any kind of information and data on computers. All orders in respect of teacher recruitment, posting and transfer, teacher training, admissions, examinations and any other aspects of educational activity are now sent through the information technology medium.

The e-governance initiative is mainly undertaken by *IT@School Project* to make the transfer and posting of Headmasters and Assistant Educational Officers, teachers of all Government High Schools/TTI in Kerala online to ensure completion of the entire transfer and posting process, in the general category, within weeks. The move, initiated by the Department of General Education, aims at imparting an element of transparency to the entire process. Every year, the department receives hundreds of applications from teachers requesting for transfer to a place of their choice. Through computerised counselling, all the requests are now prioritised, as per the reasons indicated.

Vacancy details of government schools are entered online well in advance, enabling the applicant to view the vacancies even before the application form for transfer and posting is set off. Thus, the applicant can request for transfer, based on the vacancy that exists. Each candidate can choose upto 10 options of schools for transfer in the order of preference. Transfer and posting of teachers is done based purely on the priority opted for by them and taking into account merit in terms of their seniority. Since the computerised process enables a candidate to learn about the vacancies well in advance, only one order can be issued for every transfer aspirant. Moreover, since the conventional mode of transfer and postings was notorious for the corruption involved, a provisional list is made available on the website in order to ensure transparency.

Some of the other e-governance initiatives of the project include the Noon-meal distribution computerisation, Youth festival software, Pre-matric scholarship online, Centralised Online Textbook system, Implementation of SPARK (Service Payroll Administrative Repository for Kerala) within General Education department, Total Physical Fitness Programme software etc. SPARK is, incidentally, a programme of Department of Information Technology (DIT) of Government of Kerala for digitizing the service book details of all employees of the State so that the database could be used by decision-makers for the welfare of employees. Through this process implemented by the project, details of as many as 72,256 service books from 2,266 schools were entered in the database. Moreover, currently 107 schools are using this software to generate the monthly salary bills of teachers and staff on a regular basis. Apart from this, the decision-making process in educational planning and management is based on DISE data available online. The preparation of Annual Work Plan and Budget of SSA and RMSA is entirely dependent on information technology.

Karnataka

Karnataka Reforms Committee Report (December 2001), of Harnahalli Ramaswamy, recommended that all allocations for computerisation/e-governance be shown for each department under the head "Computerisation". Further, it was recommended that common software for common administrative purposes for all departments should be developed and all the government employees, including elected representatives, be given regular, systematic training. Keeping this in view, a great deal of automation has taken place in the government over the past couple of years. The use of computers has dramatically reduced repetitive work in many departments, especially in the Finance department. Use of PCs, E-mails, Fax-facilities, creation of official websites for all the departments and periodical upload of revised information has made the administration effective.

The Department of Education has extensively trained all its personnel in the lower offices, including school teachers, with the latest knowledge, developed by the department in the field of information technology, for the smooth running of administration. The ministerial staff are given computer training by the District Training Institutes of the respective districts and by the DIETs. The academic staff are provided computer training by the CTEs and DIETs. Karnataka is one of the few States which is in the forefront of using technology and has been applying its know-how, even in administration and personnel management. Primary and secondary teachers and head masters are all posted to the places of work directly through online counselling during their first appointment and promotions.

The transfers of primary and high school teachers and all head masters are effected only through online counselling every year during the months of April-May. All the transfers are based on the request by the teacher concerned. Eligible teachers, who apply for transfer through counselling, are transferred only to available vacant posts. The number of such request transfers are restricted to 3-5per cent of the working strength of the cadre concerned, giving due consideration to the number of years of service in rural /urban areas, spouses working in the defence services, widow cases, severe medical cases, physical disability, office bearers of approved associations etc.

Better Communication by G.Os and Circulars

Manipur

It has been widely and effectively used as a communication tool in administration and management of education since the past decade. Both the Secretariat: Education(S) and Directorate of Education(S) are electronically linked to the internet through V-Sat installed by the NIC. The Department of Education(S) maintains its dynamic official website in which all important orders, notifications, Office Memorandum are uploaded regularly. The official website is known to most officers, heads of institutions and teachers who access the website regularly.

Most officers at the Secretariat Education(S) and the Directorate of Education(S) maintain official e-mail addresses and urgent matters are communicated through electronic medium in a routine manner. As such, communication between the Secretariat Education(S) and the Directorate of Education(S) and among officers of these two offices is quick and efficient. All Zonal Educational Officers, Principals of Higher Secondary

Schools and Headmasters of High Schools are also linked electronically with the Directorate of Education(S) through e-mails. This mode of communication is, particularly, effective in dissemination of information to offices and schools located in the hills and remote areas. The Department of Education(S) is working on a mechanism to track files and proposals electronically so as to make the movement and processing of files and proposals more transparent and also to enable the head of department and subordinate officers monitor the efficiency in processing of files and proposals at different levels.

Nagaland

Electronic governance (E-governance) is the use of information and communication technologies (ICT) for the planning, implementation, and monitoring of programs, projects, and activities. Use of ICTs in educational administration facilitates an efficient, speedy and transparent process for disseminating information and actions for providing services and performing administrative activities. E-governance solutions in the educational sector incorporates the latest technology to evolve a system that combines administrative and academic management systems necessary for successful handling of all issues relating to the academic or non-academic affairs of an educational institution. Computers are extensively used for educational administration and almost every school has computers in the office. Some common areas where e-governance is used for effective educational administration include:

- General Administration.
- Pay Roll and Financial Accounting.
- Administration of Student Data.
- Employees Personnel Records' Maintenance.
- Records for moveable and immovable properties.
- Library System etc.

E-governance solution in the educational sector has enabled institutions to incorporate data into a unified system, making the process well-organised and error-proof. Computerisation of educational institutions in areas such as students' enrolment, admission, attendance, library, salary and expenses, examinations, performance, grades, hostels, etc. has revolutionised educational administration in the State even though many institutions are yet to fully avail the benefits of ICT.

Online communication between the directorate and schools, through emails, saves time and reduces the costs of administrative services. Use of smartphones and mobile technology is also replacing the conventional system of information exchange and dissemination while also enhancing administrative efficiency. Online collaboration tools, such as *Google Apps,* allow students and instructors share documents online, edit them in real time, and project them on a screen. Presentation software, such as *PowerPoint,* also enables instructors to embed high-resolution photographs, diagrams, videos, and sound files to augment text and verbal lecture content.

Computer Aided Learning (CAL), initiated under SSA, covers around 42,000 students from 700 government middle schools in the State. Initially, the program was implemented through outsourcing to four outside consultancy agencies. However, since March 2013, the outsourcing arrangement was discontinued and the program is implemented in collaboration with SCERT.

Maharashtra

E-governance is very much in use in Maharashtra, particularly in teacher management. Right from the intensive use of Information and Communication Technology in SSA and RMSA for preparation of annual plans, coordination and monitoring and in other activities with data available through UDISE, all the processes in teacher management are undertaken online. Staff approval camps are arranged by the primary and secondary education officers in the months of July and August. These camps are arranged at block level. The staff approval is made in accordance with RTE 2009 and Maharashtra Rules 2010. The norm of 1.5 teachers per division for Standards VIII to X, 1.3 teachers per division for Standard V to VII and one teacher per division for Standard I to V is followed. There is a division of 40 students at the secondary and 30 students at the primary level. There are posts of one head master and graduate teachers for the upper primary schools. A special software (SARAL) has been developed now for this procedure. The District Pay unit disburses salaries of approved staff through their bank accounts.

In Maharashtra, Information and Communication Technology is used as a tool in teaching-learning process, training, development of text and supplementary material, besides collection and dissemination of information and statistics. With this aim in view, groups of techno-savy teachers are formed in each block. The group members prepare teaching aids in electronic media. The videos are uploaded on the website. The teachers can download it for use in classroom teaching. These groups maintain rapport with each other. They discuss and find solutions in case of difficulties. The electronic material is made available with the help of stakeholders, NGOs and local body members. The expenditure can be met from the local development fund viz. MLA/MP fund.

Punjab

The Government of Punjab duly recognises the significance of e-governance as an important vehicle of growth and development. To promote efficiency, reduce delays, enhance accountability, and transparency and objectivity in the functioning of the government, the State government framed its information technology policy in 2001. The IT policy focuses on, inter alia, e-education and intends:

- to improve the quality, reach, effectiveness and delivery of education systems through the use of IT;
- to enhance the value and, thus, employability of the youth of the state by equipping them with the knowledge of IT, both at school and college levels, thus leading to creation of an IT enabled workforce; and,
- to create an IT-friendly culture through education enabling knowledge-based society.

Duly recognising that e-governance is playing an increasingly important role in efficient delivery of services in a convenient and transparent way, the Department of School Education of Punjab has taken many initiatives in the area of school education in the State, mainly through the following institutions:

- Punjab Information and Communication Technology Education Society (PICTES),
- Punjab Edusat Society (PES),
- Management Information System (MIS) Wing of Sarv Shiksha Abhiyan/ Rashtriya Madhyamik Shiksha Abhiyan (SSA/RMSA) Authority of Punjab, and
- State Council of Educational Research and Training (SCERT) Punjab.

While the two societies, as mentioned above, make focussed efforts to improve the teaching and learning and facilitate capacity building of teachers through telecast, the MIS wing looks after the task of data management and administrative matters of the department of school education, particularly in planning and decision-making at block, district and State levels. The SCERT provides academic support to PICTES and PES and conducts piloting of projects, experimentations, try-outs and evaluation. PICTES, PES, SCERT and MIS work hand in hand and are mutually supportive.

Data Management for SSA, RMSA and Other Programmes

Tamil Nadu

In Tamil Nadu, Geographical Information System (GIS) is a computer-based system for storage, retrieval, manipulation, analysis and display of geographic data. Geographic data includes spatial and descriptive data. It includes Spatial (map) data deals with location, shape and relationships among physical and human features; and descriptive (non-map) data deals with the characteristics of the features (attributes). The GIS is an effective tool that manages and monitors school-related activities in Tamil Nadu, with focus on the children and the facilities provided to them in their schools. Instant availability of an entire range of data on schools in remote areas of Tamil Nadu enables effective planning and implementation. The GIS mapping has various other benefits too. It ensures that all children, who cannot access school due to social, cultural and economic reasons, are enabled to do so. It determines the requisite changes that are indispensable in schools, such as infrastructure, equipment and faculty members. The GIS mapping facilitates viewing, understanding, questioning, interpreting and visualising data in numerous ways that reveal relationships, patterns and trends in the form of maps, reports and charts. It also helps answer questions and solve problems by examining a data in a manner that is quickly understood and easily shared. The GIS database, at present, encompasses the entire State of Tamil Nadu and has given a major impetus to accurate planning while enabling solutions based on analytical outcomes.

Online Tracking Software: Exclusive software has been developed and installed for the purpose of tracking the status of out-of-school children online. This software programme furnishes information in three categories: 1. The Profile of the Child; 2. The Monitoring Report; and 3. The Assessment Report. Special training interventions to address the needs of more than 50,000 out-of-school children, are in place. This has been made possible with the help of online tracking software.

Use of U-DISE: The U-DISE is the most comprehensive database containing school-related indicators, facilities in schools, enrolment-based indicators and teacher-related indicators. With the help of these indicators, Tamil Nadu has effectively been able to generate reports vital for improvement of the school system which are: Extensive usage of AWP & B; In addition – as a management tool some activities are as follows: to ascertain the distance of high schools from nearest middle schools as per norms; to focus on appointment of teachers against vacancies in government high and higher secondary schools; to monitor the school level visits and inspections made by the officials; to identify the teachers with higher qualification for resource persons; to use UDISE data for policy note; and to share enrollment of schools, teachers data with departments of State Government.

EMIS: Educational Management Information System comprises a common online portal, education content service, SMS-based attendance monitoring system and intra-departmental communication services system. At the common website (www.tnschools.gov.in), details of primary, high, higher secondary schools will be provided, containing details of headmasters, teachers and non-teaching staff, besides number of students studying in each school, pass percentage, exam details and other important information.

Madhya Pradesh

Education Portal: E-Governance has been a major initiative of the school education department. In collaboration with NIC, the Rajya Shiksha Kendra has developed an educational portal consisting of a suite of online applications for School Education and Tribal Development departments. The portal provides not only a common platform for interaction and information sharing for all school employees related to school education, but is also serving as a platform for dissemination of information, taking decisions based on support systems and exchange of ideas.

Stakeholders and Beneficiaries: The major stakeholders and beneficiaries of the project are over 3.50 lakh teachers and support staff of education sector; over 1.60 crore students studying in government schools in more than 1.1 lakh government schools; officers and staff of State-level offices (RSK, CPI, TWD etc.); all Drawing and Disbursing Officers (DDOs) and their accounts staff; 51 District Education Officers, District Project Officers, BEOs, BRCs; and over 10,000 supervisory functionaries at Sankul and JSK level.

Online Payroll and Human Resource Management Application: This module has been designed for employees belonging to Education and Tribal Welfare Department working in the education sector. Use of online pay bill, generated from this software, has been made mandatory by the Finance Department for submission to Treasuries for clearance. Monthly use of online pay roll system, involving schools, teachers and staff, ensures the monthly and live updation of the databases. This application also facilitates various HR functions like transfers and generation of pay bills and various related schedules and bank advices. The system is being actively used by DDOs, District Education Officers, Block Education Officers, DPCs and BRCs.

Services to DDOs and Payment Authorities: The School Education

Department has a large number of Drawing and Disbursing Officers (DDOs). These officers are responsible for drawing salary of their own school as well as of the schools in their jurisdiction or cluster. Thus, each DDO has to draw salary of more than 100 to 250 school teachers. The services made available to these DDOs are effortless and online preparation and generation of all types of pay-bills and related schedules; Elimination of existing repetitive and time-consuming manual system of preparation of pay bills; Automation of various processes; timely processing and payment of salaries to staff and continuous updation of the database of the schools, teachers and staff as it has been linked with the pay.

Services to DEOs, DPCs and other Field Staff/Authorities: The District Education Officers are responsible for all the school education related activities of the district. Similarly, the DPCs are responsible for coordinating all the activities of SSA in the district. In order to facilitate district officers, the facilities made available to them through e-governance are facility to monitor and manage teachers, employees and schools; Facility to view and process transfer applications of the staff; Facility to effect and endorse transfers; Tracking the distribution of textbooks; and facility to view circulars, orders, training announcements and other information uploaded by the Government, CPI, CTWD and RSK, and upload the same for the staff.

Services to Students and Parents: The citizen component of e-governance has been addressed to students, teachers and the community. The information available relates to online availability of various welfare schemes of the Government and the procedure to be followed are: online submission of service-related grievances; details of the teachers and other related staff in the school; Details of the infrastructure and facilities available in the school; effective learning and empowered monitoring of students (G2C) and enhancing achievement levels of students (G2C).

Financial Management

E-Transfer of Funds up to Grassroots' Level

Under SSA, enormous funds in different sectors are sanctioned by GOI. These funds are spent by different people at different levels. In a decentralised mode of governance and social participation in decision-making, most of these funds are spent by the SMCs/SMDCs and panchayats. Earlier, the transfer of funds was a lengthy process, originating from the State office, went through district office, then to block level office and then to SMC/SMDC and Gram Panchayats. This process consumed a lot of time, with the lengthy procedures resulting in delay funds reaching the grassroot level. Similarly, the expenditure progress, furnished by the district offices and block offices, was not timely and accurate. In order to deal with such problems, a system of dissemination of funds directly to the grassroot level has been developed. An MoU has been signed with the State Bank of India. All districts and block offices of SSA have SBI accounts. In lieu of account with SBI, the Bank disseminates funds to Panchayats and SMCs, through core banking within a span of seven days. One added advantage of this facility is that e-transfer and Internet banking has allowed the RSK to monitor Panchayat and SMC accounts instantaneously. Similarly, district and block-level accounts are also being monitored instantaneously. This facility has enabled RSK to monitor 24x7 real-time monitoring of funds available and spent by Panchayat, block and district office accounts. The monthly opening and closing balance of the district and block-level offices is furnished by SBI.

The system has proved to be very effective. One of the major benefits is the crediting of bank accounts of SMCs and Panchayats with funds instantaneously, as and when there is requisition from the SPO, thereby preventing the loss of time in transit and achieving transparency. Other major benefits are: monthly opening and closing balances are available in field-level offices; monthly list of funding to each SMC, panchayat and bank is available; and transparency and monitoring at district and State levels. It also provides the facility to access bank account details at the State level.

New Contributory Pension Scheme: The system has been enhanced to facilitate the seamless implementation of the New Contributory Pension scheme for the Adhyapak cadre through NSDL. Portal-generated application format is used for the allotment of PRAN numbers, integration of the pay-roll for deduction of employee share and Government contribution has been carried out and also integration with NSDL for uploading the subscription details and release of the amount to NSDL.

Teacher's Promotion and Transfer System: Online counselling system has been designed and developed to facilitate the posting of employees in various schools of the State where positions are lying vacant. The objective of the system is to ensure transparency in the process and minimise the travel and grievances of the employees regarding the posting/ allotment of schools. The places of vacancies and related information are provided to the teachers and they are allowed to place their choice online. This facility brings transparency in the system.

Teacher's Grievances Management: In order to solve the teacher's administrative and financial grievances online, a system has been set up in the educational portal, with the objective of saving the time of teachers.

They can devote more time to teaching by registering their grievances online and having the same sorted out by higher authorities.

Gujarat

The Government of Gujarat has established the Bhaskaracharya Institute for Space Applications and Geo-informatics (BISAG) in the year 1997. Teacher training across the districts is conducted through this facility, whereby important topics relating to pedagogy, administration, etc. are addressed. Besides this the 'Management Information System' (MIS) has been set up online to collect the DISE data, relating to school education, from the various districts. Grievance redressal, child tracking system, employee management system, school directory, online circulars, migration monitoring system etc. have been developed to facilitate sharing of information and maintaining transparency in the system.

At the Directorate of Primary Education, the process of admission to the different courses, such as Primary Teachers Training Certificate, Diploma in Elementary Education, etc. are offered online. Other details, such as Official Ordinances etc., are put up on the website. The Department of Secondary and Higher Secondary Education has the provision of registering new schools, accessing of online examination forms by students, conducting examinations through CCTV watch, online registrations of teachers etc. At the district and block levels, appropriate software and hardware are provided to collect data for the DISE as well as the internet to facilitate communication between the various government channels. The State Examination Board provides the facility to students to check results online for standards 10 and 12. Candidates appearing for other exams, such as TAT, TET, CP.ed, DP.ed, HTAT, GCC, etc., can also access exam application forms as also their results online. The board also uses various softwares for paper-checking and appointment of subject-wise examiners.

The GCERT conducts video conferencing and tele-conferencing in its training programmes across the State. A tele-conference for all PTTI students was held as orientation for the School Readiness Programme. All 26 DIETs and BRCs in the State are connected with internet and video conferencing facilities. The DIETs have launched their own websites under MHRD guidelines and NCTE norms. All offices falling under the education department from State to district to block level viz, schools, BRCs, CRCs, DEO office, DPEOs office, etc. are equipped with internet so that the sharing of information and data becomes easy and transparent.

The Gujarat State Disaster Management Authority (GSDMA), as part of the World Bank funded GEERP, initiated two programs, such as Gujarat School Safety Initiative (GSSI). All Government schools in

Gujarat have been provided with ISI marked portable Fire Extinguisher (31746 Government schools covered, of which 31336 are primary and 410 are secondary and higher secondary schools). For the necessary guidance/instruction for use of fire extinguishers, the GSDMA has prepared an 18-minute short education film in Gujarati on fire safety for schools. This was shown to all government primary schools through the satellite network.

Mizoram

The Department of School Education in Mizoram has made enormous changes in structure, administration and management during the last two decades. The mode of collection of data and information from various sources in a meaningful way has been done through modern electronic and technical facilities. The ability to acquire and manage information in a systematic way is crucial for educational planning and administration. The success of educational development mainly depends on the process of acquiring information and systems of its management at all levels.

Before the introduction of modern system of communication and information technology, collection of required information was done in a written form and disseminated to the appropriate destination through postal facilities. This poor system of communication, especially in rural areas, led to slow collection and compilation of data and, in turn, to delay in subsequent dissemination of information. This adversely affected the process of educational planning and administration in the State.

Since the introduction of modern system of electronic communication, especially in block / sub-division, district and State headquarters, there is a smooth flow of information from Block Level to State level and vice versa. Proper use of electronic facilities, like Computer, Telephones/ Mobile phones, Fax, e-mail etc. has led to significant improvements in educational planning and administration.

There are some schools selected for providing computer education under SSA programmes (for elementary), and under RMSA (for secondary schools). Besides, there are also some select schools which received computer set for providing computer education under SCERT, Mizoram. These schools, which are provided with computers, can easily furnish the required information to higher levels of administration, even at the secretariat level.

There are some schools in remote areas without computers and their applications, where proper collection of information and furnishing the same is not possible. These schools furnish the required information through postal system to the appropriate place (BRC/SDEO/DPC/DEO etc. office), leading to delay in compilation and, subsequently, dissemination to higher authorities.

Andhra Pradesh

The following activities are conducted through Information and Communication Technology.

- **Integrated U-DISE and Child Information:** Data of 60,462 schools were collected online. Student's and teacher's data were authenticated due to integration.
- **Digital Classroom Learning:** Digital Class is a teacher-led educational content solution that intensely improves learning outcomes in schools. The programme supplements the existing curriculum in both English and Telugu medium to make the learning experience in classrooms exciting, meaningful and enjoyable – translating into better learning and results for students, teachers, parents and the school. The system is equipped with a learning application for the classroom that contains digital content (Standards I – XII), as per the AP State Board Syllabus in both English and Telugu media. The syllabus covers the subjects of Mathematics, Physical and Biological Science and Social Studies through live videos, animations (2D & 3D), illustrations, experiments, Continuous Comprehensive Evaluation (CCE)-based question bank and virtual activities which can be used by the teacher, both within the classroom and during the lesson planning.

The Government is considering implementing the project in all Government schools in the State after the huge success achieved in the pilot projects. The following are the on-going projects:

- 352 KGBVs with Digital classrooms/ICT Lab
- 155 model schools with Digital classrooms/ICT Lab
- 51 APREI Schools
- 768 ICT Phase II Schools with Digital classrooms/ICT Lab
- 300 Virtual classrooms Reliance CSR
- 204 ERNET India Digital classrooms in Srikakulam District
- 280 ERNET India Virtual classrooms
- 1043 CAL Schools with ICT Lab
- 260 Model Primary Schools with Digital Classroom
- 226 Model Primary Schools with ICT Lab
- 1300 e-Pragati Schools with Digital Classrooms
- 10 Schools HP PoC for 9 months in Guntur District

A total of 4939 schools will be ready with either digital classrooms or ICT labs for the academic year 2016-17 from various projects mentioned above. Video conferences, Tele-conferences, uploading and making the information available on the website, sending/receiving information through mails have been introduced at various levels.

E-governance in the Educational Administration: The following activities are conducted through e-governance:

- Plans & Budgets for all CSS programmes – SSA, RMSA, MDM
- Text Books, Uniforms, MDM Supply
- Rationalisation & consolidation of schools
- Teacher Transfers – Performance points for enrolment
- Teacher Transfers – 2015
- Inter-district Teacher Transfers – 2016
- Teacher Award Proposals.
- Teacher Database

Review meetings, redressal of grievances, inspections, meetings for progress of activities are in practice in educational administration for e-governance. Information on response of the administration in respect of disaster management, political interference and corruption in administration, without mentioning individual names, is also tapped.

Biometric Attendance

- Monitoring the schools with regard to its primary functions on student and teacher attendance provides a strong input for analysis of school administration. In this context, establishing a flawless biometric attendance system is imperative to drive the school in shaping the future of students in the interest of the latter and also the State of AP.
- For this purpose, the State of AP has to be practically re-imagined and reconstructed in a planned manner, if the hopes and aspirations of its people have to be fulfilled.
- Andhra Pradesh, the 'Sunrise State of India', has 68, 86,580 students enrolled in 60,462 schools. In order to deliver granular level of administration in schools and to provide better services to its students, it is necessary for the government of Andhra Pradesh to monitor the enrolment of students and also track their attendance.
- To address this issue, Commissioner School Education has decided to implement biometric attendance monitoring system across schools in Andhra Pradesh.

- This data will not only help in making effective intervention at the school level but also help in plugging the leaks in the welfare programs. These biometric systems will also ensure that the schemes are more effective within a shorter time span for the student and teacher community as the result of an organised monitoring mechanism of their attendance.

Telangana

E-governance in the Educational Administration

Sarva Shiksha Abhiyan (SSA) and Rashtriya Madhyamik Shiksha Abhiyan (RMSA) are national flagship programmes for the Universalisation of elementary education and enhanced access to secondary education respectively. Through these programmes, the Government of India provides financial and technical assistance to States to achieve the objectives of providing quality education to children. The Department of Education, under the Ministry of Human Resource Development, has developed an online portal to collect and manage education information to facilitate effective planning, monitoring, review and evaluation of the interventions. The online data management system, developed in collaboration with the National Informatics Centre (NIC), meets the requirements of decentralised programme management catering to the needs of all stakeholders from the Central to the district level. It facilitates access for all users to the information required for setting and monitoring annual targets, both physical and financial. This enables the district, State and national level stakeholders to track and monitor progress and take suitable management decisions to improve the programme impact.

School level: Headmasters of high schools upload details of each child of their respective schools in the childinfo portal of SSA. The details include Admission number, name of the student, class, names of his/her parents, residential address, AADHAR number, photo, details of previous class, previous school, date of birth, date of joining the school etc. The data is updated from time to time. If a child leaves the school, an online Transfer Certificate is issued, without which the child's particulars cannot be uploaded in his new school. The information related to teachers also is uploaded onto the website and updated from time to time. In other words, online admission register and service registers are maintained. The Mandal Educational Officer uploads the details of children of primary and upper primary schools of the Mandal. Besides these, the details of school visits by CRPs, SCHMs and MEOs are also uploaded. The DEOs and Deputy DEOs upload reports of their visits of schools in the portal. This system helps any officer from the state headquarters to monitor the functioning of the schools. All the important information related to district educational administration is placed on the official website of the DEO.

Uttar Pradesh

E-governance is a means for government to introduce new technologies to provide people with more convenient access to government information and services as also to provide greater opportunities to participate in democratic institutions and processes. The following initiatives have been taken by the government to promote e-governance in the State:

- Web-based system is in place for online submission of applications.
- An online information system has been created for communication between the education department at State, district and block level.
- Web-based monitoring system has been developed for effective monitoring of various programmes and schemes. The system has helped in creating strong communication between State and districts.
- Fully functional computerised MIS (UDISE) for educational statistics is in place to ascertain the educational status of school, clusters, block, district and State.
- All funds are transferred electronically to all SMCs of the State.

Major Issues

Though several States have started e-governance in educational administration, especially in communication, data and information management, examinations' management and posting and transfers, some States are still in the process of implementing e-governance in educational administration. Barring a few, majority of the States have not introduced the system for monitoring of educational programmes at the school level. Service conditions of teachers have not been recorded in computers, and, as such, welfare schemes, promotion of teachers, appraisal system and teacher training information alongwith grievance redressal, which have hitherto not been part of e-governance, may be included in e-governance. This may lead to enhancing teacher effectiveness and strengthening the teaching-learning process. For recruitment of teachers, the preparation of five-year teacher recruitment plans is necessary. Only a few States have started the recruitment, posting and transfers of teachers through e-governance which has an impact on effectiveness, transparency and accountability in the administration.

4
Teacher Management

Teacher management has always been one of the important concerns of the department of education. Efficient teacher management is directly linked with the quality of school education and successful implementation of education policy. Teacher management practices are different in various States, as the trends from Third Survey of Educational Administration indicate. This chapter highlights the reforms that have taken place in the recruitment process, posting and transfer issues, welfare and career advancement schemes, the grievance redressal mechanism and role of teacher unions in different States. The following are the major reforms that have taken place in teacher management in the country.

Impact of Reforms in Education Administration

Right from the National Policy on Education, 1986, Jomtein Conference 1990 and Programme of Action 1992, tremendous changes have taken place in the administrative structures and functions of school education and in teacher management as well to make the delivery of educational programmes more effective. Teachers were considered as the hub of educational activity at all levels of education. The emphasis was on decentralisation and participatory management in all educational activities. Subsequently, there have been reforms in recruitment and selection, including recruitment agencies and teacher qualifications, posting and transfers, training and capacity-building programmes for teachers and accountability and responsibility of teachers.

Changes in Recruitment and Selection Pattern

Earlier, recruitment and selection of teachers was done by the State-level agencies, like Directorate of Education. Following decentralisation, this process was assigned to local level agencies like district and block-level education officers. These agencies recruited teachers with the help of VECs/SMCs. Instead of recruiting regular teachers, para teachers, with different designations like Gurujis/Shiksha Mitra/Vidya Shikshaks, were recruited on contract basis for the academic session of schools on consolidated salaries. As a result of the continuous policy reforms, the contract teachers have now been absorbed by the different States as regular teachers. Teachers' recruitment, on contract basis, makes the process of timely filling the teachers' vacancies necessary to avoid any gap in studies of children in schools. Another development in the teacher recruitment process is the involvement of local bodies in the selection committees so that the local situations are kept in mind while conducting the recruitment process. The States follow different patterns for recruitment of teachers at different levels—primary, upper primary and secondary. Trends indicate that in some of the States, teachers are recruited by the directorate of school education, while in a few States, teachers are recruited by their own Public Service Commissions as in the case of Odisha, Sikkim, Mizoram and Kerala. Some States like Uttar Pradesh have the Teacher Recruitment Commission at the state level for recruitment of teachers in private-aided secondary and senior secondary schools.

Changes in the Eligibility Conditions

In most of the States, the requisite qualification for primary and upper primary teachers is Class XII pass with two years' professional diploma in teaching like JBT, BTC or D.Ed. It is also necessary that they should have passed the Teacher Eligibility Test (TET). The exception in this context is Uttar Pradesh where graduate degree with two years of teacher training professional diploma, alongwith the TET, is the criterion to become a teacher. In the case of secondary and senior secondary school teachers, candidates need to be a graduate/post graduate from a recognised university and also hold a B.Ed./M.Ed. or have equivalent Teacher Training. Variations in recruitment process indicate that the State of Sikkim allows relaxation in professional training requirement in view of the shortage of trained candidates in the State. However, they are appointed on the condition that they have to complete B.Ed. and D.El.Ed. within the stipulated time.

Changes in Posting and Transfers

Teachers are posted within the district in most of the States and even at block level in some of the States, as per their preferences listed with regard to place of posting. Transfer of teachers is not done for the sake of transfers by the government in several States like Bihar, Maharashtra, Karnataka and Tamil Nadu. Only mutual transfers are done, and also if any kind of exigency arises with the teacher. However, transfers are done by the State government in most of the States after the stay of teachers in one place for a fixed time limit.

The following are the teacher management practices in different States:

Recruitment and Selection

Arunachal Pradesh

In Arunachal Pradesh, recruitment of school teachers is done separately for secondary and elementary stages by the Director of School Education (DSE) and Director of Elementary Education (DEE) respectively through advertisement and on the basis of recommendations of duly constituted selection boards. Only candidates capable of teaching in the English medium and willing to serve in the remote areas of the State are eligible to apply.

At the elementary level, the candidates have to be APTET/CTET qualified and clear the written test/viva-voce to qualify for selection. The posts of teachers under various categories are reserved as per the government norms (80% for APST and 20% for general category). The Director of Secondary Education recruits the Senior Teachers (PGTs) and Junior Teachers (TGTs) for serving in Higher Secondary and Secondary Schools respectively. On the other hand, the Director of Elementary Education recruits TGTs and Assistant Teachers (PRTs) for government upper primary and primary stages of schooling.

The minimum academic and professional qualification required for candidates to be recruited for various categories of teachers are as under;

(a) Senior Teacher (PGT): Second Class Master's degree in subject concerned with B.Ed.
(b) Junior Teacher (TGT): Second Class Bachelor's degree in subject concerned with B.Ed. (for secondary stage) and D.El.Ed. or B.Ed. (Elementary) and APTET/CTET qualified at elementary stage.
(c) Assistant Teacher (PRT): Class XII pass in Second division with D.El.Ed. and APTET/CTET qualified.
(d) Junior Teacher (Music): Second Class Bachelor's degree in Music with second class in B.Ed.
(e) Junior Librarian: Second Class Graduate from a recognised university with degree or diploma in Library Science.
(f) Laboratory Assistant: Second Class Bachelor's degree in Science from a recognised university.
(g) Craft Teacher: Class XII pass (Class X pass for APST) with Diploma in Craftsmanship.
(h) Physical Education Teacher (PET): Second class Bachelor's degree in Physical Education (B.P.Ed.).

Age limit for direct recruitment to the above posts is normally 21 to 28 years with five years' relaxation for APST candidates. There is normally 50 per cent reservation of posts for direct recruitment.

Odisha

In Odisha, teachers at the senior secondary level are known as junior lecturers. Department of Higher Education posts junior lecturers in the Junior Colleges to teach senior secondary classes. The selection to the post of junior lecturers in different subjects is done by Odisha Public Service Commission (OPSC) through a written test, followed by a viva-voce. OPSC recruitment to the posts are as per the vacancy notified by the Higher Education Department. At the secondary level, teachers are posted on contractual basis since 2003-04 against vacant posts by abolishing an equal number of scale-bearing posts. The contractual teachers are regularised in their respective posts only on completion of a minimum six years of continuous and satisfactory engagement. The performance and eligibility for appointment as regular teacher is scrutinised by a Steering Committee, headed by the District Collector.

The teachers for elementary schools have been appointed on contractual basis since 2000-01. The scheme of "Swechhasevi Shiksha Sahayak (SSS)" was introduced in the State. The recruitment and posting was done by a committee headed by the Collector. The recruitment to the post of Swechhasevi Siksha Sahayak (SSS) was done purely on the basis of career marks. From time to time, the State Government changed the norms of recruitment of teachers for elementary schools. As per recent order in 2014, recruitment is done in accordance with the guidelines issued by NCTE, as the Academic Authority and Chief Executive Officer, Zila Parishad is the authority to issue the order of engagement. After the regularisation of the Shiksha Sahayaks, Gana Sahayak as regular elementary teachers, administrative control of these teachers vests with Director, Elementary Education and their names are reflected in the gradation list.

Mizoram

In Mizoram, all recruitments of teachers, from primary to higher secondary stages, are done through Mizoram Public Service Commission (MPSC). The MPSC notifies the vacancy of teachers. Those candidates, who are qualified candidates, apply for the post in a prescribed application format obtained from the MPSC. The recruitment process includes both written test and interview. MPSC normally selects two candidates for one post to face personal interview and the names of successful candidates in the interview are sent to Secretariat of School Education Department for appointment. The requisite qualifications for primary and upper primary teachers are Class XII pass (minimum for primary) and graduation degree from a recognised university for upper primary, two years' diploma in primary education, and also Mizoram Teacher Eligibility Test (MTET). In the case of Secondary and Senior Secondary Teachers, candidates need to have a graduation from a recognised university and B. Ed. or equivalent teacher training.

Karnataka

The posts of assistant teachers i.e I language teacher / English language teacher / III language teacher / PCM teacher/ CBZ teacher/ Arts teacher/ Physical Education teacher in Karnataka are filled through direct recruitment at the divisional level on merit and on roster basis through competitive examinations. Special teachers in Craft/ Horticulture/ Tailoring/ Drawing/Music etc. also work in high schools. Eligible teachers, serving in primary schools, are also promoted to secondary school teachers, as per the norms of recruitment and selection. In primary schools, teachers for primary schools are recruited at district level based on the merit in competitive examination and roster. Teachers have to undergo the counselling process for final allotment of the school.

Andhra Pradesh

In Andhra Pradesh, primary, upper primary and secondary school teachers are selected and recruited by the District Selection Committee (DSC), headed by the District Collector. As per Right to Education Act-2009, Teacher Eligibility Test (TET) is mandatory for every candidate to qualify in order to become a teacher. All the teachers are selected and recruited through a written test. The candidates are selected purely on merit, with reservations provided candidates belonging to SC/ST. The DEO is the appointing authority upto the school assistant level, whereas the regional joint director of school education is the competent authority to appoint head masters of secondary schools. With regard to promotions, the DEO is the competent authority to accord promotions upto school assistant level. For this, the promotion is purely based on seniority/merit. For the posting and transfer of teachers, it is entirely through counseling only. The DEO is the competent authority to transfer teachers upto school assistant level, subject to the condition that prior permission for transfer through counselling is accorded by the government. The DEO has no powers to transfer a single teacher without counselling and without the permission of the government.

The candidates must have completed the age of 18 years and must not have completed the age of 36/40 years as on 1st July of the year in which notification for recruitment is made. However, in the case of Backward Classes, the maximum age limit is 40 years and, in the case of Scheduled Caste and Scheduled Tribes, it is 41 years, while in the case of Physically Handicapped candidates, the maximum age limit is 45 years. In the case of ex-servicemen, the maximum age limit for eligibility is determined by allowing a deduction from his age of a period of three years in addition to the length of service rendered by him or her in the Armed Forces. This is, however, subject to the rider or proviso that after making the deduction from his or her age, the person concerned shall not exceed the maximum age limit prescribed for the post.

Maharashtra

In Maharashtra, the primary education sector is mainly with local self-government. Secondary, higher secondary and higher and technical and vocational education are with private managements. The primary teachers, working in schools run by local self-government are recruited as per procedure laid down by the government. The government conducts Teachers Eligibility Test (TET) which enables them to work as teachers in primary and upper primary schools. The government also conducts Common Entrance Test (CET) for actual recruitment of teachers. Only the candidates who are successful in TET can appear for CET. There are very few secondary and higher secondary schools that are run by local self-government. The recruitment procedure and conditions of service and emoluments and perks are as prescribed by the government from time to time.

Nagaland

In Nagaland, the Department of School Education sends requisition to the Nagaland Public Service Commission (NPSC) for direct recruitment to the post of Post-Graduate Teacher from among candidates having Master's Degree with B.Ed in the respective discipline or who are professionals. The department also makes ad hoc and contractual appointment as stop-gap arrangement and mostly the services of such appointees are regularised by the government provided they fulfil the criteria for regularisation. Thirty percent of the posts of Post-Graduate Teachers are reserved for in-service graduate teachers, having the requisite qualification of master's degree with B.Ed and who have put in a minimum of seven years of continuous regular service as graduate teachers. In the case of graduate teachers, the department rarely sends requisition to the NPSC, except in a few cases. As such, the graduate teachers and primary teachers in the State are recruited through departmental examination. All other appointments of teachers, such as teachers under SSA, RMSA and

Hindi Teachers etc., are carried out through examinations conducted by the department.

Uttarakhand

In Uttarakhand, recruitment and selection of teachers at the elementary level takes place through Uttarakhand Teacher Eligibility Test (UTET-1). Teachers qualifying UTET-1 undergo induction training, known as D.El.Ed. (Diploma in Elementary Education), in order to make them aware of teaching skills at the primary level. They are placed through promotion of Primary School Assistant Teachers. Teachers at secondary level are selected through common entrance test after qualifying TET-2 (eligibility for teaching in elementary level). Selection of lecturers to teach at senior secondary level is done either through promotion of secondary teachers or direct recruitment through Public Service Commission. Promotion is based on vacancies in each subject as well as seniority list.

Uttar Pradesh

In Uttar Pradesh, Assistant Teachers of primary schools under Basic Shiksha Parishad are selected by BSA, according to the manual 1981 with upto date modification of basic school teacher service. The prescribed qualifications of those to be appointed as teachers are that they should have graduation degree with two-year BTC training/special BTC/Urdu BTC training, and should have passed Teachers Eligibility Test (TET) organised by the Central or State Government. After the introduction of Right to Education Act, 2009, teachers are being appointed on a large scale so that the objective of qualitative education can be achieved by making teachers available in all the schools, as per the prescribed norms.

Tamil Nadu

In Tamil Nadu, Teachers Recruitment Board recruits teachers of various categories through appropriate mode of selection. It is the nodal agency for conducting Tamil Nadu Teacher Eligibility Test (TET) to appoint Secondary Grade Teachers and B.T. Assistants. For all subjects and languages for Higher Secondary Schools, Post-Graduate Teachers are recruited through two different modes: (i) By direct recruitment (50%) through TRB and (ii) by way of promotion (50%) of eligible, senior B.T. Assistants. The B.T. Assistants in high schools and higher secondary schools are either directly recruited through TRB or by means of promotion from eligible Secondary Grade Assistants and Special Teachers. The B.T. Assistants in middle schools, on the other hand, are recruited from the following four options:

- Direct Recruitment by Teachers Recruitment Board
- Promotion from the post of primary school headmasters
- Promotion from the post of secondary grade assistants
- Promotion from the post of special teachers

Of the above four modes of selection, 50 per cent is reserved for direct recruitment, while the other 50 per cent is reserved for recruitment on promotion. The appointing authority for the post of Post Graduate Assistants in higher secondary schools is the Joint Director of School Education. Likewise, the appointing authority for the post of School Assistants (B.T. Assistant) in the high and higher secondary schools is the Joint Director (Personnel). For all other posts pertaining to elementary education, the appointing authority is the Director of Elementary Education.

Assam

In Assam, the teachers of lower primary (LP), upper primary (UP), high school and subject teachers are recruited by conducting TET centrally at the State level for the respective levels. Presently, the required qualification to be a teacher in lower primary school is higher secondary pass, with 50 per cent marks, and D.El.Ed. or graduate, irrespective of marks, with D.El.Ed. For upper primary teacher, the required minimum qualification is graduation with D.El.Ed./ B.Ed. or its equivalent degree from a recognised university. Presently, teacher of all categories for secondary schools have to qualify the TET examination, conducted by the TET Empowered Committee constituted by the Government. The School Teacher Selection Committee conducts interviews of the TET qualified candidates and prepares a panel of selected teachers and forwards the same through the Inspector of Schools to the District Approval Committee for approval. The district-level list is approved by the District Approval Committee and is submitted to the Director of Secondary Education. The list is finalised and published by Director of Secondary Education and, finally, the appointment letters are issued.

The teachers in the schools, under the Social Welfare Department, are recruited by the Social Welfare Department. The norms prescribed by NCTE. D.EL.Ed. or B.Ed. are not mandatory to become teachers in these schools. Instead, the course/training under Rehabilitation Council of India (RCI) for special schools are essential. The teachers of these schools need to take Continuing Rehabilitation Education (CRE) training of RCI from time to time and have to acquire 100 points within five years, failing which the teacher's registration is liable to be cancelled by RCI. The teachers of Guwahati Municipal Corporation (GMC) schools are recruited by GMC, as per the existing Rules of the Government for elementary and secondary schools, through public advertisement.

Sikkim

Recruitment and selection of teachers in Sikkim is done through written test and interview conducted by Sikkim Public Service Commission (SPSC), as per NCTE norms. For the post of post-graduate teachers and language teachers, in view of insufficient trained manpower, the required qualification is relaxed and the teachers appointed with the rider that they have to complete B.Ed and D.El.Ed, as the case may be, within five years from the date of appointment and till then they would not be given annual increments. For rest of the posts, one must be trained like B.Ed and D.El.Ed and also have to pass Teacher's Eligibility Test, before one can apply for the post of graduate and primary teachers.

Goa

Teachers of higher secondary schools in **Goa** are designated as Post-Graduate Teachers or Teachers Grade-I. Fifty per cent of the posts are filled through direct recruitment and the remaining by promotion, failing which the posts are filled by direct recruitment. The entire selection process of Teachers Grade-I, by direct recruitment, is done by GPSC. The candidate has to obtain post-graduate degree from a recognised university with bachelor's degree in teaching/education or equivalent from a recognised university and have knowledge of Konkani to be eligible to apply for the post of higher secondary teacher. In case of appointment by promotion, the candidate needs to have minimum three years of regular service as a primary school Headmaster/Headmistress/ Assistant Teacher/ Junior Instructor besides possessing all the qualifications prescribed for direct recruitment to the post. The Departmental Promotion Committee (DPC) for promotion to the post of Teacher Grade-I consists of three members, viz. the Director of Education as Chairperson of DPC, DDE of the Education Zone and the Principal of Government Multi-purpose Higher Secondary school.

The teachers in Government high schools are designated as Assistant Teachers (trained graduate teachers). Fifty percent of the posts are filled by promotion, failing which by direct recruitment, and the remaining 50 per cent exclusively by direct recruitment. The prescribed qualifications for the post of Assistant Teacher are Bachelor's degree or equivalent from a recognised university in the stream concerned i.e. Arts, Science or Commerce and Bachelor's degree in teaching/education or equivalent from a recognised university with proficiency in English and knowledge of Konkani. For direct recruitment, the posts of Assistant Teachers are advertised in local newspapers and candidates are also called from the regional employment exchange. The selection of candidate is done by group C Departmental Selection Committee. Generally, candidates are selected, based on their performance at the interview.

With regard to the posts of Government primary school teacher, 10 per cent are filled by promotion failing which by direct recruitment and 90 per cent by direct recruitment. The candidates, having the required qualifications, are called from the regional employment exchange and also the posts are advertised in local newspapers. Selection of candidates is done by the Group 'C' Departmental Selection Committee. The prescribed qualifications for the post of Government primary school teachers are higher secondary school certificate, two-year diploma in education, and knowledge of Konkani. The Government pre-primary school teachers, with five years of regular service in that grade and possessing all the qualifications prescribed for direct recruitment, are eligible for promotion as Government primary school teacher.

Gujarat

For the recruitment and selection of elementary level teachers, the State government in Gujarat has constituted a state-level committee called Gujarat State Primary Teacher Selection Committee for the recruitment of teachers (Vidyasahayak). The teacher recruitment committee is headed by the Director of Primary Education with Deputy Secretary (Primary Education) and Director, GCERT. Deputy Director of Primary Education is the Member Secretary of this committee. This committee publishes an advertisement for the recruitment of teachers. Applications are invited online on the dedicated website of the recruitment committee. The candidate has to pass TET exam, conducted by the State Examination Board, before applying for the post of teacher. The state-level committee prepares a merit list by scrutinising the applications received. Candidates can choose their work district as per their merit. Selection committee provides a merit list of selected candidates to the DPEO concerned. DPEO is the Member-Secretary of District-level Selection Committee, which is headed by the chairman of District Education Committee with District Education Officer (Secondary) and Principal DIET as the members. As per the merit list, this Committee calls the candidate to choose their school and appoints them as per their choice. This Committee appoints the teacher in the school run by District Panchayat Education Committee. For Municipality and Municipal Corporation schools, there is a Committee headed by the Chairman of Education Committee, with DEO and Principal DIET as members and A.O. as Member Secretary. The recruited teachers are called Vidhyasahayak, who have to work for five years on a fixed pay of Rs. 10000 per month. The Vidhyasahayak is considered as regular teacher and gets the Pay scale on completion of five years' service.

The recruitment of secondary school teachers in grant-in-aid schools is carried out by the office of commissioner of schools. The qualified candidates are required to appear and pass the TAT examination conducted by the State Examination Board. The merit is calculated in two parts viz. the result of TAT and educational qualifications. The weightage of TAT result and educational qualifications is 70-30 per cent respectively. The candidates are required to apply online on the dedicated website of the education department. The Management Information System calculates the merits and prepares the category-wise merit list. The merit list of candidates is provided to the respective districts by the State-level Committee. The choice is given to the candidates to select the district in which they want to work. Thereafter, they are given choicc to select the school. Finally, the DEO allots the candidate to the school. The teachers in government schools as well as the aided schools are also recruited by the government. These recruited teachers are called Shikshan Sahayak who have to work for five years on a fixed pay. This Shikshan Sahayak is considered as a regular teacher and gets the Payscale on completion of five' years service.

Himachal Pradesh

To look at the required minimum qualification in Himachal Pradesh, a candidate, with a two-year JBT diploma from the District Institute of Education and Training (DIET)/ from some recognised institutions, is eligible to be appointed as JBT Teacher. But before his appointment, he/ she is required to qualify in the Teacher Eligibility Test (TET) meant for the JBT Teachers, and, on the basis of TET merit, he/she is selected as JBT teacher and posted in the district concerned, as per requirement of the Deputy Director of Elementary Education. Similarly, a graduate candidate, after qualifying in the one-year B.Ed. training from a recognised institute and passing the Teacher Eligibility Test (TET) meant for the TGTs, is eligible to be appointed as TGT. The selection of a TGT is done by the Subordinate Services Selection Board at Hamirpur or, for filling up the Departmental Quota on seniority basis, the selection is done by the Director of Elementary Education. But, for the appointment of TGT, the candidate must have the one year B. Ed. degree from a recognised University and must also have qualified in the TET. The appointment of school lecturer is done through the Subordinate Services Selection Board, Hamirpur. A candidate having a Master's degree in the respective subject from a recognised university and a one-year B. Ed. Degree from a recognised institute is eligible to appear in the competitive exams, conducted by the Subordinate Services Selection Board, Hamirpur, for the post of Lecturer (School Cadre).

Kerala

In Kerala, the recruitment of teachers of Government primary, upper primary, high school and higher secondary schools is done through the Kerala Public Service Commission (KPSC). In accordance with the number of vacancies for teachers, KPSC calls for applications from eligible candidates, as per the required qualifications, and Teacher Eligibility Test (TET) pass students. The process of recruitment involves calling of applicant candidates for a written test by KPSC, after scrutiny of their applications to determine their eligibility. After the written test, the KPSC prepares a list of candidates, who have qualified for the interview. The interview board is constituted by a member or Chairman from KPSC, a subject expert and the deputy director of the district concerned. KPSC selects the candidates, as per the number of vacancies in the State, on the basis of the merit, list is prepared. The KPSC issues advice memo to the selected eligible candidates and gives the list to the concerned deputy director of education of the district. On being furnished the list of selected candidates, the deputy director appoints the teachers. The stipulated educational qualifications for being a teacher of secondary school is a degree in the subject concerned alongwith a B.Ed degree.

Haryana

The norms for recruitment of elementary and secondary school teachers are fixed by the State government from time to time and the selection is made by Haryana Staff Selection Board. The selection of teachers for government schools is done through the Haryana Public Service Commission / Subordinate Services Selection Board, Haryana. Private managements have their own recruitment system, subject to governmental regulation. Selections are made through a duly constituted committee. One member of the selection committee is required to be an experienced educationist. Selections are made by the department on the basis of pre-determined criteria. This is done to avoid delay in recruitment. There is also a provision for age relaxation in case of scheduled castes, backward castes, ex-servicemen, differently-abled persons and women (widow, legally separated, divorcee and deserted by husbands).

Senior Secondary Level: Teachers at the senior secondary level are known as the school lecturers in the State. HPSC/SSB recruits school lecturers in the school to teach students of Classes 9 -12. Normally, the selection to the post of school lecturer in different subjects is done by

Haryana Staff Selection Commission. H.T.E.T is compulsory for the appointment of school lecturer. In the year 2012, candidates, with four years' teaching experience, were made eligible to apply for the post of school lecturer, subject to the condition that they had to pass H.T.E.T within four years of joining. Transfer of these lecturers is controlled by the School Education Department.

Secondary Level: Prior to 2003, Masters in secondary school were recruited on regular basis. The recruitments were conducted by the Subordinate Staff Selection Commission, Haryana on being appraised the vacancy position by the Directorate of Elementary Education. Engagement of teachers as Guest teachers, on temporary basis, in different Government High and Sr. Sec. Schools of the State was introduced in 2005. The Head of school was authorised to appoint teachers on contractual basis.

Elementary level: Teachers for elementary (on regular basis) are selected by the Staff Selection Commission, Haryana and are appointed by the District Elementary Education Officer of the district concerned. Elementary teachers were appointed in the State in 2008 and 2011. Approximately 3600 teachers were appointed in 2008 and 8700 teachers in 2011.

Appointment of Part-time Teachers/Contractual Teachers: The part-time teachers are appointed on period basis. These appointments were made purely on the basis of local requirements. They were called Guest teachers and the Head of Institute was empowered to make appointments of Guest teachers from the same village or locality. These appointments were banned by the government in November 2007. After that, from 2009, Guest teachers were converted into contractual teachers and their remuneration revised from time to time.

Readjustment of Contractual Teachers: In case a regular teacher, by transfer or posting or by promotion, joins against a contractual or guest teacher's post in school, the affected guest/contractual teacher is readjusted in a vacant and required post by the Director on the recommendation of DEO or DEEO of the district concerned. In case there is no vacancy in the district, the candidate may be adjusted in some other district on the recommendation of the DEO/ DEEO concerned.

Posting and Transfer

In the case of initial posting and transfer of school teachers, generally all the States have fixed a minimum period of posting for teachers after which a teacher can be transferred. For example, in Assam, a candidate needs to complete three years, while in Goa, one needs to complete five years of compulsory service in a particular place of posting. States having hill regions, like Manipur and Mizoram, ensure compulsory service of Hill and Valley as a prerequisite for getting next transfer. Inter-district transfers are not generally preferred. However, in Goa, inter-district transfers are done: a) only if a vacancy exists in the district and the same is recorded by the Director of Education in writing and approved by the government; or b) to remote areas in another district with the condition that those who have transferred inter-district will have no right to seek another transfer for a period of five years. Similarly, in Uttar Pradesh, in the case of inter-district transfer, seniority benefits are not given to the candidates in the next posting. States like UP also have separate rural and urban cadre of teachers. Kerala, Karnataka and Gujarat have started online transfers to bring more transparency into the system. The detailed description of posting and transfer norms in different States are discussed hereunder.

In the case of lecturers of Higher Secondary Schools and graduate teachers of Higher Secondary/ High/ Junior High Schools in **Manipur**, a teacher is liable to serve in the schools anywhere in the State of Manipur. Normally, a teacher shall serve from three to six years at a place of posting. The period of one term of posting at one place in the hills shall be three years, and the intervening period between two terms of posting in the hill areas should not be less than six years. As far as their transfers are concerned, no transfers shall be effected before the person concerned has completed three years in a school in the hills and five years in a school in the valley, unless there are compelling reasons to do so, such as ill-health, old-age, handicapped due to accident, etc. A teacher who has put in 30 years of service may not necessarily serve three years in the hill areas. However, such teacher shall serve normally for three years at any place of posting other than the hill areas and shall also be transferable at three year intervals.

In the case of Ad-hoc/Substitute Lecturers/Teachers appointed against short/regular vacancies, they shall not be transferred from their present schools to another school. Normally, lecturers/ teachers on the verge of their retirement from service on superannuation i.e. lecturers/teacher having only three years or less service before retirement should not be transferred to another school, subject to the proviso that if their present posting is more than 3 km from their home, they should be given the option of posting in other schools nearer their homes. The National Awardee teachers shall be posted at the schools of their choice. In the case of lecturers/teachers who are physically handicapped /disabled, they shall be posted in schools nearest to their homes.

In **Odisha**, in the case of transfer of the secondary teachers within the districts (intra-district), the District Education Officer is the authority. The district-level transfer committee finalises the transfer of secondary teachers. Ultimately, the Collector of the district is the final approval authority for the transfers. For inter-district transfers of secondary teachers in the State, a committee is constituted, headed by the Director, Secondary Education and Director, RMSA. Additional Secretary of S & ME Department and senior-most Joint Director (School Education) are the members of the committee. The Commissioner-cum-Secretary, S and ME Department is the Appellate Authority to dispose of the grievances/ petitions related to the transfer committee at State level.

For the transfer of elementary teachers/Zila Parishad Teachers/ Shiksha Sahayaks/Gana Shikshakas in government primary and upper primary schools, the government has constituted the transfer committee at the district level under the chairmanship of the District Magistrate. The committee decides the transfer of all categories of elementary teachers within the district. While transferring the teachers, the transfer committee should consult the M.P./M.L.As of the district. The transfer policy primarily considers the rationalisation of all categories of elementary teachers to comply with the provisions of the RTE Act, pupil-teacher ratio at primary and upper primary level. As reported by the DEOs, the BEOs are directed to invite applications from teachers for transfer. Thereafter, the BEO, after consultations with the local people's representatives, submits the proposals to the DEO. The DEO places all the proposals before the district-level Transfer Committee which is convened by the Collector as the Chairman of the district-level Transfer Committee. The district-level Transfer Committee finalises the list of teachers to be transferred from one school to another within that revenue district.

In **Arunachal Pradesh,** the norms for posting and transfer of teachers were prescribed vide executive orders issued by the Secretary (Education), Government of Arunachal Pradesh and the Director of Public Instruction. Further, the norms for posting and transfers are now provided in the Arunachal Pradesh Education Rules-2010. The policy of posting and transfer was formulated with a view to restricting inter-district transfers of all categories of teachers and ensuring qualitative improvement of teaching and effective supervision of schools. In exceptional circumstances, on compassionate grounds, inter-district transfer of teacher is considered. Teachers appointed under SSA are normally posted to remote area schools where vacancy exists and are not transferred, save in exceptional circumstances. Transfer of teachers within the district is effected by a committee under the chairmanship of the Deputy Commissioner, whereas inter-district transfers are made by a committee under the chairmanship or with the approval of the Secretary (Education).

The normal tenure of service of teachers, for effective transfer to hard, middle and soft belts (areas) of the State are two, three and five years respectively, taking into account the communication difficulties and harsh topographical and geographical conditions in the State. For transfer and posting, there is no provision of consideration for APST teachers. However, due consideration is given to women and differently-abled teachers and they are posted in well connected schools. During the survey, it was revealed that transfer and posting policy of the education department is comprehensive and takes into account all vital issues in this context. Private and government-aided schools follow their own policies of transfer and posting. The transfer policy/norms, as per the Arunachal Pradesh Education Rules-2010, are fixed for teachers in a cycle of two, three and five years in hard, middle and easy belts.

In **Mizoram**, the State Government has divided the schools into four categories—A, B, C and D, depending on their location, based on easy accessibility by road communication and remoteness and distance from the State and district headquarters.[1] These categories are taken into consideration for posting and transfer of teachers. In case of posting of the teachers, the State ensures that no teacher shall be deployed in a school in excess of the sanctioned strength. From time to time, the government fixes a minimum tenure in a post, on completion of which a teacher is liable to be transferred. A different minimum tenure may be fixed depending on the category/ grade (A, B, C, D) of the school. As per the transfer policy, a teacher posted in a school of 'any Category' may be considered for transfer to a school of other categories on completion of a minimum tenure and subject to availability of a vacant post. For example, a teacher posted in a school of 'C' category may be considered for transfer to a school of 'A' or 'B' category on his own application or to a school of 'D' category,. according to the requirement as decided by the appropriate authority, after the teacher has completed his minimum tenure in his present school. In the case of a married female teacher with family, she may be considered for exemption from such transfer even after completion of the minimum tenure, except on her own volition. On the commencement

1. All schools within the limit of Aizawl and Lunglei may be graded as 'A Category' with a minimum tenure of six years.
   Schools in District Headquarters other than Aizawl and Lunglei, towns and villages along NH 54 may be graded as 'B Category' with a minimum tenure of 5 years.
   Schools in villages connected by all-weather truckable roads may be graded as 'C Category' with a minimum tenure of 4 years.
   Schools in villages not mentioned above in clause (a), (b) and (c) of Sub-Rule (1) may be graded as 'D Category' with a minimum tenure of 3 years.

of these rules, the minimum tenure or otherwise shall be made effective from the date of posting of teacher in his/her existing category of school. In a cycle of 18 years from the date of commencement of these Rules, a teacher may be required to serve at least one stint of minimum tenure at a school located in D category.

In transfer and posting of teachers a) for inter-district deployment, the Director of School Education, b) for inter-sub-division deployment of elementary school teachers, the District Education Officer, c) intra-district deployment of secondary school teachers, the District Education Officer, d) intra-sub-division deployment of elementary school teachers, the Sub-Divisional Education Officer shall be the appropriate authorities. Any application for transfer must be submitted by a teacher himself/herself though proper channel only. The officers concerned shall scrutinise the application with reference to the teacher's service particulars and category under which the transfer application has been made. In the Annual Confidential Reports of Teachers, the fact that they have completed their minimum tenure in D and C categories of schools shall be specially mentioned.

In **Haryana**, a transfer policy has been formulated for government teachers by the education department. Posting and transfer of secondary teacher is done by Director Secondary Education, Haryana. For elementary teachers at primary and upper primary school level, transfers are done by Director, Elementary education only. Teachers of primary level are of district cadre and they are transferred within the district. If they wish to be transferred out of the district, they have to lose their seniority. On joining service, the first posting of a teacher is in a rural area for at least five years. In special cases, such as for widows, divorcee women, unmarried women, couple case, deserted women, chronic disease patients, differently-abled, ex-servicemen, there is a provision for relaxation in the policy.

All transfers are done under relevant rules and regulations of the government. There are different ways for transfer. Some are as under:

- Through application, which can be offline or online;
- Mutual arrangement between teachers;
- On administrative grounds, such as complaints against the employee; and
- Transfer in public interest.

In the case of the first appointment, counselling procedure is adopted by the department for allotment of place of posting. Few categories such as widows, divorcee women, unmarried women, couples, deserted women, chronic disease patients, differently-abled, ex-servicemen are considered preferential categories. First posting is made in rural areas for five years. In special cases, one can be appointed in urban area only on the basis of relaxation in policy by the State Chief Minister. On promotion at each level from JBT/ Masters/School Lecturer/ Headmaster and Principal, one has to serve in rural area for a minimum period of three years. Relaxation of policies is also allowed in the case of transfers and promotions.

Karnataka is one of the few States which is in the forefront of the country in using technology. It has been applying its technological prowess even in the spheres of administration and personnel management. Primary and secondary teachers and also head masters are all posted to the places of work directly through online counselling during their first appointment and promotions. The transfers of all school teachers are done through online counselling every year during the months of April-May. All the transfers are based on the request of the teacher concerned. Eligible teachers, who apply for transfer through counselling, are considered for transfer to available vacant posts only. The number of such request transfers is restricted to 3-5 per cent of the working strength of the cadre concerned, giving due consideration to the number of years of service in rural /urban areas, spouses in defence service, widow cases, severe medical cases, cases of physical disability, office bearers of approved associations etc.

In **Andhra Pradesh,** the transfers of teachers in schools under Mandal Praja Parishads, Zila Praja Parishads and the State government are regulated. All the applications are then organised according to category (SGT/SA (Maths)/SA (Social Studies) etc.,). The applicant teacher, with highest entitlement points, is placed first in the list and others in descending order as per their respective entitlement points. The list of qualified applicant teachers is displayed on the notice board of Zila Parishad/ Mandal Parishad/ DEO office, as the case may be, as per the schedule communicated by the DSE or State government, along with an indication of the dates for counselling and issue of related orders.

The applicant teachers are then called in person, as per a pre-drawn programme by the competent committee to choose any of the vacant posts available at that time. Immediately pursuant to the choice of posts by the applicant, the committee, through its convenor, issues a transfer order to the applicant teacher, and delete that vacancy from the list of vacant posts. This exercise is continued till all the applicants have been posted, as per time frame/schedule communicated by the DSE.

As per Rule 3 of the Andhra Pradesh Panchayat Raj and Government Teachers (Regulation of Transfer) Rules, 1999, all inter-district transfers in respect of Panchayat Raj teachers are made by the State government, in consultation with the Chief Executive Officer (CEO) concerned, and no transfers are allowed unless the applicant completes two years of service in the respective section. Other than the transfers effected according to the schedule communicated by the D.S.E/State Government, there are no transfers of teachers during the academic year. However, there are certain exceptions such as: (a) in the event of disciplinary action; (b) consequent upon promotion (c) consequent upon the readjustment of surplus posts, if any; and (d) inter-district transfers in which the DEOs and CEOs concerned of both the ZPs agree, under orders of the State government.

The **Nagaland** government has not framed any proper norms or policies for the transfer of teachers as of now. There are no established norms for transfers and postings, but, as a convention, as far as possible, teachers are posted within their own district. Many employees do not like to serve in interior areas or remote places due to communication issues and lack of basic amenities. Therefore, appropriate policy could be put in place to make it compulsory for teachers/ administrator to serve in interior areas for a particular period of time.

As per the survey data in **Uttar Pradesh**, teachers of lecturer grade are posted by the Additional Director of Education (Secondary). High School teachers are posted by Director of Education (Secondary). Teachers of L.T. Grade are appointed by Regional Joint Director of Education on receipt of the recommendation given by the commission through Director of Education. Teachers of lecturer grade are transferred within U.P. by Additional Director of Education after the prescribed period, while teachers of L.T. grade work under the administrative control of Joint Director of Education.

The State government has the power to transfer any government teacher. Teachers appointed in Parishadiya Schools have their district-level cadre; hence, these teachers cannot be transferred to other districts without their consent or request while they may be transferred within the district by the Basic Shiksha Adhikari (BSA), in accordance with the transfer policy of the government. No teacher is transferred during the session without the permission of Secretary, Basic Shiksha Parishad. As per the new scheme of selection of teachers working under the Basic Shiksha Parishad, teachers are also posted in districts different from their home district. In such circumstances, keeping in view the demand of teachers and their convenience, the government has been according permission for their inter-district transfers from time to time.There is, however, a provision for keeping these transferred teachers in new district in the junior-most posts. A committee, constituted at the district level for the transfer of teachers, deals with the procedures of transfers. It may be noted that schools working under U.P. Basic Shiksha Parishad have their separate cadres in the Urban and Rural areas. Generally, there is no provision for transfer of a teacher from rural to urban area. As far as possible, teachers of government primary and upper primary schools are mostly posted in their own districts.

In **Uttarakhand,** transfer policy is effected each year at the end of the session, normally in the months of May and June. Under the transfer policy, rationalisation of teachers is done in accordance with the number of students (enrolment). The request transfers are effected on the basis of the topological categorisation of the schools and *Sugam, Durgam, Ati durgam* places are allocated to the applicant teachers on the basis of their Quality Marks. Transfers at each level are done on the basis of academic performance of teachers, enrolment at primary and elementary levels and on the basis of length of service in the categorised schools.

The **Tamil Nadu** State government is sensitive to the need of appointing teachers in proportion to the Teacher-Pupil ratio norms laid down by the RTE Act, 2009. At the time of issuing posting orders, the native place and native districts of the selected candidates are taken into consideration. Further, the individuals are intimated about certain requirements to be complied with, such as the last date for joining, production of agreement form, medical fitness certificate etc., failing which the offer of appointment will stand cancelled. Transfer of teaching and non-teaching personnel is another challenging task performed every year. Frequent transfers are avoided in view of functioning of schools. General transfer is carried out once a year, usually between May and June, as per the guidelines issued by the State government for transfers, in a transparent manner. Certain criteria, viz. complaints and personal requests, employment of spouse, physical handicap, health issues etc., are taken into account while effecting transfers.

In **Assam**, during the posting of elementary school teachers, due consideration is always given to SC/ST candidates and those belonging to the backward classes of the State, as per norms. Elementary school teachers in the government schools are transferred on grounds which include: a) the conversion of single-teacher schools into double teacher schools; b) the maintenance of pupil-teacher ratio at 30:1; c) mutual transfer; d) transfer on public complaints; and transfer in the interest of the public. The teachers of the schools, run by the District councils of the two Hill Districts, are transferred in accordance with the suggestions of the members of the council, as and when the need arises. There are, as yet, no specific norms for the transfer of secondary school teachers. Sometimes, teachers are transferred to accommodate the number of trained teachers in certain specific subjects. The work of posting and transfer of teachers is done both at district and state levels. A teacher may be posted anywhere in the State and transferred with the prior approval of the

Government. For secondary teachers of government secondary and higher secondary schools, the DSE is the competent authority for transfer and posting of teachers, with prior approval of the Government. The same policy is adopted in case of provincialised secondary, higher secondary and junior colleges, including the Autonomous District Councils and BTAD areas in Assam. One of the important norms for transfer of government officials and teachers is that they should normally be transferred only on completion of three years of service in a particular place of posting. The transfer of teachers working in the schools under the Social Welfare Department and Municipal Administration is limited to their schools only.

In the Government set-up in **Goa**, the newly selected/recruited teaches are posted usually in schools located in rural areas against posts falling vacant due to transfer or retirement. The candidates belonging to SC and ST communities are given preference while posting. Women teachers are given preference for posting in urban areas. Further, women teachers are usually posted in schools in localities having good transport and accommodation facilities. Teachers selected for working in government schools need to give an undertaking to serve in rural areas for at least five years. The government has framed transfer policy for government teachers of all levels. The policy is also applicable to the headmasters of government middle school, primary schools and ADEIs. Under this policy, a teacher from any school is liable for transfer in normal circumstances after five years of service in the school where he/she is posted. Generally, transfers are made at least two to three weeks before the commencement of the new academic year. However, if the situation warrants, due to unforeseen circumstances, transfers are made during any period in the academic year in public interest. As soon as a teacher becomes due for transfer, the same is effected during summer vacation before the schools reopen or in the month of July /August after the enrolment figures are scrutinised. In exceptional circumstances, transfer is effected at the time of the Diwali vacation. Mutual transfer applications are allowed, keeping in mind the contingencies.

In normal circumstances, transfer is effected only within the district of the State. The transfer can be on grounds such as a) Teachers with hardship cases b) Teachers who have served more than 10 years in remote areas c) Extra teachers in the district d) Serious disciplinary issues or for any other administrative reasons. The other administrative reasons include complaint in writing from the MLA of the area, complaints from Zila Panchayat or Panchayat through resolutions and adverse report of the ADEI. Inter-district transfer is generally not encouraged but is considered in the following circumstances: a) In case a vacancy exists in the district and the same is recorded by the Director of Education in writing and approved by the Government b) To remote areas in another District with the condition that the inter-district transferee will not have any right to seek another transfer for a period of five years. But, in the case of surplus teachers, the general policy does not apply. They are transferred and posted as and when the need arises and at any time of the year. Also, in case of death or long leave, transfer is done any time as per the need. Besides these guidelines, as far as transfer of high school and higher secondary teachers are concerned, the list of teachers is prepared as per the subjects of teaching and teachers are transferred taking into account the subjects taught by the teacher.

In **Gujarat**, in primary schools, run by Government/District Panchyat, the transfer policy for teachers is very transparent. The online transfer system is being implemented across the State. The advertisement is published in the newspapers seeking applications for transfer from interested teachers. The interested candidates are required to apply online within the stipulated time period. The online forms, filled up by the teachers, are validated by the Taluka Panchayat Eduction Officer (TPEO) and confirmed by the DPEO. The MIS generates the transfer order on the basis of seniority. In the case of the secondary teachers, DEO can transfer the teacher working in government schools, as per the requirement of the school or as applied by the teacher in the schools of the district. District transfers are carried out by the office of Commissioner of Schools. The post of teacher in a Grant-in-Aid school is non-transferable.

Since the year 2010, the **Kerala** government has adopted online transfer policy. The move by the Department of General Education aims at infusing the element of transparency in the entire process. Vacancy details of government schools are entered online well in advance, enabling the applicant to view the vacancies even before the application form for transfer and posting is set off. Through the online process, teachers can get transferred to convenient schools of their choice. The Director of Public Instruction (DPI) releases a detailed Circular every year at the end of the academic year. On the basis of the Circular, the Deputy Director of Education concerned uploads the vacancies in the L.P, U.P, H.S categories of teachers and issues appropriate instructions therein to teachers seeking transfer. According to the directive of Deputy Director of Education, teachers select 10 schools in the order of priority. In the case of L.P., U.P., H.S. school teachers, the Assistant Educational Officers concerned and, in the case of H.S. teachers, the District Educational Officers (D.E.O) uploads the applications of the teachers and sends to the Deputy Director of Education. On completion of verification, the Deputy Directors of Education concerned upload the revenue district-wise transfer application and forwarded to the Director of Public Instruction. The Director of Public Instruction scrutinises the seniority of the teachers vis-a-vis the priorities opted for by them in terms of their choice of schools for posting. After the scrutiny by the Director of Public Instruction, the verified applications are returned to all Deputy Directors concerned to clarify and remove the anomalies, if any. The Deputy Directors of Education, in turn, issue the necessary instructions to the applicants to recheck their options, review and, if required, rectify their seniority and revisit their options for any final changes. On completion of final verification and scrutiny, the Deputy Directors again upload the application to Director of Public Instruction. On receipt of the rectified applications from all Deputy Directors, the Director of Public Instruction locks the online facility before finally issuing the transfer orders online in April.

Promotion and Career Advancement

Promotional aspects are considered very important for career development of the employees in any department. The State reports indicate that all States have developed their own norms and rules for promoting their teachers at different levels. Generally, the first promotional provision to teachers is provided on their completion of a certain level of regular and satisfactory services. To cite an example, in **Odisha**, at the elementary level, a Shiksha Sahayak and junior lecturer, after completion of three and eight years respectively of continuous satisfactory engagement/ service, become eligible for promotion. Similarly, in Manipur, all teachers on completion of eight years in the entry grade are upgraded to senior grade and again upgraded to selection grade on completion of eight years in the senior grade, while in Goa, teachers need to complete 12 years of regular service to become eligible for promotion. In the case of contractual positions, the regularisation of the posts also happens after completion of a certain number of years. Contract teachers in Odisha are regularised with regular scale of pay attached to their respective posts after completion of six years.

While the filling up of vacant posts is done by direct recruitment, many States have a provision for filling up the vacancies through promotion from lower grades. To mention the case of Manipur, one-third (1/3) of the vacancies of lecturers of higher secondary schools are filled by promotion from among eligible graduate teachers. Similarly, in Uttarakhand, elementary level teachers are promoted to TGT or LT grade, while senior secondary teachers and lecturers are promoted to headmasters of high schools in the ratio of 55:45.

As a part of the promotion policy, teachers become eligible for administrative posts, such as in Nagaland where high and higher secondary school teachers could be promoted to the post of Director and the senior-most Directors to the post of Principal Director. In some cases, where teachers are unable to get promoted due to unavailability of posts, the State has made provision for providing incremental benefits to those eligible for promotion. To mention an example, in Uttar Pradesh eligible teachers and principals, who are unable to get promotion, are provided first promotion scale after satisfactory completion of regular service of 10 years, second promotion scale after 16 years and third promotion scale after 26 years. Despite all these provisions, it is essential that to be eligible for the promotions, the employee concerned must have the prescribed qualifications as laid down by the government. There are some States like Nagaland and Assam where the primary teachers remain at a disadvantage as they have no chance for promotion, they retire as primary teachers. The detailed description of promotion and career advancement policy is given below.

Some States provide ample opportunities for career advancement and professional growth to their teachers. To cite the case of Karnataka, teachers in the education department have been provided opportunities for career advancement and professional growth. At the primary level, teachers are deputed for higher studies like B.A., B.Sc., B.Ed, and B.P.Ed as regular students with salary. Both primary and secondary teachers are permitted to pursue their higher studies in any recognised university through distance mode. In case of Assam, the secondary teachers are deputed to CTEs/ NCTE recognised B.Ed. colleges for obtaining B.Ed. degree. Government also issues No Objection Certificate (NOC) to teachers who wish to pursue higher studies like M.Ed./ Ph.D. etc. for enhancement of their professional qualifications.

In **Manipur**, Recruitment Rules for all teaching posts have the provision for promotion from among eligible teachers in the feeder posts. Fifty per cent of the vacancies of Graduate Teachers are filled through promotion on merit-cum-seniority basis from among eligible primary teachers having minimum five years of regular service. All vacancies of Assistant Headmasters of High Schools and Headmasters of Junior High Schools are filled by promotion on merit-cum-seniority basis from among eligible graduate teachers having three years of regular service. Assistant Headmasters of High Schools and Headmaster of Junior High Schools are, in turn, promoted to the posts of Headmaster of High Schools as per eligibility criteria and vacancy position. One-third (1/3) of the vacancies of lecturers of higher secondary schools are filled on promotion from among eligible graduate teachers. All vacancies of Vice-Principals of Higher Secondary Schools are filled on promotion from among lecturers having eight years of regular service in the grade. Vice-Principals, having five years of regular service in the grade, are likewise eligible for promotion to the posts of Principals of Higher Secondary Schools. On failure to get sufficient number of Vice-Principals, lecturers, with 10 years' regular service, are also eligible for promotion to the post of Principals of Higher Secondary Schools.

In **Odisha, t**he Higher Education Department formulated policy for career advancement and promotion of the junior lecturers to the next higher posts. A junior lecturer, after completion of eight years of service with satisfactory performance, shall be eligible for promotion to the grade of lecturer on Junior Class-I (State Scale). The School and Mass Education Department framed the career advancement policy for contract teachers of the government high schools. Under this policy, the contract teachers are regularised, with regular scale of pay attached to their respective posts after completion of six years of continuous and satisfactory service. Further, they are eligible for all service benefits as admissible to regular employees under the State government with effect from the date of such regularisation.

The teachers, after regularisation in high schools, are treated as Junior Subordinate Education Services (Jr. SES) cadre and their gradation is maintained by Director, Secondary Education as a State Cadre post. In the Jr. SES Cadre, assistant teachers are promoted to headmaster (Sr. SES), on the basis of seniority and Confidential Character Roll (CCR), and posted as headmasters in Type – B high schools. When they are promoted to Sr. SES cadre, they belong to the State Cadre. The Director, Secondary Education does the posting of those headmasters. The Director, Secondary Education is also the competent authority to transfer those headmasters. The Senior SES Cadre teachers are promoted to the next higher rank i.e. OES-II (School Branch) and posted as either BEO or headmaster of Type-A High Schools.

At elementary level, with the Career Advancement Policy of Shiksha Sahayaks (SS) / junior teachers, on completion of three years of continuous satisfactory engagement as SS, s/he is eligible for appointment as junior teacher by Zila Parisad on contractual basis, with consolidated monthly remuneration as decided by Government from time to time. S/he must also have ensured 90 per cent attendance of children in respective schools in all classes and it must be certified by the authority concerned. The SS must have reduced the drop-out rate to below 10 per cent and they must have performed all other duties assigned to them successfully

In **Mizoram**, all teachers, on completion of eight years in the entry grade, are upgraded to senior grade and again upgraded to selection grade on completion of eight years in the senior grade. The teachers in primary schools (trained undergraduate), on graduation, are allowed the benefit of trained graduate scale of pay. Promotion avenue for a teacher in the school is very limited where senior-most teachers of a particular school are not always appointed to the post of headmaster in the same school since promotion for school headmaster is decided on State-level seniority. State-level senior teachers are given offer of appointment to the post of headmaster, depending on the number of available vacancies.

In **Karnataka**, there is ample scope for teachers at various levels for promotion to higher posts in the department, depending upon their qualifications and experience. A primary teacher can be promoted as a headmaster of a primary school and a high school teacher. Similarly, a high school teacher can be a high school headmaster and lecturer in a Pre-University College. These promotions and other employees' promotions in the education department are given, after taking into account the seniority and qualification, Roster system and also the vacancy position in the department. All the employees will get an additional increment in the form of monetary benefit for a period of 10 years as time-bound increment. Similarly, those employees, who have completed 15 years of service in the same cadre, will get another additional increment as automatic promotion. Those who have completed 20 and 25 years of service are also eligible to get additional increments in the form of monetary benefits. In Karnataka, at the primary level, teachers are deputed for higher studies like B.A., B.Sc., B.Ed, and B.P.Ed as regular students with salary. Both primary and secondary teachers are permitted to pursue their higher studies in any recognised University through distance-mode.

In **Maharashtra**, the promotion of teachers in Z.P. primary schools is given on the basis of experience and qualifications. The process of promotions from assistant teacher lead to Graduate Teacher – Headmaster – Cluster Head– Extension Officer – Class II – Class I which is serially followed. The secondary teachers, working in Z.P. high schools, are promoted to class-II cadre taking into consideration state-level seniority. Teachers, provided they fulfil the norms and conditions laid down, are eligible to appear for the examinations conducted by State Public Service Commission for direct recruitment as Gazetted Officers in Maharashtra Educational Service Group-A (Education Officer or equivalent) or Group-B (Deputy Education Officer or equivalent).

Promotions in **Nagaland** are made through the Departmental Promotion Committee on the basis of seniority in service, as per standing rules and regulations. A separate list of seniority is maintained for the post-graduate teachers and graduate teachers. They could be promoted to Director and the senior-most Director to Principal Director. The promotional chances of primary teachers are not very bright as they retire as primary teachers, while Hindi and physical education teachers can be promoted to the rank of Deputy Director.

In **Uttar Pradesh,** opportunities for promotion are provided for each category of personnel. Generally, an employee gets two promotions in the Education Department. Seniority of the employee and his service records are the major norms for promotion. Those teachers and principals who do not get promotion due to unavailability of posts, are provided first promotion scale after completion of satisfactory regular service of 10 years, second promotion scale after 16 years and third promotion scale after 26 years. Despite all these provisions, it is essential that for all the promotions, the employee must have prescribed qualifications, as laid down by the government. For the teachers of secondary level, there is the provision for promotion of L.T. grade teachers to the posts of lecturers and headmasters (Gazetted Scale). Similarly lecturers get promotions to the posts of headmasters (Gazetted) and then become principals. Among the Parishadiya Teachers working under the Basic Shiksha Parishad, the assistant teachers of primary schools get promotion as headmaster in primary school or assistant teacher in upper primary school, while head teachers of primary schools or assistant teachers of upper primary schools are promoted to the posts of headmasters of upper primary schools after their promotion.

In **Uttarakhand,** promotion of teachers at the primary level is made on the basis of vacancies available at subsequent higher levels, such as the post of head teachers of the primary school and assistant teachers in upper primary schools. Vacancies for promotion at upper primary level are calculated on the enrolment and vacancies per subject such as social studies, science/mathematics language. Elementary level teachers are also promoted to TGT or LT grade in the ratio of 25 per cent and 50 per cent consequently. Senior secondary teachers and lectures are promoted to headmasters of high schools in the ratio of 55:45. These headmasters are further promoted to principals subsequently. Teachers also impart their services on deputation basis in educational projects such as SSA, RMSA and Mid-Day Meal etc.

In **Tamil Nadu**, the teachers working in the lower category can qualify and become eligible for promotion to 50 per cent of the vacant posts (reserved for promotees) in the categories of graduate and post-graduate teachers. A panel of qualified and eligible teachers is prepared and promotion to the higher category of teacher's post is offered purely on seniority basis.

In **Assam,** there are no promotional avenues for LP teachers. The posts of headmaster of LP schools are yet to be created. The assistant teachers of ME/MV Schools are promoted to the post of headmaster, as per the seniority list of the DEE, Assam. Similarly, the assistant teachers of high school/ higher secondary schools are promoted to the post of headmaster and principal, as per seniority basis from the DSE, Assam. As per the State notification regarding procedure for promotion to the post of headmaster of M.E./ M.E. Madrassa/ M.V. and senior basic schools, the teachers having less than 10 years of continuous service shall not be considered for promotion. The teachers, who have passed at least matric/ HSLC, or have at least intermediate or its equivalent qualification or above and have successfully undergone necessary training, as may be prescribed by the department, shall only be considered for promotion.

However, the teachers, who have completed minimum 15 years of continuous service but no facilities have been provided to them for the prescribed training, may also be considered for promotion provided there is nothing adverse against them. A panel of selected teachers, prepared by the committee, shall remain valid for one year from the date of selection. Hindi/ Classical/ Language teachers, having required minimum educational qualification and training, may also be considered for promotion. Government of Assam has introduced Assured Career Progression Scheme (ACPS) for all the State government employees, including teachers, from 2011, with the two provisions – i) ACPS involves two financial upgradations for the employees of the Government of Assam ii) The benefit under the scheme is given twice in their service period – the first one, after completion of 10 years, and the second one, after completion of 24 years of service if they do not get one regular promotion within the first 10 years of regular service and two regular promotions within 24 years of regular service. The ACPS is designed only to provide upgradation. It is neither a regular promotion nor requires creation of new post(s) for this purpose. Government of Assam provides ample opportunities to teachers for career advancement. The secondary teachers are deputed in CTEs/ NCTE recognised B.Ed. Colleges for obtaining B.Ed. degree. Government also provides No Objection Certificate (NOC) to teachers who wish to go for higher studies like M.Ed. Ph.D. etc. for enhancement of their professional qualifications.

In **Goa**, the same guidelines are followed with regard to promotion and career advancement of teachers of both Government and aided schools. All teachers are considered for two promotions in their career, subject to fulfilment of certain requirements. A teacher, after completion of 12 years of regular service in the grade, can be promoted and placed in senior scale provided he/she has attended/participated in in-service programs, conducted by national and State-level institutions/ organisations, for a total of not less than 21 days.

In **Kerala**, teachers, on the basis of their experience, are designated as lower primary school associate (LPSA) in case of lower primary school, upper primary school associate (UPSA) in the case of upper primary school and high school associate (HAS) in the case of high school. On the basis of seniority, they are promoted and appointed as heads of schools. In the case of high school, the senior HSA is appointed as head of the high school, a post that is equal to the Assistant Educational Officer (AEO) Cadre.

Welfare Services for Teachers

It is the general consensus that no amount of educational reforms or progress is possible in the real sense without adequately addressing the reasonable demands of the teachers. Having realised the importance of the welfare of teachers, almost all the States, besides the allowances, leave, medical facilities, teachers guest houses, have started many schemes that extend due benefits to them with care and concern. National and State awards to teachers are among the schemes to acknowledge and honour the teachers. The awardees are mostly given two advance increments in the form of pay alongwith a one-time choice of posting by the State government, besides the benefits. A State like Odisha also gives cash award of Rs. 25000. States like Mizoram and Odisha have established Teacher Welfare Fund to provide assistance to teachers in different kinds of distress situations. Most of the States have the provision of providing a job to family member/son/daughter in case of death of the in-service teacher.

Manipur State provides two advance increments in the form of pay alongwith a one-time choice of posting by the State government to the National Teacher Awardee besides the benefits given by the Union Government. The State Cabinet has recently approved the proposal of the Department of Education(S) for extension of services of the National Teacher Awardees by two years. Likewise, the State Government instituted the State Teachers Award which carries cash prize of Rs. 10,000 with incentives of one –time choice of posting and extension of service by one year, as approved by the State Cabinet recently. The State has also implemented the scheme of *Die-in-harness* wherein a family member of an employee, who expires during his/her service tenure, is given employment (Class-III/IV) under the Government. On the eve of Teachers' Day, principals/headmasters of schools, which produce toppers in the high school (Class X) and the higher secondary examination (Class XII), are acknowledged and honoured for their contribution and efforts to bring quality education.

In **Odisha**, Teacher's Welfare Fund is maintained under the charge of Director, Secondary Education. This fund is used for welfare of the teachers in case of disability, treatment of fatal diseases and sustenance of the family of the deceased teacher. In case of death, the son/daughter of the teachers is provided employment in the Department of School and Mass Education under Rehabilitation Assistance Scheme. National and State awards to teachers are two main incentives to encourage teachers to excel in their professional areas. A Cash Award of Rs. 25000 is provided to each State awardee teacher. Besides, in order to encourage the noble teachers working in the remote areas of the State, District Award has been instituted from the year 2014 for 314 blocks of the State.

In **Mizoram**, National and State level awards are presented annually to the deserve teachers, based on their academic performances and activities relating to educational developments undertaken by the teachers. Special provision from teachers' welfare fund is made for teachers suffering from chronic illness on their submitting an application or on proper recommendation from competent authorities @ Rs. 5000 per teacher in the State and Rs. 7000 outside the State. Medical expenses for teachers, who are treated on referred cases outside the State in recognised hospitals, are also provided reimbursement, as per State medical and attendance rules. Besides these, the State government provides other facilities in the form of medical reimbursement, HRA 10 per cent of basic pay + GP, DCRG for teachers completing five years qualifying service, and study tours are arranged for selected group of teachers, as well as facility of Teachers' Inn at Aizawl City and Lunglei Town is provided.

In **Karnataka,** all the teachers in the Karnataka government service are entitled to the incentives and allowances applicable to government servants. However, teachers, who are enrolled for the Karnataka State Teachers Benefit Fund, are eligible to get many welfare schemes. Medical assistance to teachers and their dependents is one of the important welfare measures where Medical Assistance, ranging from Rs. 6,000 upto a maximum of Rs. 50,000, is sanctioned to teachers and their dependents for medical treatment, based on the severity of the illness. The State also has a scheme for providing 'Financial Assistance for Family Maintenance to the families of the deceased teachers'. In the event of the death of a teacher while in service and where the family pension is yet to be settled, a financial assistance of Rs. 10,000 is sanctioned to the family of the deceased. An amount of Rs. 5,000 is sanctioned to the families of teachers who die after retirement. Financial assistance, ranging from Rs. 1000 to Rs. 3000, for the higher education of the children of the teachers, merit scholarships in the range of Rs. 2000 to Rs. 6000 to the children securing highest marks in SSLC, PUC, Degree and Post-Graduation examinations.

Conduct of literary and cultural activities for teachers at taluk, district and State levels are some other schemes implemented by the State government for the benefit of teachers. Under the 'Grants for construction of Gurubhavans', a minimum grant of Rs. 12 lakhs upto a maximum of Rs. 30 lakhs is sanctioned for construction of GURUBHAVANS at taluk and district levels. The motive behind this is to provide respectable dormitory facilities to teachers visiting places of historical importance. Meritorious awards are presented to teachers who have rendered meritorious service in their fields. District Awards, Special Awards and Best Science Teacher Awards are given.Under the Teacher's Safety Assistance Scheme, in order to provide compensation to the families of teachers, who become victims of accidents and other natural calamities, the Karnataka State Teachers' Benefit Fund has introduced "Teachers Safety Scheme" from the year 2001-02, with provision for a compensation of Rs. 50, 000 to the family of the deceased teacher.

In **Maharashtra,** the primary, secondary and higher secondary teachers working in the schools run by the local Self Government and the schools run by private management receiving grant-in-aid are eligible to grade pay, perks and other benefits as available to Government servants. It includes pensionary benefits, gratuity, earned leave, leave on medical grounds, reimbursement of medical expenses of family, payment of Travelling and Daily Allowances while on tour for office work, reimbursement of expenses towards education of children, Leave Travel Concessions and other facilities available to Government servants.

In **Nagaland,** government teacher appointed on regular basis avail all facilities, like the other State employees, but private teachers are not covered by any regulations, hence their service benefits are not legally protected. Benefits available to government teachers are leave as per leave rules, medical allowance and reimbursement, government accommodation or 10 per cent of the basic pay as HRA, GPF/GIS/CPF/NPS, gratuity and pension, training facilities, selection grade/MACP on completion of 10 years.

In **Uttar Pradesh** also, the scheme of providing State and National awards to teachers on the basis of their distinguished service and identification of talent is in practice. Under the State award, cash amount, a woollen shawl, medal and certificate are provided to every selected teacher. The National and the State awardees get the benefit of extension of two years in service and one advance increment in pay. The incentive amount of Rs. 25000 is fixed for National award. The awardee teachers are given the benefit of free travel upto 4000 km. by the State Transport Corporation every year. A Teachers' Welfare Corporation has been established that manages money for teacher's medical treatment and other requirements. Provisions for provident fund, pension and other benefits have been made. All the government teachers get gratuity and the facility of journey on leave. During service, in case there is sudden death of any teacher, his ward is provided employment for the sustenance of his family members. In the event of death of any teacher working under the Basic Shiksha Parishad, while earlier their wards were appointed as untrained teachers, but after the introduction of RTE Act 2009, the wards are appointed as class IV employee or junior clerk in case the vacant post is available.

In **Uttarakhand**, GPF Encashment, Medical, Leave Travel Concession, subsidised Home Loan, Vehicle Loan etc. are provided as welfare services to teachers by the School Education Department. Government has made provision for various incentives for the welfare of Teachers such as Subsidised Home Loan scheme, Leave Travel Concession, Medical Leave, Childcare Leave for female teachers, Maternity Leave, extension of the superannuation period and two-year extension of services for awardee teachers etc.

In **Tamil Nadu**, all the regular teachers, teachers of non-government (aided schools) and local body schools are covered under pension scheme. The Contributory Pension Scheme (CPS) has been introduced for the employees appointed on or after 1st April 2003. The Tamil Nadu Special Provident Fund-cum-Gratuity Scheme has been extended to the staff of all aided educational institutions from 1st April 1984. The teachers of aided schools, whether serving or retired and receiving pension, are being provided a medical allowance of Rs. 15 per month, with effect from 1st April 1990. National Teachers Welfare Fund – Medical Aid to Teachers (grant of 75 per cent of medical expenditure or Rs. 50,000, whichever is less), stipend of Rs. 5,000 and Rs. 2,500 under educational assistance to children of teachers, housing facilities are other schemes available for teachers. Teachers, who provide efficient services, are honoured with Dr. Radhakrishnan Award' with a cash prize of Rs. 5,000 each, a silver medal and a Certificate of Appreciation, and National Award which consists of a cash prize of Rs. 25, 000-, a Silver Medal and a Certificate of Appreciation. Youth Welfare and Sports Development Department presents the Chief Minister's Award to two coaches and two physical education teachers with proven excellence in training and producing outstanding sportspersons. Each awardee is presented a cash prize of Rs.one lakh and a citation. Till date, four coaches and three physical education teachers have been recipients of the Chief Minister's Award. With the amount allocated under the National Teacher Welfare Fund, 'Teacher's Home' is being built in Tiruchirappalli for teachers commuting to Chennai and other cities on personal and official engagements.

In **Assam,** as in the case of other employees of the State overnment, the teaching and non-teaching staff of the education department receive the benefits of pension after retirement. They have GPF, GIS, facility of medical reimbursement, LTC, appointment under compassionate grounds. Regarding the new pension scheme of all the employees, including the teachers, the Government of Assam, vide its Notification No. AEE.384/2005/Pt./105 Dated 20th May 2009, clearly states that for the Provincialisation of Assam (Elementary) Education, Provincialization Act, 1974 will be applicable in terms of MOU dated 01-04-1995 as well as OM No. HAD-57/95/316 dated 11-12-1996, the new pension rule will be applicable to the newly appointed employees of Karbi Anglong Autonomous Council if and when Government of Assam introduces new pension rules. The power of appointment of teachers will be exercised by the KAAC. The State government will not bear any additional liability of funds. The trained teachers of the schools under the Social Welfare Department get additional 15 per cent of their basic pay as training allowance for being considered as teachers of special schools.

In **Goa**, there is no difference between the Government and aided school teachers with regard to the benefits and privileges enjoyed by them. The pay scales of the teachers in Goa are at par with that of the teachers of schools under the Central government. The teachers are given a fixed amount as medical allowance every month. Besides, they are allowed re-imbursement of medical expenses incurred on the treatment of certain diseases. In case of housing facilities, in urban areas where government accommodation is available, government school teachers are treated at par with other government servants of the same rank for allocation of government quarters at their place of posting. Teachers and others, who are not provided government accommodation, draw house rent allowance as stipulated by the government from time to time. At present, 20 per cent of the basic pay (Band Pay plus Grade Pay) is given as HRA. Teachers are also eligible to draw house building advance, as per the rules laid down by the Government for the purpose. The facility of housing loan is also available to the teachers of aided schools. Teachers are given travelling allowance every month, as applicable to other Government employees placed in equivalent position and at the rate recommended by Sixth Central Pay Commission. Loan/Advances are given for the purpose of construction of house, purchase of two-wheelers, cars, computers, laptops etc. Interest-free loans are sanctioned for purchase of laptops by teachers. Loans advanced to teachers are recovered in instalments from their salaries. Children's Education Allowance Scheme (upto ? 18,000 per annum per child for two eldest surviving children), Leave Travel Concession (LTC), Casual and Earned Leave, Provident

Fund and Pension Scheme (under new Pension Scheme called PPAN introduced by the Government of India) are other benefits available for teacher welfare.

Grievance Redressal and Litigation Cases

In **Karnataka**, litigation cases in the various courts are looked after by the offices concerned across the State. Legal cell in the office of the Commissioner for Public Instruction monitors, the process, through Court Case Monitoring System which is an online system. Karnataka has a well-established structure for redressal of the employee's grievances. Under the grievance-redressal mechanism, educational administration hierarchy deals with the cases as per their respective jurisdictions. In the case of primary teachers, the headmaster, BEO, DDPI and commissioner perform the role of Redressal Authority at their respective stages of administration. Similarly, in the case of high school teacher, the headmaster, DDPI and commissioner act as the redressal authority at different stages. The department also conducts 'Shikshana Adalat' at block, district and state levels once a year to redress the problems of all its employees. The government has started the KGS (Sakala Programme) under which the services get done within a stipulated time. The Government of Karnataka has implemented the Right to Information Act (RTI) as per the directions of the Central Government. Women's Grievance Cell is also active in the State and takes up issues related to women employees of the department. Grievances can be submitted through proper channel to the authorities concerned for redressal.

More than 5000 cases, related to teachers' issues, are pending in High Court, District/Taluk Court and School Tribunal in **Maharashtra**. These cases generally deal with issues related to pension, transfers, land requisitions, changes in birth date and caste, reinstatement in service, Demand payment of arrears, objections in selection list, recovery sanctions of teachers posts, promotions, seniority list etc. The primary responsibilities of redressal of individual grievances of teachers in schools run by local Self-Government are with the officer in-charge of the Education Department. An appeal against the decision lies with Chief Executive Officer of Zila Parishad send to the Commissioner of the Revenue Division in case of teachers of Zila Parishad and to the Regional Deputy Director of Education in case of teachers of Municipalities and Municipal Corporations. The final appellate authority is Director of Education. The teachers may approach the Court if they are not satisfied with the redressal by the authorities concerned.

As reported by the Directorate of Secondary Education, in **Odisha**, more than 5000 cases are pending in different courts, such as Supreme Court, Odisha High Court, State Administrative Tribunal at Bhubaneswar and Cuttack Bench. These cases pertain to redressal of teachers' grievances and other matters relating to management, recognition of institution etc. Similarly, over 400 cases are pending before different courts relating to DTE and SCERT, Odisha. In recent years, there has been a significant increase in the number of court cases in Department of School and Mass Education and in different directorates. A large number of cases is pending for many years. In order to expedite the cases, the government has established a special cell at Cuttack and one at OAT, Bhubaneswar and posted standing counsels there. The State has a clear and robust grievance redressal system for the teachers and other employees of the education department. As per government order, every officer, from the Commissioner-cum-Secretary to the Block Education Officers, holds grievance day on every Monday. If any teacher/employee does not get justice from his/her immediate authority, s/he can go to the higher authority. Besides, the Chief Minister's cell also hears grievances of the people and employees and sends these to the appropriate department and sections for speedy hearing and disposal.

In **Sikkim**, the Principal/ Vice-Principal is the grievance redressal officer at the school level, while at the district level, it is the district head. It was proposed that a grievance register will be maintained in the schools and offices concerned in the name and address of the petitioner, and the nature and date of the petition are required to be entered in it. This register will also contain a column on the action taken. The register will be monitored by the senior authorities as well as PRIs. Once a grievance has been disposed off, the date and nature of disposal should be communicated to the petitioner. These details are to be made available on notice boards of the schools and office to which they relate and also on their website as far as possible. Data generated by classifying petitions are to be analysed each month for reason and type, so that it becomes a tool for identifying areas that require senior management attention and redesigning of systems. All grievances are to be disposed off within the time limit prescribed by the State government. The PRIs will provide a forum for public hearings so that grievances may be quickly redressed. The State government may designate an alternative grievances redressal authority at the block, district and State levels. The State government may also consider setting up an ombudsman system at the district level, manned by people of proven integrity. Action taken on the complaints received by the principal and district head will be placed before the meetings of the panchayats and the urban local bodies (ULBs) respectively.

Prior to 2004, the primary forum that heard grievances of teachers from government schools in **Tamil Nadu** was the Tamil Nadu Administrative Services Tribunal. However, the tribunal was abolished in 2004. Hence, the High Court is now the first forum and the court of original jurisdiction under Article 226 of the Constitution take up for all grievances of teachers from both government and government-aided schools. This situation has caused strain on the resources of the High Court. As a result, the amount of time lapsed between the filing of a writ petition and the first hearing has become a cause of concern. Another concern raised by the lawyers was that a number of petitions on service-related matters were filed in the High Court because the competent officials of the Education Department were often unwilling to decide on issues in the absence of a court order. For example, there were a number of pension-related grievances with minor technical defects that, according to some lawyers, could have been easily resolved by the District Education Officers but, instead, ended up in the High Court. Despite the High Court being the first dispute resolution forum for most teachers with grievances, in practice, teachers generally exhaust all other remedies before approaching the High Court. The first competent authority that a teacher with a grievance may approach is the Education Officer at the block level, Assistant Elementary Education Officer or AEEO in the case of primary schools and aided schools up to the eighth grade and the headmaster of the respective school in the case of secondary schools. In addition, teachers also tend to seek help from teacher's associations as Tamil Nadu is a State where the teacher's associations are quite active in offering assistance to teachers for resolution of their grievances.

The Tamil Nadu government has also instituted a regular grievance redressal forum at block and district levels, where sessions are held by AEEOs on the first Saturday of each month, at which a grievance is either resolved by the AEEO, by passing relevant orders or the matter is passed on to the District Education Officer, who takes up grievances on a district-wise basis on the second Saturday of every month. The grievances that cannot be resolved at the district level are passed on to the Directorate for further consideration. While these grievance-redressal sessions are a good starting point for improving the efficiency of dealing with teacher-related grievances, they are plagued by certain limitations. First, this grievance redressal mechanism is not applicable to teachers of secondary schools. The only avenue for grievance redressal is to approach the headmaster of the school concerned, failing which they have to file a petition in the High Court. Secondly, even in the case of primary school teachers, only a very limited number of grievances can be addressed at these fora. The officers at the block and district levels cannot resolve issues related to eligibility criteria for appointments or other issues that require an interpretation of the relevant rules. In addition, any challenge to the existing government orders (for example, an order on promotion or pay scale) will have to be made in the High Court. Thus, these grievance redressal sessions end up being able to address only a small percentage of overall grievances related to very straightforward matters such as salary arrears or leave encashment, and they do not replicate the role of a dispute resolution tribunal.

In **Uttarakhand,** the Legal cell of the Directorate of School Education has a total 6124 cases pending of teaching and non-teaching staff. Cases are mostly related to personal matters of functionaries, such as monetary and retirement benefits, promotions, seniority, transfers etc. Some of these cases are filed against the administrative decision taken by higher officials. The State has introduced the counselling system in postings and transfers which can be considered as a grievance redressal mechanism having positive impact on the attitude of functionaries. All information, directions and government orders and list of transfers, postings are uploaded on the education portal of directorate of school education to make the system more transparent. Use of ICT and portal has made a big attitudinal change in teachers.

In so far as the ground level redressal system in **Andhra Pradesh** is concerned, School Management Committee is the first redressal authority for school teachers. A committee, constituted at Mandal Parishad level, with Mandal Parishad Development Officer (MPDO) as the chairman and the Mandal Educational Officer as convener, is the next level for unresolved cases. At district level, a committee, comprising District Collector as Chairman, Superintendent of Police, Chief Executive Officer, Zila Parishad, District Medical and Health Officer, Commissioner or Chief Municipal Officers of local urban body at the district headquarters, Assistant Commissioner Tribal Welfare and District Educational Officer, functions to redress the grievances of the teachers. Any teacher of the school, established, owned or controlled by the State government or the local authority, may submit his/her grievance, in writing, to the convener of the committee. The grievance may also be submitted through education portal maintained by the SSA. The committee may, after such enquiry as it deems fit, will redress the grievance. The convener of the committee will communicate its decision to the teacher.

In **Mizoram**, there have been 26 court cases during the last three years, of which five cases are still pending. The cases are mainly of inter-se seniority and related matters. Complaint Boxes are prominently displayed in all offices of the Director, DEO, SDEO, DPC (SSA and RMSA) and they are opened every week to see whether there are any complaints and grievances. If there are, the same is examined and considered as deemed appropriate at different levels concerned. A telephone number of Deputy Director (Administration) is notified to all schools for any complaints and grievances of teachers and staff.

In so far as **Nagaland** is concerned, there are many cases of litigation pending in the High Court and Supreme Court. Most of the litigations are related to promotions and seniority among officers of the department, Modified Assured Career Progression schemes (MACP), salaries and arrears etc. The principal and vice-principals are the Grievances Redressal officer at the school level and the District Programme Coordinator at the district level. Grievances registers are maintained in all schools and offices in which the name and address of the petitioner, and nature and date of the petition are to be entered. The registers are monitored by the senior authorities. The State government designated an alternative Grievances Redressal Authority at the block, district and State levels. Action taken on the complaint received by the principals and district programme coordinator are placed before the meeting of the SMDC/VEC. However, the grievances of teachers are not effectively redressed in the department. There is no separate cell in the School Education Department to attend to the grievances of teachers.

With regard to **Manipur**, there are around 650 cases of civil nature, pending in the Manipur High Court besides 10-15 cases in the Supreme Court. All these cases are related to service matters of employees of the department. The nature of cases varies such as ad hoc employee related cases and those related to management and recognition of Aided schools, time-scale, recruitment, pension, appointments under Die-in-Harness and Meritorious Sportspersons Scheme, upgradation of posts and grant of Qualification Scale of pay, recruitment related cases, claims for scale of pay of headmaster (Primary School), seniority list for various categories of teaching posts etc. There is no grievance redressal cell, as such, either at the secretariat or at the directorate or district-level offices. However, teachers and other non-teaching staff normally submit their grievances, in written or verbal form, to the head of department through proper channel. The representations on grievances of employees are dealt with at the directorate. The grievances are addressed at the directorate level. The grievances for which redressal requires approval of the government are submitted to the government for necessary action. Redressal of grievances of employees is normally given priority at different levels of the government.

The **Kerala** State has 6,500 litigation cases pending with different courts. These cases are related to appointments, retrenchment, promotion, leave, pension, seniority of teachers and management disputes between the manager and management of the school, teachers, non-teaching staff of government and aided schools. Court cases take a substantial time of teachers and administrators at sub-educational district, district, regional and State levels and, ultimately, the studies of children suffer. It was found that Additional Director of Public Instruction and even Director of Public Instruction had to devote much time in hearing of cases of teachers and management disputes. Sometimes, they have to face contempt of court issues also. In case of any dispute, the first appellate authority for primary and upper primary schools is Assistant Educational Officer. If the matter is not solved, then appeal is made to the District Education Officer. The subsequent authorities in the chain of command respectively are Deputy Director of Education, Director of Public Instruction and Secretary of the General Education Department. When the case is not solved then it goes to the court. Sometimes, the court again refers the case to the General Education Department, which assigns it to the Directorate of Public Instruction. It was observed that senior officers like Additional Director of Public Instruction, remain busy with the hearings of the appellate party for at least three days in the week.

In **Goa**, teaching and administrative/non-teaching staff, as and when aggrieved, file cases in various courts, including State Administrative Tribunal and High Court of Bombay at Goa. Petitions / Appeals are filed relating to the cases of appointments, transfers, promotions, claiming of benefits like senior scale/selection grade, extension in service, seniority, termination of service and against major penalties imposed. They also file petitions before the State Human Rights Commissions and Women's Commission relating to harassment by school management. Out of 20 cases pending before different Courts, 13 (65%) relate to seniority list alone. Six out of 20 cases relate to termination from service. Most of the cases are filed by teaching staff only.

There is no separate cell at the directorate or zonal or taluka level to redress the grievances of the teachers or the administrative/non-teaching staff or the public. In addition, no official at any of the three levels (directorate, zonal and taluka) is specifically designated to redress the grievances of teachers. However, grievances are redressed at all three levels, following certain unwritten procedures. At the taluka level, grievances are redressed by the ADEIs. In case the ADEI is unable to do so or if the matter is beyond his powers, then the ADEI may forward/refer the matter to the DDE of the concerned zone, giving the details of the case. The Director of Education is the next authority if the petitioner remains unsatisfied. The Director, in turn, refers the matter to the DDE/ADE/Section concerned to study the case and report the matter to him.

Based on the report, the Director takes the appropriate decision/action. If needed, the Director invites the party for a personal hearing.

The situation in respect of court cases is very grim in **Uttar Pradesh** as it hampers the smooth functioning of school and studies of children in the class. Most of the time of DEOs is spent in attending the cases. Sometimes, education officers have to face contempt of court proceedings. Details of litigation cases related to education department, with category, are given in the Table 4.1.

Table 4.1: Litigation Cases in Uttar Pradesh

S. No.	*Department*	*Pending Cases with the Courts*	*Disposed*
1.	Basic Education	17973	37089
2.	Secondary Education	21324	34100
3.	Higher Education	6034	11701
	Total	**45331**	**82890**

Source: Third Survey of Educational Administration, Uttar Pradesh.

Role of Teachers' Unions

Teachers' unions are expected to play a significantly positive role in promoting professional standards, upholding professional integrity, enhancing the dignity of teachers and in curbing professional misconduct. These associations/unions are very active. They play an important role in protecting the interests of their respective members. They act as pressure groups to ensure that the government implements the pay scales in time, as and when a Central Pay Commission recommends a new pay structure for teachers. More importantly, the associations/unions work sincerely for quality improvement in education in the State and, towards this end, devote their time for the professional development of their members/ teachers. Some teachers'/headmasters' unions design question papers for use by different schools for their school examinations. Some unions also conduct in-service programmes for professional development of their members. The associations/unions also organise seminars/workshops/ conferences for the benefit of teachers.

As it is common in the other States of India, **Karnataka** also has a number of associations/organisations for the protection of the rights of its members. Teachers of different categories such as primary, secondary, physical education, and head of schools have their unions and associations at block, district and state levels. All associations are formed with the main purpose of providing moral support to the aggrieved employee, when required. They extend moral and legal support to the aggrieved employee whenever he/she approaches it. Some teacher associations, at the block and district levels, go to the support of their respective level officers while organising functions like workshops, seminars and training programmes. Some associations also take part in honouring the retiring or awardee teachers. They also bring to the notice of the Pay Commission the demands of the employees through their associations.

In **Odisha**, there are many Teachers' Unions that look after the rights and welfare of the teaching community. These unions also make efforts for professional and academic development and optimum use of the talents of the teaching community in achieving the goal of education towards the students' learning in the school. In Odisha, some of the leading teachers' unions are Odisha Secondary Teachers' Association (OSSTA), All Odisha Government School Teachers' Union, Odisha Elementary Trained Graduate Teachers' Association, United Teachers' and Employees Association (UTEA), Government Teachers' & Employees Association (GTEA), Block Grant School Teachers Association (BGSTA).

In **Sikkim**, different teacher unions are active in the areas of salary structures and transfers etc.

In **Tamil Nadu**, Teachers' Service Associations or Unions exist for elementary, secondary, higher secondary, matriculation, SSA, RMSA, Aided School and Municipal teachers. In recent days, associations for the welfare of DEOs and CEOs have also been formed. It is a common accusation that these Unions focus only on teachers' welfare and do not bestow much attention on the students. In other words, teachers and their unions are intent only on advocating and demanding better service conditions, congenial working environment and enhancement of remuneration. The intense focus on these aspects obscures the core objective of education—the need to enhance learning outcomes.

In **Uttarakhand,** primary and secondary teachers' associations are the biggest among all employee associations on account of the large number of teachers. It comprises approximately 40 per cent strength of the total State-level unions. These unions try to solve the problems of teachers and coordinate with higher level educational administrators. Union leaders are also nominated as the member of counseling committee.

In **Andhra Pradesh**, teachers' unions work at three levels – Mandal, District and State. Mandal unit is elected by the primary members of that particular Mandal. In general body meeting of the Mandal unit of the union, the president and secretary and other executive members of the Mandal unit are elected either by way of election or through unanimous opinion. District-level executive body is formed by direct or indirect election as per the bye-laws of the union. The same procedure is adopted for State unit. The State president and secretaries of recognised unions are provided on-duty facility. They can reside in the State Capital for representing the teachers' problems at the State level. The district president and secretaries of recognised unions have some special casual leaves for representing the teachers' problems at the district level. They are also given some entitled points in counselling for transfers. The unions play a vital role in representing teachers' problems at various levels, conducting educational seminars, submitting recommendations to the Government/Commissions on pay scales, striving for reforms in educational policies, and motivating teachers for quality education. Teachers' representatives are elected in the Upper House of the State – the State Legislative Council. Only the teachers of high school have the right to cast their vote to elect their representative as MLC (Member, Legislative Council). The representative MLCs of teachers raise the issues in the House, on behalf of teachers, and the issues related to school education and teachers are brought to the notice of the government, through discussions in the House, and decisions are taken.

All **Nagaland** School Teachers Association (ANSTA), Nagaland Government Higher Secondary School Employees Association (NGHSSEA) are the main teachers' unions under the School Education Department. All Nagaland Private School Association (ANPSA) represents the private schools in the State. Mostly, the unions work for promotion of effective teaching process while preserving the principles of State education policy and play a supportive and constructive role towards the department in implementing educational policies. They also make efforts to create better understanding and coordination among their bonafide members.

In **Goa**, the State also has the presence of a large number of registered teachers' unions. There are separate teachers' unions of primary school teachers, secondary school teachers and higher secondary teachers. There are Association of Headmasters of Secondary schools and also a Principals' Forum formed by the Principals of Higher Secondary Schools. There are many taluka level associations of teachers. The government and aided schools teachers have also formed separate associations/unions. Besides, there are subject-wise associations of higher secondary school teachers. The subject-specific associations, formed by the higher secondary school teachers of different subjects, conduct academic programmes for the benefit of their teachers. These associations collect funds from the members and utilise the same to organise professional development programs. They also sometimes make representations to different agencies/ organisations like SCERT, Directorate of Education and Goa Board of Secondary and Higher Secondary Education (GBSHSE) to sanction funds/organise need-based in-service programmes for teachers.

Major Issues and Challenges

It has been found that the departments of education intend to give at least two to three promotions to an employee in his/her career. However, it was observed that most teachers do not get even one promotion throughout their career. This may be because of the large number of teachers present at the primary and secondary school levels. Promotions are not done and even sometimes out-of-turn promotions are done. These promotions should be given, after taking into account the seniority and qualification, roster system and the vacancy position in the department. The arrangement should be made to facilitate teachers with timely promotions.

Another issue, related to promotion of teachers, is "Merit-based Promotion". At present, only service seniority is taken into account for promotional purposes. However, it is reflected in the State reports that merit should also be recognised and rewarded at all stages. Therefore, it is suggested that the department should conduct an examination or a screening test for all the eligible employees due for promotion and only the meritorious of those should be promoted alongwith seniority-based promotion to the next designation. This will definitely bring in the quality consciousness among the employees. If this is strictly introduced, it will definitely make all the employees of the department keep themselves well aware of the recent developments in the field of education and keep themselves fit for the demands of the job.

In the context of transfers of teachers, it has been observed that teachers generally prefer urban area transfers. When teachers get any metropolitan town school, they do not vacate their places at all. The other rural teachers are, in the process, deprived of the opportunity of coming to urban areas. In line with Kerala, Karnataka and Gujarat, other States should also be encouraged to start "online transfer" to bring about transparency in their transfer policy and it will also help to reduce other anomalies and delays in the transfer procedure. In a State like Nagaland, there are no established norms for transfer and posting, but conventionally, teachers are posted within their own district as far as possible. In the absence of transfer norms, interior areas have shortage of teachers as many employees do not like to serve in interior areas or remote places due to communication problems and lack of basic amenities. Similarly, in Assam, there are no specific norms for the transfer of secondary school teachers. Therefore, it is strongly recommended to frame proper policy and rules for transfers as are in practice in other North East States like Manipur and Sikkim.

Regarding the litigation cases and grievances, most of the States reported that large number of litigations cases are pending in different courts and tribunals. These cases waste department resources and adversely impact teaching time as well. Efforts should be made to bring transparency in the system and the grievance-redressal system should be made stronger to expedite the redressal process. In States like Goa and Manipur, there is no separate grievance redressal cell at the secretariat, directorate, zonal, taluka/district level to deal with such cases. As no official at any of these levels is specifically designated to redress the grievances of teachers, unwritten procedures are followed to solve the cases. It results in further delays and lack of transparency. Therefore, it is suggested that proper redressal cell, with clear rules, should be set up at school, block, district and directorate level.

5
Inspection and Supervision

Inspection and supervision across the world has been considered a process of assessing the quality and performance of schools by internal and external evaluations. In recent years, many countries have re-examined their inspection and supervision systems in the face of demands that schools should be made more transparently accountable for the outcomes and standards that they achieve and, therefore, responsible for continuously assessing their performance. School supervision, since its origin in the early nineteenth century in Britain, has been the main instrument for facilitating and ensuring quality improvement in schools. It started in the form of systems' tool for monitoring by Her Majesty's Inspectors of Schools that was based on top-to-down authority and control model, as well as on rules, regulations, acts and codes. In the new system now available, the Office of Standard in Education (Ofsted) and the Office of Her Majesty's Chief Inspector in Wales ensure that schools are inspected by teams put together by private companies, which focus upon the parents' opinions about the school.

In India, the system of inspection came in vogue with the recommendations of Wood's Despatch of 1854, mainly for regulating the private-aided and missionary schools. Studies have shown that the purpose was to control and maintain the education system rather than improve and develop it. Its nature was authoritative, autocratic and unscientific. In the beginning of the 20th Century, the concept of inspection was modified and came to be known as supervision. In 1930s, however, the emphasis was shifted from rigid inspection to democratic supervision, and, subsequently, on human relations and cooperative efforts of supervisors and teachers to bring about improvement in all activities of the school. Research studies have shown that teachers and other educational functionaries perceived term-inspection and supervision differently. Inspection has been referred to the system-based assessment and evaluation of schools, of teachers and students. It could be seen as a review and reporting on a school's work by the local authority, personnel, inspectors and advisors who play an important role in reviewing performance, with varying combinations of audit and support. Supervision, however, is more concerned with the assessment of academic aspects of an institution. However, school supervision, since its origin in the early nineteenth century, has been the main instrument of quality improvement in schools. Tremendous changes have taken place over the years in its organisation, functions and objectives.

The old concept of inspection was, to some extent, rigid. It primarily emphasised on the enforcement of control and authority over the school with less professional guidance to teachers. Secondary Education Commission (1952-53) describes the contemporary condition of those days and remarked that inspections were perfunctory, that the time spent by the inspector at any particular place was insufficient and that the greater part of his time was taken up with routine administration. The Kothari Commission (1964-1966) recommended separating administrative and academic inspection, so that the inspecting officer could pay more attention to supervision of the class. The Commission laid emphasis on dynamic inspection system for accelerating educational reforms while analysing the reason for weaknesses of programme of supervision. It stated that a sympathetic and imaginative system of supervision and administration can initiate and accelerate educational reform. On the other hand, a rigid, autocratic approach stifles all experimentation and creativity and makes any educational reconstruction almost impossible.

Thus, the concept of supervision was added with inspection to improve the quality of performance of the students by monitoring the instructional processes and by evaluating the teaching-learning processes. Thus, by guiding teachers to improve teaching, the inspectors and supervisors help in maintaining as well as upgrading performance standards.

Present System of Inspection and Supervision in India

Third Educational Administrative Survey on school education, conducted by NIEPA across the States in India, shows that all the States have elaborate arrangements for inspection and supervision of educational institutions from primary to secondary stages, in the country. In India, primary responsibility of inspection and supervision lies with the Ministry of Education. Specific guidelines are prescribed, and from time to time, the instructions are issued for inspection and supervision. In each State, an organisational set-up for inspection and supervision exists at different levels of education to ensure smooth and effective functioning. These are at the regional/division, district, sub-division, block and circle levels. However, the set-up differs from State to State. In Assam, inspectorate is set up at all the six levels i.e. regional, district, sub-division, block, circle and cluster levels. In Kerala, Tamil Nadu and Uttar Pradesh, the inspectorates have been set up at three levels—regional, district and block. In Tamil Nadu, the inspection code specifies the principles and procedures to be followed by inspecting officers. The department gives guidelines and fixes target for inspection and supervision from primary to higher secondary level. The inspection and supervision responsibilities are delegated to specific officers. The Chief Education Officers (CEOs) are responsible for higher secondary schools, DEOs for high schools, District and Assistant Elementary Education Officers (AEEOs) for primary and upper primary. For inspection and supervision of SSA and RMSA, in some States, the parallel structure of education has been abolished after implementation of RTE 2009.

A total 11 States, viz. Assam, Bihar, Kerala, Uttarakhand, Odisha, Madhya Pradesh, Mizoram, West Bengal, Uttar Pradesh, Maharashtra and Andhra Pradesh have given responsibility to their respective regional offices for efficient supervision. District and block have emerged as important units for performing the function of inspection and supervision as all the States have district-level administrative set-up. The variations are found at the sub-division and block levels.

In Andhra Pradesh (Dy. Education Officer), Maharashtra (Dy. Education Officer), West Bengal (Additional District Inspectors), Uttarakhand (Block Education Officers and District Education Officers), Nagaland and Assam (Deputy Inspectors) officials at sub-district/division level have been assigned duties. District and block-level officials play an important role, as all the States have made block-level arrangements for effective inspection and supervision in primary and upper primary schools. Assam, Nagaland, Mizoram, West Bengal and Maharashtra have sub/assistant inspectors or Circle Education Officers to perform inspection duty. Assam, Bihar, Uttarakhand, Odisha, M.P., Mizoram, West Bengal, Tamil Nadu and Maharashtra have made the cluster as the lowest unit for the task of inspection and supervision. In States like Bihar, Odisha, M.P. and Mizoram, the Cluster Resource Center (CRC) under SSA, perform this task while States like Uttarakhand and Maharashtra have Deputy Education Officer and Cluster Heads for inspection duties. The Table 5.1 indicates the administrative machinery for inspection and supervision.

Parameters of School Assessment

In most of the States, listed broadly, the following points are to be inspected during visits to educational institutions by the designated personnel at various levels:

Table 5.1: Organisational Set-up of Inspectorate in Different States

	State	Region/ Division	District	Sub-division	Block	Circle	Cluster
1.	Assam	Inspectors of Schools (IS)	DEEO (5% schools within district)	Deputy Inspector of Schools (10% schools in sub-division)	BEEO (20% elementary schools in block)	Sub-Inspector of Schools (200 elementary schools in sub- division)	AIS (200 elementary schools in sub- division)
2.	Bihar	RDDE	DEO		BEO		BRCC/CRCC
3.	Kerala	DDE	DEO		AEO		
4.	Uttarakhand	CEO	DEO/DPO	DC	BEO/BRP		Deputy Education Officer
5.	Odisha	Regional Directors	DEO (all HS in academic year and test the work of subordinate inspecting officers by visiting 10 high schools/UP and primary schools every month		BEO (all high schools, UP and Sanskrit)		CRCC
6.	Nagaland		DEO	DDEO (assist DEO in Supervision)	SDEO (all UP schools of his/ her jurisdiction of sub-division and primary schools)	SIS/IEO (5-10 primary schools and assist DEO in supervision)	
7.	Madhya Pradesh	OIC (district allotted by commissioner)	DEO/Assist. Commissioners of tribal welfare/DIET Principal, Lecturer/CTE Principal Lecturer)		BEO		CRCC & BRCC
8.	Mizoram	Officers of Directorate (whole State)	DEO		SDEO (All elementary schools)	CEO (Elementary schools – 15 days in a month)	CRCC-under SSA to visit al schools; BRCC & subject- specific expert under RMSA

(*Contd.*)

Table 5.1: (*Cond.*)

	State	*Region/ Division*	*District*	*Sub-division*	*Block*	*Circle*	*Cluster*
9.	Tamil Nadu		CEO (Hr. Sec.), DEO (HS), Deputy Inspectors (secondary schools)		AEEO		CRCC
10.	West Bengal	Dy. Directors (posted in Bikas Bhawan)	District Inspectors of schools (Primary and Secondary) DPO (SSA)	Sub/Additional District Inspectors of Schools (PE)		Assistant Inspectors of Schools (PE)	CRCC (Shiksha Bandhu)
11.	Uttar Pradesh	Regional Deputy Director	District Inspector of Schools/ Basic Shiksha Adhikari		Block Education Officer		
12.	Maharashtra	Deputy Director	District Education Officer (Primary and Secondary)	Dy. Education Officer	BEO (Primary and Secondary)	Extension Officer	Cluster Head (Kendra Pramukh)
13.	Arunachal Pradesh		Dy. Director of School Education (for Sec and Hr. sec)		BEO (for EE)		
14.	Andhra Pradesh	Regional Director	District Education Officer	Dy. Education Officer	Mandal Education Officer		
15.	Gujarat		DPEO, DEO		Taluka Primary Education Officer, Assistant Education Inspector, Education Inspector		
16.	Himachal Pradesh		Deputy Director of Education. for Middle and Deputy Director of Higher Education for High Schools		BEEO (Primary only)		
17.	Chhattisgarh		DEO		BEO		
18.	Karnataka				BEO (High Schools/ Secondary)	Sub- Block Educational Supervisors (primary)	

Note: In some States, percentage and number of schools to be supervised have been mentioned.
Source: Third All India Survey of Educational Administration.

- Suitability of the building.
- The sanitary condition.
- The arrangement and organisation of classes.
- The furniture and apparatus.
- Accounts and registers.
- Order and discipline.
- The relation between the teachers and the taught and, specially, the method of teaching, examination of pupils (when on inspection) means the process of testing.
- Whether the teaching and discipline are such as to exert a right influence on the manners, the conduct and the character of the pupil.
- To see whether faults detected by failure in examination have been or are being corrected.
- To see how far subordinate officers have made suitable reports
- Attendance of teachers and students.
- Readiness of teachers covering preparation of lesson plans, teaching diary, teaching learning material.
- CCE and classroom observation.
- Observation of drinking water facility and toilet facility.
- Quality and quantity of Mid-Day Meal.
- Library and science labs.
- Implementation of innovation programmes.
- Facilities for CWSN student education.
- Functioning of SDMC, SMC, PTA.
- Verification of Student Welfare Schemes.

In Odisha, under its monitoring progmamme, 'SAMIKSHA', monitoring is done through prescribed formats. The monitoring formats contain 51 indicators under six heads. Besides, one part of the format on the demonstration in class and school observation is to be filled by the CRCC, while another part of the format is to be filled by the DEOs, DPCs, BEOs, ABEOs, BRCCs. The six components include: a) teacher and student attendance, a) school environment, curricular component, other curricular components, school community linkages, school management, Mid-Day Meal, c) Demo-Class and School Observation, d) Observation of inspecting personnel e) Progress made after previous monitoring visit.

In Madhya Pradesh, a school monitoring tool called "Shala Darpan" has been developed with UNICEF support as a follow-up measure of the headmasters' training in the State. The Shala Darpan has been designed as a reflexive index of the status of elementary schools on key indicators/ standards which a school is supposed to maintain. Information in Shala Darpan is furnished by the headmasters on monthly basis.

In Maharashtra, inspection and supervision is done with the help of a five-point scale ranging from A to E. The academic efficiency is decided on the basis of this gradation tool, which was developed by Maharashtra State Council of Educational Research and Training in 2012 for primary schools as 'Mazi Samruddha Shala' (My Enriched School). The schools, with grades E, D, C, which show low performance in the inspection and supervision, are under the vigilance of supervising authority.

Norms of Inspection and Supervision

There are specific norms and guidelines, prescribed by the Education Department of every State, regarding the number of institutions to be visited in an academic year by the inspecting officers posted at different levels of the administrative hierarchy.

All the education officers at district level have to inspect and monitor every school at least once in a year. The inspection is followed by visits for a specific purpose, as prescribed by the department. For all the levels of education i.e. for the senior secondary, secondary, primary and upper primary levels, these norms are different in different States. At the district level, major responsibility of inspection and supervision lies with DEOs, with the support of block or sub-district level inspecting officers. The inspection report is to be reviewed by the immediate superior officer who instructs the institution inspected to rectify defects, if any, pointed out in the inspection report. The follow-up action is verified in the course of the next inspection by which the completion report is needed to be sent by the heads of institutions to the reporting and reviewing officers. Tables 5.2 and 5.3 present norms of inspection and supervision in elementary and secondary schools respectively

All the States have developed very detailed norms for inspection and supervision of schools. In case of elementary level supervision, regional level officials are not assigned duty for inspecting the schools. In this regard, Uttarakhand and Uttar Pradesh remain exceptions where Chief Education Officer (10 schools per month) and Assistant Director perform the inspection duty. In Assam, Mizoram, Uttarakhand, Odisha, Maharashtra, West Bengal, Uttar Pradesh and Andhra Pradesh, district level officials have been given the responsibility to visit a fixed number of schools for inspection duties.

The number of schools to be visited varies from State to State. Most of the States recommend their inspecting officers to visit and inspect all schools in their jurisdiction every year. For example, in Uttar Pradesh, all the Nyaya Panchayat Resource Centres (NPRC) and schools of their area are definitely supervised at least twice in a month. In the context of subject experts, their single visit should be planned in such a way that all

Table 5.2: Norms of Inspection and Supervision (Elementary Level)

State	*RDDE/Chief Education Officer (Schools)*	*DEO/DPO/DIs./ DEEO*	*ADEO/ADIs/ SDEO*	*BEO/AIS/ Additional Block Resource officers/ABEO/SIS*	*Deputy Education Officer/ ABEO/SIS*	*BRCC/CRCC (Shiksha Bandhu)*
(1)	(2)	(3)	(4)	(5)	(6)	(7)
Assam		5% of the schools within district	10% schools in sub-division	BEEOs 20% of the elementary schools	Sub-Inspector of schools/ Assistant of schools 200 schools	
Bihar		Not fixed		Once in a year all the schools		
Kerala		All schools under jurisdiction		All schools under jurisdiction		
Odisha		10	Not spelt out, only to assist DEO	All UPS, Primary schools, Sanskrit schools and madarsas		10 schools per month
Nagaland			All UP schools (Depends upon no. of schools in sub-Division)	All Primary schools	5-10 primary schools	
Mizoram		8 days in a month	8 days in a month	20 days in a month		
Madhya Pradesh				30 schools (20 PS & 10 UPS)		2 times each schools in month, competency evaluation of minimum 5 students in a month

(Contd.)

Table 5.2: (*Cond.*)

(1)	(2)	(3)	(4)	(5)	(6)	(7)
Tamil Nadu			AEEO visit to each school every year, 12-15 Elementary schools every month and few nursery schools.	Every month 5 schools and super-vise visit 18		Weekly and monthly meetings are fixed for BRCCs and CRCCs
Uttarakhand	10 schools per month	10 schools per month		15 schools per month	15 schools per month	
Maharashtra		10 tribal/ 20 non-tribal areas		All primary and UP schools, 40 schools in tribal and non-tribal areas		10-20 schools, run by local bodies, and private schools
West Bengal			20 primary schools in month		10 primary schools in a month	All the primary schools in the circle
Uttar Pradesh	AD (Basic Edu) create one team for inspecting 5 schools in each tehsil.	20 school in a month by District Coordinator		One time inspection in every school in block, at least 20 school inspections in a month		
Arunachal Pradesh				1. Posted at head quarters: minimum 5 schools in a month 2. posted at block: minimum 10 schools		

(*Contd.*)

Table 5.2: (*Cond.*)

(1)	(2)	(3)	(4)	(5)	(6)	(7)
Andhra Pradesh		20 schools by DEO in a month (Juris-diction not clear)		20 schools by MEO in a month		
Gujarat				Assistant Education Inspector (Bit Nirik-shak) have to ins-pect 50-60 schools		
Himachal Pradesh	Each inspecting officer is required to inspect at least 8 schools per month i.e. 3 regular and 5 surprise inspections.					
Karnataka				15 school visits, 8 school inspections		
Sikkim	12 schools annually from all categories jurisdiction, at least 30% should be from remote area. Joint Directors: 12 schools annually from all categories jurisdiction, of which at least 30% should be from remote area. District Joint Directors: 36 schools annually from all categories jurisdiction, of which 30% from remote area. District deputy Directors: All schools from all categories jurisdiction, of which 30% from remote area. Deputy Director attached to HQ: 12 schools annually from all categories jurisdiction of which at least 30% should be from remote area. District Asstt. Director: All school from all categories under their jurisdiction.					

Source: Third All India Survey of Educational Administration.

Nyaya Panchayats of the block are supervised and given support every month. Similarly, in Kerala, all the arrangements for inspection of schools are based on the principle that each school be inspected thoroughly at least once in each school year and visited at other times as frequently as circumstances permit.

In some States, the norms are laid down in terms of the number of schools to be inspected by inspecting officers every year/month, such as 10 schools per month in Uttarakhand and 10 tribal/ 20 non-tribal areas in Maharashtra, while some other States prescribed the norms of inspection in percentage of schools to be inspected in a year. In Assam, the State report mentions that DEOs are supposed to cover 5 per cent of district schools per month. Similarly, in Arunachal Pradesh, each inspecting officer is supposed to inspect 25 per cent of the total schools under his/her jurisdiction in one quarter, with coverage of all primary and upper primary schools during the session. As per the Primary Education Act in Gujarat, 10 per cent of the total number of primary schools in the district needs to be inspected by education inspectors of DEOs office.

In some States, norms are also set in terms of the minimum number of days spent in the field, like the Block Resource Academic Persons are expected to spend at least 18 days on the field wherein they visit at least three schools in a day or three classrooms in a day. In Mizoram, according to the norms issued by the Directorate of School Education, every District Education Officer and Sub-divisional Education Officer have to spend eight days in a month for inspection of schools. Circle Education Officer (CEO) has to spend 15 days in a month for inspection of Elementary Schools.

The Table 5.3 indicates the norms for inspection and supervision in secondary and higher secondary schools in the States.

In comparison to elementary school inspection, regional level officers are given the responsibility to monitor the specific number of high schools and higher secondary schools in some States such as Uttarakhand, Maharashtra, Bihar and Kerala. Regional Education Officer in Uttarakhand inspects 10 secondary and higher secondary schools in a month. Deputy Director in Kerala inspects five secondary and higher secondary schools in a month. Without specifying the number of school to be inspected, the Maharashtra report mentions that the Deputy Director of Education conducts supervision and inspection in primary and secondary schools with the help of Education officers and his subordinates. Although norms vary from State to State in terms of inspection duty of district education officers, however, the district remains a very important unit of administration in the context of monitoring, supervision and inspection of schools. In comparison to elementary schools, in secondary and higher secondary schools, the sub-district and block-level officials have mostly the assisting role. These officials assist the regional and district-level officials in their task.

Table 5.3: Norms for Inspection and Supervision (Secondary and Higher Secondary School)

State	*Chief Education Officer/ RDDE/IS*	*DEO/DIS, Dy. EO/DEEO/ CEO, DEO (HS), Inspectors (Secondary schools)*	*ADIs/ SDEOs*	*BEOs/ABEOs/AIs/Circle Education Officer*	*Deputy Education Officer/ Extn. Officer/High schools head master/Sis*
(1)	(2)	(3)	(4)	(5)	(6)
Assam	Inspector of Schools (twice a year)	DEEO (5% of the schools)	DIS & ADIS 10% schools in sub-division		All high school, aided HS
Bihar	Offices of DEOs, 5 offices of subordinate, one primary teachers education college in each district	Once in a year all the schools 33% private high and higher secondary schools			
Kerala	5 HS & Hr. Sc				
Odisha		1. All high schools in every academic year. 2. 10 high schools/UP and primary school per month to test work of subordinate		Assist work assigned by DEO	Assist work assigned by ABEO
Nagaland		All GHSS and GHS	All the GHS (depends upon no. of schools in sub-division)		
Mizoram		8 days in a month (all level)			
Madhya Pradesh			DEO-20 Schools DPC-30 schools APC- 30 schools DIET principal 30, DIET lecturer- 20, Assist. Director-20, once in three months in KGBV CTE principal/ lecturer 10	BEEO	BRCC CRCC

(*Contd.*)

Table 5.3: (*Contd.*)

(1)	(2)	(3)	(4)	(5)	(6)
Tamil Nadu		CEO & DEOs to 5 schools in month and surprise visit 18; DIS to 50-60 schools			
Uttarakhand	10 secondary and higher secondary school per month	10 secondary and higher secondary school per month			
Maharashtra	20	10 schools in tribal and 20 school in non-tribal area		20 Schools	20 (ZP high schools)/ Head Masters
West Bengal		DISs 10 secondary schools in a month			
Uttar Pradesh	About 200 schools by DIOs				
Arunachal Pradesh		Dy Director: at least 3 schools			
Andhra Pradesh		20 schools by DEO in a month	20 schools by Dy DEO in a month		
Gujarat				2 Academic Inspectors (Kelvani Nirikshak) need to inspect 50 schools	
HP	Each inspecting officer is required to inspect at least 8 schools per month i.e. 3 regular and 5 surprise inspections.				
Karnataka		5 school visits (not inspection)			
Sikkim		12 schools			

Source: Third All India Survey of Educational Administration.

Besides the regular administrative structure-wise (Regional, District, Block, Cluster) supervision, some specific arrangements have also been made. In the case of Kerala, the Inspector of Muslims Education is responsible for the supervision of instruction in all Arabic schools. It is his duty to watch the progress of the education of the Muslims, in general, and suggest measures for improvement. In Odisha, the schools under the control of the SC and ST development department have separate inspecting officers. While the District Welfare Officer (DWO) is the overall authority of those schools, there are Circle Inspectors (CI) of Schools and District Inspector (DI) of Schools for the schools of the department. Seven CIs and 18 DIs are entrusted the task of supervision and inspection of the schools under SC and ST department. They have to supervise 15 schools per month.

In Assam, the field level study revealed a wide gap between the norms and actual situation. The Inspector of Schools, DEEOs, DISs, BEEOs and SISs visit school in a year and about two to four hours are spent on each visit. In the case of primary schools, the inspecting officers, generally, record their observations and highlight the strengths and weaknesses of a particular school, alongwith their suggestions in the inspection book maintained by the headmaster. On the next inspection, the previous inspection records are generally followed up.

Availability of Vehicles

Availability of vehicles is a crucial factor for inspection and supervision of the schools by the inspecting officers. In all the States, vehicles for inspection and supervision are provided to regional and district level officer. For the sub-district, block and circle-level officials, vehicle facility is not provided in any State, except in Karnataka, where BEOs have vehicle facility. In Karnataka, out of 28 different posts for inspection, 12 cadres are given vehicles, BEO being one of them. In most of the States, they are provided a fixed amount annually to meet the travel expenditure to monitor and supervise the schools. In Odisha Rs. 30,000/ per annum is given to ABEO-cum-BRCC. Similarly, each CRCC is provided a fixed amount of Rs. 12000 per annum to meet the travel expenditure to visit schools. In Mizoram, due to privatisation of government vehicles, the DEO, SDEO and CEO are not allotted vehicles. The State has made alternative arrangements, and from the funds of RMSA, the DEO is provided one vehicle. In Sikkim, Assistant Directors and Assistant Education Officers are given travelling allowance, as per the State government norms, for visiting schools. In Tamil Nadu, at the block level, Assistant Elementary Education Officer and Additional Assistant Elementary Educational Officers are provided Travelling Allowance and Dearness Allowance, subject to a maximum of 10 per cent of Basic pay, towards meeting conveyance expenditure for visiting schools. In Goa, each Zonal office is provided with one vehicle to be used for visiting schools, while there are four Zonal officers in one zone. As a result, on many occasions when the vehicle is used by one officer, other officers visit the school by claiming T.A. as per their entitlement. In Arunachal Pradesh, though the Dy. Director of school education in the district is entitled to have a government vehicle for visiting the schools, a number of DDSEs, particularly in the newly-created districts, do not have government vehicles for the purpose. This restricts the movement of the DDSEs for regular inspection of schools. They use vehicles from RMSA funds.

Process of Supervision

The supervision in the schools in the country can broadly be categorised by surprise visits, panel inspection and informed visits.

In the case of **panel inspection**, schools are given ample time to prepare for the inspection. Teams of experts of various subjects are deputed by the district authorities for meticulous monitoring. To cite the case of Uttar Pradesh, the inspection programme is chalked out with Basic Shiksha Adhikari (BAS), Principal of the DIET, Associate Coordinator and Mentor/District Coordinator.

In the case of Arunachal Pradesh, different panels are formed for secondary and elementary schools' supervision. In the case of secondary schools, Dy. Director alongwith principal/headmaster of various schools and subject expert from DIET or higher secondary schools comprise the panel of inspection. On the other hand, for elementary schools, the panel comprises co-coordinator of Block Resource Centers and Cluster Resource Centers alongwith Block Education Officers. Besides panel / team visit, in case of UP, the BEO has to prepare a monthly single inspection/supervision plan of the block.

In respect of **surprise visit**, random visits are paid by the inspector without informing school-level officials to check school functioning and academic activities. In the case of U.P., BEO has to take up the programme of casual inspection/supervision of schools located at far-off places to strengthen and give right direction to the process of implementation of provisions. This type of working maintains awareness and zeal for performance of duties among the functionaries serving the fundamental right to education of children. In Maharashtra, surprise visit to school has to be conducted by the educational officers at least once in an academic year. Its aim is to visit school in its normal condition without special preparation for inspection.

In the case of informed visits, schools are informed prior to conducting the inspection. In Uttarakhand, nine or 10 State-level officials are deputed in a single district in different blocks for checking of a large number of schools on the same day. This process of monitoring concludes through sharing and decision-making on the next day to improve school functioning, taken immediately. In Kerala, seven days' notice of the date of an annual inspection is given by the educational officers to the headmaster of the school concerned, with the intimation that work in the school should be carried on in accordance with and within the usual routine on the day of inspection so that the educational officers may have the opportunity of seeing how the school is managed. A notice is required to be sent to the manager in case of private schools. The notice is to be accompanied by a blank inspection report form in triplicate, with a request that the statistical information, required for the inspection report, be entered in the forms.

In Maharashtra, there is also one 'pre-inspection visit' to school. In this visit, the Extension Officer (Education) conducts a short meeting and discusses the school needs, difficulties faced by the teachers in teaching-learning process, curriculum implementation etc. S/he assesses the effectiveness of the school, without actually grading it. S/he also goes through the process of institutional planning and guides the teachers, including the institutional head, wherever necessary. S/he discusses the academic and administrative expectations from teachers and headmasters.

Madhya Pradesh has presented a unique example of multi-type inspection by making maximum use of technology. In M.P., a three-fold "Monitoring and Supervision" approach has been adopted, where data-based monitoring remains very significant and successful. The data-based monitoring is conducted for enrolment in Class VIII, teachers in position, functioning of SMDC, distribution of free bicycles and free textbooks and quality of teaching activities.

Community-based monitoring is also taken up in all the schools. Capacity building of SMC members is done for this purpose. This includes a system of community-based monitoring mechanism for RTE, with focus on standard of quality.

Process of Academic Supervision

The mechanism for academic supervision is almost unattended in majority of the States. At the district level, this responsibility is entrusted with district-level authorities and school head and, at the sub-district level, BEO, with the help of CRC, carries out the inspection upto elementary schools. Few States have developed their own performa to carry out inspection in a systematic way. However, the inspector, while doing the normal inspection, observes the classroom process in one or more classes and discusses the results of his observation with the school authorities. The school is assessed on the basis of academic standard, conditions of the school building, provision of sanitary facilities, implementation of MDM, distribution of text books and free uniforms, smart classes, utilisation of Grants, punctuality of teachers and students, etc.

In most of the States, the head of the school is primarily responsible for all the academic activities of the school, which include classroom process, use of TLM by teachers, and evaluation. In Maharashtra, the process of academic supervision includes administering short written test, followed by discussions with students, to assess the achievement level. The headmaster is supposed to observe at least one lesson of every teacher in a month and record his/her observation in the log book. S/he is to discuss the discrepancies in the teaching work of the teacher in person. S/he is supposed to organise day-to-day teaching-learning process in the school and ensure that the prescribed standards in academics are achieved.

In Nagaland, SCERT is empowered to process academic supervision from pre-primary school upto Class VIII. The Nagaland Board of School Education monitors and supervises the academic section of the secondary and senior secondary school from Classes 9 to 12. The academic section of NBSE mainly deals with developing curriculum and syllabus, preparing and prescribing textbooks, method of teaching and evaluation and organising teacher development programmes etc. In MP, under project Gyanpunj, onsite process of institutionalising subject-specific training and school-based teacher support is provided through a pool of resource teachers.

In many States, SMDC is also responsible for control and supervision of academic and physical development of schools. SMDCs have to supervise attendance of students, their scholastic performance, school discipline, curricular and co-curricular activities, school management, planning of available funds etc.

Number of Supervision in the Sample Survey in Different States

Most of the States' reports fail to mention the number of inspections carried out in the sample districts and blocks. Only three States, Maharashtra, Odisha and Uttar Pradesh, have given this information. In Maharashtra, only the number of inspections done is provided and the expected number of inspections and the total number of schools in the sample area is not provided. Hence, the gap between actual number of supervisions and the expected number of supervision cannot be calculated. As per the data provided by Education Officer (Primary and Secondary) of sample survey of the three districts in the year 2013-14 and 2014-15, the number of inspections done of schools is shown in Table 5.4.

In **Odisha**, as per the information supplied by the DEOs, in Kandhamal, 39 per cent secondary schools i.e. 56 secondary schools out

Table 5.4: Maharashtra—Inspections of Schools in Sample Survey Districts

	Primary			*Upper primary*			*Secondary*			*Higher Secondary*		
District / Year	Satara	Sindhudurg	Yawatmal	Satara	Sindhudurg	Yawatmal	Satara	Sindhudurg	Yawatmal	Satara	Sindhudurg	Yavatmal
2013-14	1823	963	1416	716	511	918	208	106	359	16	-	139
2014-15	1703	953	1416	590	515	918	147	70	403	12	-	198

Source: Third All India Survey of Educational Administration.

of 141 secondary schools (87 government and 54 aided secondary schools) had been inspected by DEO. However, the DEO in Cuttack had inspected and supervised 14 per cent of secondary schools (62 out of 440 secondary schools, 292 government and 148 aided high schools) under his jurisdiction.

From the Table 5.5, it can be seen that the number of elementary schools in Balasore Sadar block is 397, which is the highest among the 12 blocks, while that of 116 in Tikabali block of Kandhamal district is the lowest number of schools among the three districts. Thus, the number of elementary schools per inspecting officer varies to a larger extent.

In **Uttar Pradesh**, at the State-level, inspection and supervision in all schools is observed to be 65 per cent whereas the inspection and supervision percentage for primary, upper primary, high school and intermediate level separately is 70.64 per cent, 62.20 per cent, 44.76 per cent and 41.74 per cent respectively. It may also be mentioned that education officers seem to inflate the inspection figures since they are busy more with their office work and litigation cases, as also in meetings. The Tables 5.6 and 5.7 indicates the Inspection and Supervision in Sample District taken for conducting Third Survey in Uttar Pradesh.

In Assam, every Inspector of School should inspect at least 10 schools a month and submit action taken report on the basis of the inspection to the Director, Secondary Education. DEEO should inspect at least 10 schools a month and submit action taken report on the findings of inspection to the Director, Elementary Education. DI of school should inspect at least 20 schools a month and submit report to DEEO. BEEO should inspect at least 20 schools in a month and the SI of schools should inspect at least 25 schools in a month and submit the compiled report to DEEO for taking necessary action.

Table 5.5: Number of Schools per Inspecting Authority in Odisha

District	*Name of the Block*	*No. of Schools per Inspecting Authority*
Cuttack	Cuttack Sadar	230
	Tangi-Choudwar	195
	Niali	200
	Baranga	125
Balasore	Oupada	154
	Remuna	230
	Simulia	167
	Balasore Sadar	397
Kandhamal	Kotagad	170
	Tikabali	116
	Phulbani	139
	Baliguda	176

Table 5.6: Percentage of Sample Schools Inspected and Supervised in Sample Districts during 2013-14 in Uttar Pradesh

District Name	*Type of School*	*Number of Sample Schools*	*Schools Inspected and Supervised*	
			Number	Percentage
Mirzapur	Primary	1610	1165	72.36
	Upper Primary	899	523	58.18
	High School	88	62	70.45
	Intermediate	111	52	46.85
	Total	**2708**	**1802**	**66.54**
Ghaziabad	Primary	397	220	55.42
	Upper Primary	194	130	67.01
	High School	94	27	28.72
	Intermediate	101	32	31.68
	Total	**786**	**409**	**52.04**
Shravasti	Primary	888	660	74.32
	Upper Primary	391	270	69.05
	High School	66	22	33.33
	Intermediate	109	50	45.87
	Total	**1454**	**1002**	**68.91**
State of Uttar Pradesh	Primary	2895	2045	70.64
	Upper Primary	1484	923	62.20
	High School	248	111	44.76
	Intermediate	321	134	41.74
	Total	**4948**	**3213**	**64.94**

Source: Third All India Survey of Educational Administration.

Table 5.7: Number of Schools for Inspection and Supervision per DIOS/ Associate DIOS in Uttar Pradesh

District	*Number of Schools in Sample District*		*Total Schools*	*No. of Sanctioned Posts of DIOS+ADIOSs*	*Average No. of Schools per Inspecting Officer*
	High School	*Inter-mediate*			
1	2	3	4	5	6
Mirzapur	88	111	199	1	199
Ghaziabad	94	101	195	1	195
Shravasti	66	109	172	1	172
State of Uttar Pradesh	248	321	566	3	187

Source: Third All India Survey of Educational Administration.

The Tables 5.8 and 5.9 indicates the Inspection and Supervision in Tamil Nadu.

Table 5.8: Inspection and Supervision in Primary and Upper Primary Schools in Tamil Nadu

Designation of the Officer	*Schools under control*	*Visits*	*Inspection*
AEEO, Mannargudi, Thiruvarur District	81	Each school	All schools
AEEO, Thiruvarur, Thiruvarur District			
AEEO, Nannilam, Thiruvarur District	40	Once in 2 months	Not furnished
AEEO, Koradacheri, Thiruvarur District	38	Once in 3 months	Not furnished
AAEEO, Salem Urban	44	Once in 3 months	All schools
AEEO, Thalaivasal, Salem Urban	41	Regularly	All schools
AAEEO, Thalaivasal, Salem District	39	Regularly	All schools
AEEO, Attur, Salem District	41	Once in a month	Not furnished
Additional AEEO, Attur, Salem District	40	Once in a month	Not furnished
AEEO, Chitalapakkam, Kancheepuram District	69	Once in a month	All schools
AEEO, including Additional AEEO, Kattankolathur, Kancheepuram District	103	Thrice in a month	All schools
AAEEO, Walajabad, Kancheepuram District	56	Twice in 3 months	All schools
AAEEO, Kancheepuram District	68	Once in 3 months	All schools

Source: Third All India Survey of Educational Administration.

Table 5.9: Inspection and Supervision in Secondary and Senior Secondary Schools in Tamil Nadu

Designation of the Officer	Schools under control	Visits	Schools Inspection
CEO, Coimbatore District	353	Regularly	5-6
CEO, Thiruvannamalai District	367	8 in a month	40
CEO, Madurai District	282	5 in a month	38

Source: Third All India Survey of Educational Administration.

Inspection Report

In almost all the States, the same pattern is followed for preparing a report after the inspection. The inspection officer makes observations and comments on administrative and academic aspects, including teaching work, of the school concerned. In Odisha, under its Samiksha programme, the CRCC has to consolidate his monitoring outcomes in the Individual Consolidated Format (ICF) by the 21st of every month and submit the ICF to BRCC by the 22nd for block-level consolidation. The individual format, filled up by the CRCCs and BRCC, are consolidated at the block level in the Block Consolidated Format (BCF) and sent to District Project Office, SSA by the 23rd of every month. ICFs of DEO and BCFs from BRCC are consolidated in District Consolidated Format (DCF) by the MIS unit of the District Project Office of SSA and sent to State Monitoring Unit by the 25th of every month. The visiting inspector may also write notes in a note book. Inspection notes, submitted to authorities concerned, are checked and analysed for follow-up action. There are also some inspection reports which are of confidential nature and such reports are taken and considered with due care and sent to competent authorities for further action.

Supervision by the Head of the Institution

- Regular supervision is also done by the head of the institution. A case of Maharashtra can be discussed here.The supervision by the headmaster, particularly in high and higher secondary school, begins well ahead of regular school hours. The headmaster goes round the school to ensure cleanliness of the entire campus, classrooms and hygienic conditions in the mid-day meal kitchen and toilet blocks.
- The headmaster, assisted by the physical education teachers, enforces a disciplined way of arrival of the students inside the campus and orderly movement towards their respective

classrooms. The silent study sessions are also supervised by the headmaster with the help of the PETs.

- The headmaster monitors whether all the teachers and students are present during the Assembly (Prayer Meeting).
- The headmaster plans the proceedings of the Assembly, including the important announcements to be made, in advance.
- The headmaster observes the class sessions during school hours. The headmaster observes a minimum of two classes everyday and records his critical observations in the supervision diary. The observations recorded are given access to the teachers concerned for betterment of their teaching methods and other aspects noted therein.
- The headmaster offers guidance to both newly recruited and experienced teachers in scheduling their scheme of work / lessons and counsels them periodically.
- The headmaster peruses the notes of lessons of the teachers and makes brief comments on them, wherever necessary.
- The headmaster sets a vision for the school, in consultation with teachers, and plans the school activities towards realisation of the same.
- The headmaster interacts positively and constructively with teachers, students, parents and society at large and addresses their concerns related to school activities.
- The headmaster supervises the performance of teachers and students so as to achieve excellence in academic performance.
- The headmaster evinces interest and encourages the students in sports and games, creative arts and debates.
- The headmaster closes the Staff Attendance Register on time and makes alternate arrangements for the classes of the teachers who are not present on the day.
- The headmaster instructs teachers to maintain classroom discipline.
- The headmaster ensures use of teaching aids and audio-visual equipment, whenever necessary, to enhance the learning experience
- The headmaster visits the laboratories, vocational workshops and observes the practical classes being carried out. The headmaster confirms whether the safety measures are in place in chemistry and electrical laboratories.
- The headmaster interacts meaningfully with the students in order to comprehend their aspirations and concerns. Suitable action is initiated towards the fulfilment of their aspirations.

Best Practices

Odisha

The Odisha State Government has introduced a system named "*SAMIKSHA*" in 2010 for monitoring of schools through prescribed formats. The DEOs, BEOs, District Project Coordinators of SSA, ABEOs, BRCCs and CRCCs have to monitor the schools under their jurisdiction. This system is introduced to bring a uniform system of monitoring throughout the State. All the CRCCs and BRCCs have to use common formats for the purpose of school monitoring. The salient features of the SAMIKSHA are as follows:

- The CRCCs and BRCCs to observe at least 10 schools and the DEO, DPC, BEO and ABEO to visit five schools in a month.
- While the CRCC is required to spend the whole day in the school, others will spend the required time to observe and fill the prescribed format satisfactorily.
- After the completion of monitoring, the monitoring officer has to share his/her observation with the school teachers, SMC members and parents.
- The monitoring officers have to prepare two copies of the report: one for the school and one for their own office.
- The CRCC has to consolidate his monitoring outcomes as mentioned earlier and sent for upward consolidation at BRCC at block, and district level. It is further transmit to State Monitoring Unit.

The monitoring format contains 51 indicators under six heads. Besides, one part of the format is on the demonstration class and school observation by the CRCC. Another part of the format is to be filled by the DEOs, DPCs, BEOs, ABEOs, BRCCs.

Madhya Pradesh

Madhya Pradesh is reported to make maximum use of technology for monitoring and supervising its school education. The case-monitoring of schools is done with the help of collection of data through UDISE and web-based system of online monitoring. The information flow for collecting the data is from village to block level. The data-based monitoring is done for activities such as extent of enrolment, transition from Class VIII to Class IX, teachers in position, use of school grants, functioning of SMDC, distribution of free textbooks, bicycles and quality of teaching activity.

Maharashtra

Apart from the inspection and supervision of schools by block and district-level education officers, cluster heads in Maharashtra also have responsibilities of inspection and supervision of schools in the following ways.

1. To monitor and supervise the activities of headmasters and teachers in his cluster.
2. To review the activities carried out in schools in cluster-level meetings.
3. To guide teachers to keep them updated regarding teaching-learning process, evaluation, innovations etc.
4. To guide teachers to conduct the curricular and co-curricular activities successfully.
5. To supervise financial matters and monitor various government schemes in schools.
6. To pay visits to school, to attend the SMC meetings and impart guidance to the functionaries.
7. To ensure 100 per cent attendance, retention of students and quality of education.
8. To take four demonstrative lessons per week in the schools in his cluster.
9. To report to the extension officer regarding irregular findings in the school functioning.
10. To conduct teacher training programmes.
11. To pay visits and monitor the activities in pre-primary schools, Anganwadi, Mahila Prabodhan Centre, Rural libraries, Informal Education Centers, Ashram Shala, Adult Education Centers and guide the H.M. and teachers concerned.
12. To co-ordinate the activities in his cluster.
13. To arrange for the remedial teaching for the students lagging behind in learning.
14. To attend parent-teacher meetings and follow instructions of higher Officer.
15. To monitor and supervise the activities of Mid-DayMeal Programme.
16. To assist the superior authorities to carry out various functions and responsibilities.

Apart from the above duties, he has to attend Panchayat Samit meetings and the meetings of Zila Parishad as and when invited and the work according to instructions of higher authorities.

Role of BRC and CRC in Monitoring and Supervision

Each BRC has specialist staff of 5-7. Besides, there are a number of CRCs, perhaps one for every 15 villages. Between the staff of these two resource centres, it should be possible for one person to visit each school once every two months and indeed every month if the circumstances so allow. The purpose of these visits is to provide curricular support to teachers – particularly progress with syllabus, the manner in which use is being made of textbooks and other materials assess and support teachers develop teaching-learning material and the manner in which continuous and comprehensive evaluation is being put into effect. In addition, BRCs conduct workshops with subject teachers of upper primary classes and they, as well as CRCs, organise trainings expected of them. The staff from the office of BEO as well as from BRCs and CRCs ordinarily are not expected to prepare inspection/visit reports. Rather, they record their main observations in a register that may be maintained in each school. HMs/teachers take action on the visit note. In addition, computers are available in the office of BEO, and in BRCs and CRCs so that important observations (particularly points on which administrative action is to be taken) are shared through the internet.

Major Issues

The number of schools, teachers and enrolment has increased tremendously in the past few years. However, the administrative machinery has not been increased commensurately. The target of inspection, of 100 per cent schools every year, remains unachieved. Given the diverse nature of duties assigned to education officials, the officers do not get adequate time for inspection. To mention Uttar Pradesh report, as per activity profile of DEO in the State, these officials spent only 25 per cent of their time on visits and inspections, with rest of their time devoted to other activities such as travelling, receiving visitors, attending meetings and conferences and other activities. Similarly, Mizoram indicates that as DEOs and SDEOs are Drawing and Disbursing Officers (DDO), they have less time to spare for inspection. Besides, many posts of Circle Education Officer are lying vacant for a long period of time and the existing CEOs are deputed to SSA which creates problems in conducting inspection and supervision.

As such, during the last few decades, school supervision has suffered enormously due to insufficiency of staff and also administrative neglect. The efforts made under SSA, through establishment of BRCs and CRCs, have improved matters marginally, but the overall situation has remained essentially unchanged. As a result, the functioning of schools has deteriorated and quality of the teaching-learning process has shown no improvement. Improvement of quality of education is a pre-requisite for the successful implementation of the RTE Act. Periodic inspection/ supervision of schools, to take note of the infrastructure and facilities and the administrative aspects, is critical. In addition, a proper system of academic and curricular support has to be developed to serve the purpose of continuing professional upgradation of teachers and to see that school syllabi and learner evaluation system are operationalised as expected. Each Block Education Officer should have a contingent of Assistant EEOs, who would be expected to undertake at least two visits to every school each year. They should, inter alia, look at the record required to be maintained by teachers/headmasters, condition of school building and infrastructure and seating arrangements for students. They should be asked to pay particular attention to availability of potable drinking water, usability of toilets, the kitchen where the MDM is cooked and whether the school has a well-maintained boundary wall.

The capacity-building of the existing officers is also needed. As has been observed during the survey, mobility support, which is not sufficient, needs to be provided to officials (generally lower than district level). Lack of availability of vehicles remains a crucial inhibiting factor for successful implementation of inspection and supervision. It is noticed that follow-up action after the inspection is not taken seriously. This aspect needs urgent attention as the follow-up ensures as to whether the issues noticed and discussed during inspection are taken care of by the school teachers/authorities or not.

6
Institutional Management

Institutional management has been one of the most important areas of school education. Better school management not only improves the working of school but also enhances the quality of education and services to the clientele. The purpose of institutional planning and management is to identify the existing resources and ensure optimum utilisation of those resources for achieving institutional vision and objectives. It involves the process of developing plans and taking decisions for further action with a view to achieving the established goals of an institution. The head of the institution plays an important role in pooling available resources and using them optimally. The head of an institution is expected to be an able organiser, efficient administrator and, above all, a professionally competent leader. Each State has laid down its basic essentials for schools at various levels. For elementary education, management guidelines for schools are issued by the Directorate of Elementary Education and, for Secondary and Senior Secondary Schools, by the Directorate of School/ Secondary Education.

Type of Institutions and Their Management

All the States have three types of schools viz. Government schools, including Central government, State government and local bodies, Aided schools and Private schools with no financial aid. Private-aided schools are provided recognition, on the basis of fulfilling the laid down norms by the State Education Departments, and affiliated by the Board of Secondary Education. Private educational institutions (private-aided and unaided) have been established by individuals, NGOs, Voluntary organisations, educational trusts, religious and social organisations and corporate groups. The government provides grants to some of the institutions. The policy has been advantageous to the government since it promotes education without the government having to invest its resources on buildings and other infrastructural facilities. In some cases, it allows institutions to function and utilise their own resources. The grants-in-aid system has allowed the opening of schools in far-flung areas in the States.

The grants-in-aid rules have clearly spelt out detailed modalities for: requirements for establishment of a new school or upgradation of the existing one; scrutiny and grant of permission, validity of permission; recognition and conditions governing institutions; appointment of staff through staff selection committees; admission to schools; constitution of school governing body and its functions; criteria and procedure for fixing salary structure for staff; criteria for fixing fee structure and collection of revenue earned as fee; disciplinary control; and submission of annual administrative report by the educational agency.

Powers and Functions of Heads of Institutions

There are variations in the powers and functions of heads of secondary, upper primary and primary schools. This is due to the fact that their responsibilities differ widely. The head of a Government Senior Secondary School has a variety of duties and responsibilities in terms of academic and administrative matters. The head of the school can be a role model for teachers and students. As a head, s/he has to maintain discipline in the school and also can propose disciplinary action against those who violate the rules and regulations of the respective institute.

As a principal/headmaster of secondary, upper primary and primary school, s/he must be able to motivate the teachers towards their teaching profession and create an environment for improvement of learning enhancement of students. The head of an institution should have good relations with teachers, students, guardians and parents and with the local community/people. The principal/headmaster should have the capacity to deal with the official procedure and administrative machineries, both at the district and State level, for the greater interest of the school.

Implementation of Mid-Day Meal Scheme is another major activity of the head of the school. As a head of the school, s/he can exercise administrative and financial powers with academic leadership to improve the quality of education in the school. In addition to that, examination, sports, submission of information relating to U-DISE data to RMSA and SSA, convening of the School Management Committee meeting are some of the major activities of the head. As a head of the institution, principal/headmaster can supervise and monitor the teacher activities relating to classroom transactional process. The heads can call meetings of the PTA, community, youth club and other organisations in the greater interest of school development and public co-operation, considering the school as part of a social organisation.

The following are the examples of region-wise five States, indicating the powers and functions of heads of institutions.

1. Madhya Pradesh

Secondary and Higher Secondary Schools

Administrative Powers of the Head: The head of school is responsible for:

1. General administration of the school and cluster of schools in the jurisdiction;
2. Issuing of transfer certificates to students;
3. Drawing and disbursing pay and other administrative and financial claims of own-school and other schools in the cluster;
4. Sanctioning increments, GPF and leave of cluster schools;
5. Sanction and pay GPF, TA, advances, medical claims, advance for house construction and purchase of vehicles etc.;
6. Spending funds of the schools as per norms and rules;
7. Permiting the use of school building for other purposes;
8. Rusticating a student from school;
9. Purchasing books for library;
10. Sanctioning permission to appear in the examinations;
11. Arranging alternative teacher/s in schools where the teacher/s are on leave; and
12. Issuing orders for quality improvement in cluster schools.

Functions of Heads: The Head of School

1. Manages academic, administrative and financial issues;
2. Uses financial powers, as per powers mentioned in the M.P. Finance Code Vol. 1 & 2;
3. Prepares time-table of school and implement it accordingly;
4. Ensures regular attendance of teachers and students;
5. Ensures that the school opens on time;
6. Makes efforts for subject and faculty-wise availability of teachers;
7. Maintains admission, transfer, attendance registers;
8. Develops school calendar and institutional plan and ensure its implementation;
9. Monitors classroom teaching and inspect various sections of the school;
10. Organises workshops/seminars and ensure teacher participation in them;
11. Organises teaching-learning based workshops and teacher seminars;

12. Promotes educational innovations;
13. Organises SMDC/PTA meetings and make efforts for the development of school;
14. Organises cultural and educational activities and ensure student participation in them;
15. Manages the cleanliness, Science Club, Scout & Guide, NCC activities in the school;
16. Uses administrative powers for disciplinary and motivational conduct of teachers and recommend them accordingly;
17. Decides and sanctions administrative and financial issues of the subordinate staff as per powers delegated;
18. Develops a good library of books and promote its use among students;
19. Organises sports and other extra-curricular activities for students and teachers;
20. Makes provisions for disciplinary action and reward for good work;
21. Makes provision for potable water, toilets, cleanliness and other requirements of school;
22. Sends administrative and other information to the senior officer of the department within the prescribed time;
23. Draws and disburse salary of the subordinate staff on time;
24. Maintains Cash Book and other registers; and
25. Obeys and abides by the orders of the senior officers and offices.

Functions of Headmaster of Elementary School

The HM/incharge of EE school:

1. Ensures student attendance in schools;
2. Ensures school cleanliness and maintenance of school building, using funds earmarked for the purpose;
3. Organises and conduct School Management Committee and PTA meetings and ensure implementation of their decisions;
4. Ensures school activities as per school calendar;
5. Checks teacher's diary and provide guidelines to them accordingly;
6. Monitors the achievement level of students and intimate it to their parents;
7. Prepares school time-table and ensure its implementation;
8. Distributes and assign school work to teachers;
9. Ensures facilities for CWSN;
10. Inspects classrooms and teaching;

11. Ensures minimum teaching facilities in the school;
12. Ensures receipt of various incentives to students;
13. Forwards teachers' administrative and financial issues, such as TA, medical, GPF, leave etc. to the Cluster Principal;
14. Maintains cash book and other registers as per directives of the department;
15. Conducts monthly, half-yearly and annual examinations and declare results accordingly;
16. Sends any required information of the school to the Principal of the Cluster;
17. Cooperates during inspection and audit of the school;
18. Be a model for the teachers, students and the society;
19. Works for getting physical, financial or any other form of cooperation from the society; and
20. Organises functions on birth anniversaries of national celebrities and other activities, as per State School Calendar.

2. Karnataka

The government has listed out the administrative powers and functions of the heads of the institutions. He should be a good administrator, leader, guide, as well as be part and parcel of academic progress. Head of the institution has certain duties and functions to carry out. He is also given some powers and authority to discharge his functions effectively. The powers and functions of heads of schools are classified under administrative, financial and academic-powers.

Administrative Powers of Heads

- Admission of pupils.
- Issue of transfer certificates.
- Sanction of casual leave to assistant teachers not exceeding five days at a time subject to availability of teachers in the school.
- Maintaining of government and non-government cash books regularly. Sending regularly all types of data and statistical information to the higher offices.
- Submitting regularly annual teachers' performance and assets and liabilities reports to the higher officials.
- Drawing and disbursing regularly the salaries of the teachers and other staff of the institutions. Maintaining the school records efficiently and regularly.
- Acting as a secretary of S.D.M.C. Management and supervision of all teachers of the institution.

- Preparing and implementing annual institution plan and school development plan.
- Organising various national festivals, samudaydatta shala yojane, adoption programme, teacher's and children talent days.
- Mobilising resources with the help of community and S.D.M.C. for the development of the institution.
- Collecting and submitting government fees regularly to the government without misappropriation.
- Preparing annual budget.Preparing annual budget for purchasing laboratory equipment and materials, library books, sports materials, and Audio-visual educational materials by utilising the non-government fees of the students.
- Collecting the registration fees from the 10th standard students and submitting to the K.S.S.E.B and issuing receipts to the students.
- Following purchasing rules while utilising government grants.
- Giving receipts for all contributions from the public collected through S.D.M.C. and contributions in cash and kind.
- Taking the responsibility for all civil works.
- Implementing the mid-day meals with utmost care and interest.
- Disbursing all the welfare schemes of the government to the students without fail and maintaining the documents.
- Protecting all movable and immovable properties and its records of the institutions forming the S.D.M.C. in accordance with the rules framed by the government.
- Proper utilisation of the funds allotted to the schools by way of gram, taluk, zila panchayat or MLA or MP fund for the development of the school.
- Arranging for special classes. Arranging free medical check-up, maintaining medical records, and helping the students get medical aid.
- Getting benefit from school adoption programme. Receiving uniforms, books from the government and distributing them to the students.
- Providing training to students to participate in inter-school, taluk-level and district-level sports and cultural meets.
- Arranging vocational guidance courses to introduce a variety of vocational courses for the students.
- Arranging educational tours, forming school parliament to develop leadership qualities.
- Reviewing and providing guidance in students' learning and allocating work to all the teachers.

- Teaching the students—taking 12 periods per week besides lesson observation and guidance.
- Verifying regularly the yearly plan and daily lesson plans of the teachers.

Financial Powers

- Collection of fees for students of Class VIII onwards in government schools.
- Utilisation of contingency funds.
- Utilisation of non-government funds.
- Purchase of equipment.

Academic Powers

- Conduct of tests and examinations.
- Declaration of results of examinations.
- Providing academic guidance to teachers.
- Preparation of annual programme of work, time-table etc.
- Condonation of minimum attendance of pupils to the extent of 15 days.
- Lesson observation.
- Giving guidance to teachers.

Other Powers

- Observation of the quality of the construction works.
- Proper utilisation of the grants from the government.
- Supervision of the mid-day meal programme.
- Active participation as a secretary of S.D.M.C

Maintaining the school records systematically with full care and protection. In 2007-08, the head of the secondary schools were given additional powers as head of the composite high school which included academic and administrative head of the primary school which is located in the same premises as the secondary school. If both primary and secondary schools are situated in the same premises or within the same compound, then the head of the secondary school becomes the head of both the institutions, viz. the COMPOSITE HIGH SCHOOL. The head has the power to control, and supervise both the institutions and salary drawing power in the secondary section.

In 2007-08, the head of the secondary school was given the power of Cluster Assistant Education Officer [CAEO] to maintain the academic and administrative functions of his cluster. The power and responsibilities of the head included controlling, supervising, and drawing and disbursing salary besides being the leave sanctioning authority of all the LPS &

HPS of the same cluster. With the implementation of SSA and RMSA programmes, the function, responsibilities and power of the head of the institutions has been increased to a greater extent.

The powers and functions of the head of the institution at primary, secondary and senior secondary levels are summarised as follows:

Government Lower Primary: The powers and functions of the head in lower primary government school include maintenance of cleanliness within the premises and surroundings, administering mid-day meals programme, maintenance of records, implementing government schemes.

Government Upper Primary: In upper primary schools, the powers and functions of the head include enrolment of students, observation of classes, maintaining records of the school, solving teachers' and students' problems, conducting SDMC meetings. In addition, the head has to maintain a good relationship between the school, school development & betterment committee and the public.

Upper Primary – Aided: The head of upper primary in government-aided school has the powers and functions of administration and overall supervision of the school, covering school discipline, punctuality, maintaining school records and accounts, good communication with society, parents, students, staff and higher authority.

Government Secondary: The powers and functions of the head in a government secondary school include school administration work, planning (educational, physical, etc.), solving academic and administrative problems, taking decisions on academic, administrative and financial matters, conducting meetings (PTA, SDMC), maintaining records, planning and execution of academic programmes.Class observation and supervision, administering school admission work, preparing yearly action plan and timetable, formation of school committees and clubs, conducting cultural programmes, financial planning, budgeting, accounts, etc. are among the other functions.

Secondary – Aided: The powers and functions of head in secondary government-aided school include management of finances and infrastructure through effective planning, budgeting and expenditure control, guidance and development of staff-student relationship, maintaining health and hygiene in school – students, environment, etc., maintaining school property, enforcing discipline among teachers and students, maintaining school records etc.

Government Sr. Secondary: In a senior secondary institution, the powers and functions of the head include general administration, work assigned by higher authorities of the education department, financial administration, facilitate good academic environment, fulfil essential needs of teachers and students, build good rapport with teachers, parents and the public.

Sr. Secondary – Aided: The powers and function of the head in a senior secondary government-aided institution includes teaching, staff administration, coordination with stakeholders, and social interaction with parents and public.

3. Gujarat

Administrative Powers and Functions of Heads

In all primary and secondary schools in Gujarat, the headmaster is expected to do all administrative work as well as supervise school and teachers. The HM also ensures that the school is functioning as per the norms specified under the various acts. HM has to observe three lessons per day and provide guidance and suggestions to the teachers. All school principals are permanent and their pay scale is uniform throughout the State for primary and secondary schools i.e. the pay scale of 9300-34800 (grade pay 4200). The post of principal is filled by promoting working teachers and through direct recruitment. For the post of principal in primary school, candidates must have five years' experience of teaching with post-graduation and PTC / One-year degree in special education / degree in education. They are eligible to appear in HTAT examination conducted by the State Examination Board.

For the post of Principal in Secondary and Higher Secondary schools, candidate must have 15 years' experience of teaching and possess graduation degree with degree in education or seven years' experience of teaching and possess post-graduate degree with degree in education. They are eligible to appear in TAT examination held by the GSHSE Board. In Government schools, Departmental Promotion Committee (DPC) has powers to finalise the list of teachers to be promoted, keeping in view their merit, seniority etc. as prescribed by the rules and regulations of the department.

Preparation and Implementation of School Development Plan

The State has implemented RTE Act 2009. As per the provision of Act, SMC has to prepare School Development Plan (SDP) through SSA. This activity is carried out by all schools. SSA provides necessary guidance to all schools in their second term of the academic year. SMC prepares SDP, keeping in mind the enrolment of students, requirements of teachers and physical facilities available. CRC and BRC verify the School Development Plan (SDP) and submit it to DPC and DPC takes necessary action with regard to academic and infrastructural requirement to be provided to the school.

School Working Days and Number of Holidays: As specified in the RTE Act, 2009, the total number of days that a primary school is expected to function is 240, of which 14 days are utilised for conducting examinations and seven days for conducting other school functions. Hence, a school functions for a total of 240 days. However, secondary and higher secondary schools function for a total of 244 days wherein teaching days are 219, examinations are conducted over a period of 20 days and five days are utilised for other school functions. GSHSEB prepares annual activities' calendar for schools wherein activities, examinations, holidays and vacation etc. are clarified. Here it may be mentioned that Diwali vacation of three weeks and summer vacation of five weeks is finalised by the Board and it is implemented all over the State. The same period of vacation is applicable for primary schools.

4. Uttarakhand

Powers and Functions of Heads

Headmaster of the primary school is fully responsible for all activities in primary school with the help of the school management committee. He has to ensure smooth functioning of the school, supervise arrangements of Mid-day Meal scheme, distribution of scholarships, uniforms, free textbooks distribution, enrolment and monitoring of teacher attendance as well as for children. As per norms of RTE 2009, the school headmaster, as local authority, is responsible for activities of the primary school. Similarly, at the elementary level, the head teacher is also responsible for activities, as mentioned for head teacher of primary school, in spite of wide catchment area.

Headmasters at secondary school level in government and aided schools have to work as administrator or head of office and ensure the smooth functioning of the school alongwith arrangements of teachers, and implementation of various schemes of Central and State government. The headmaster is overall responsible for arrangement of laboratories, co-curriculum activities, libraries with the help of work distribution within the teaching and non-teaching staff. Being head of office at secondary school level, he is also responsible for personal records, leaves, salary of teaching and non-teaching staff and performance records.

The principal, at intermediate level in government and private-aided schools, has similar role and responsibilities as headmasters of secondary schools. They are member of school management committee and secretary of parent teacher association organised at school level. Principals and headmasters of government schools are also drawing and dispersing officers at the school level.

5. Mizoram

Powers and Functions of Heads

The administrative powers and functions of the head of an institution vary from school to school, depending on their management. The headmasters of government middle and primary schools have the power to grant three days' casual leave at a time to the staff under them. Headmasters of government high schools, who are placed in Schedule 111 of the Education Department, have been delegated the powers of drawing and disbursing authority in financial matters relating to salaries of their staff. In addition, they have the power to grant casual leave and earned leave to teaching and non-teaching staff in their respective schools. Principals of higher secondary schools have been delegated the powers to draw and disburse salaries of their staff and utilise contingency grants, as per financial rules of the department, and they also have the power to grant casual leave and earned leave to their staff. When the schools do not receive adequate grants from the State government, the headmaster/ principal has the power to mobilise community resources for the development of the school.

All heads of institutions/schools have been authorised to supervise the classroom teaching process and provide relevant suggestions, instructions and remedial measures to the teachers, depending on their performances. Head of an institution, with the help of his/her staff, looks after the maintenance of the school and its premises by utilising available resources.

Classroom teaching and its supervision constitutes a major academic function of the principal/headmaster. He/she supervises the performance of teachers and other staff in the school by maintaining daily attendance registers. For academic improvement of the school, the head of an institution involves in coordination work with parents and public leaders and constitutes parents-teachers association. Students are also encouraged to participate in the school development plans and implementation works and establish students' association, under the guidance and control of the principal/headmaster.

Some of the powers and functions vested in the head of the institution are:

Functions

a. To maintain and check the institution record books, students' register, teachers' attendance and school facilities etc.
b. To check and observe the performance and teaching mode of the teachers.
c. To maintain good relationship with the teachers.
d. To finalise or decide any matter relating to the institution.

***Powers*:**

e. To tell the staff and students to obey the rules.
f. To punish those who are against the school rules.
g. To give orders to be obeyed by the staff and students for the betterment of the school.
h. To look into financial management.
a. To develop cordial relations between parents-teachers.
b. To be a good manager and a good administrator.
c. To impress upon the staff and students the need for punctuality.
d. To make a good democratic education.
e. To make a classroom better.
f. To get a good academic goal.

The head of institution is the key figure, on whom the success or the failure of the school depends. Everything in the school plan, the staff, method of teaching, co-curricular activities, human relationships, good cooperation are the products of his personality. He/she is also responsible for carrying out the policy and programme of the education department. No scheme of educational reconstruction will produce the desired result unless it is administered with the right vision and efficiency.

Norms of Establishment of Institutions

Universal education primarily requires the provision of schools in the vicinity or within close proximity to the habitation of all the children to enable them to easily access the facilities. The RTE Act has laid down the principles of neighbourhood norms, such as the distance within which every habitation should have a primary and an upper primary school, though the norms of establishing secondary/higher secondary schools differ from primary and upper primary and also from State to State. The following are the examples of the norms for establishment and upgradation of institutions in two selected States:

Norms of Establishment and Upgradation of Institutions in Odisha

At present, the norms of establishment of primary schools and upgradation of primary schools to upper primary schools are governed by the norms prescribed in the RTE Act, 2009. During 1989, the government, in erstwhile Education and Youth Services Department, vide Resolution No 33891 dated 03.08.1989, stipulated that primary schools will be opened in all habitations having population of more than 200 in hilly and tribal areas and 300 in other areas. The government, through School and Mass

Education Department, vide letter no.25423/SME dated 09.08.1995, advised all Collectors to maintain a distance of one kilometre between the existing primary school and a new primary school and similarly maintain a distance of three km between the existing upper primary school and the proposed upper primary school.

In 2009, the government relaxed the norms of opening of new primary schools under SSA in order to ensure access to elementary education and in line with the government's commitment for universalisation of elementary education in the State. The Government's decisions are as follows:

1. In KBK districts and tribal sub-plan areas, new primary schools will be opened in habitations having at least 25 children in the 6-11 years' age group, provided there is no primary school within 1 km of such habitations.
2. In all the districts, the distance norm for opening of new primary and upper primary schools will be relaxed in case of natural barriers like river, hilly terrain, dense forest etc.

The Odisha Right of Children to Free and Compulsory Education Rule, 2010 that specifies the areas/limits of neighbourhood within which a school should be established by the government or Local Authority provides as follows:

- In respect of children in Classes I–V, a school shall be established within a walking distance of one km of the neighbourhood.
- In respect of children in Classes VI-VIII, a school shall be established within a walking distance of 3 km of the neighbourhood.
- Wherever required, the government shall upgrade existing schools with Classes I-V to include Classes VI-VIII. In respect of schools, that start from Class VI onwards, the government shall endeavour to add Classes I-V, if necessary.

In pursuance of Section 6 of the RCFCE Act, 2009 and Rule 6 (4) of Odisha Right of Children to Free and Compulsory Education Rule, 2010, the State government, vide Notification No.22554/SME dated26.09.2013, which superseded the earlier Resolution No. 9599/SME dated 18.06.2009, made the following provisions for opening of new primary and upper primary schools in the State by adding the number of children norm with the limits of distance specified in the State Rule.

1. Opening of New Primary School:

- In non-KBK districts or non-Tribal sub-plan areas, a new primary school will be opened in habitations, having at least 40 children in the 6-11 years' age group, provided there is no primary school within a walking distance of 1 km of such habitations.
- In KBK districts and Tribal sub-plan areas, a new primary school will be opened in habitations/cluster of habitations, having at least 25 children in the 6-11 years' age group, provided there is no primary school within a walking distance of 1 km of such habitations.

2. Opening of New Upper Primary School: In all districts, a new upper primary school will be opened in habitations/cluster of habitations, having at least 25 children in the 6-14 years' age group, provided there is no upper primary school within a walking distance of 3 km. of such habitations.

3. In all districts, the distance norm for opening of new primary and upper primary schools will be relaxed in case of natural barriers like river, hilly terrain, dense forest etc.

The criterion for establishment of a secondary school is that there shall be at least a high school in every gram panchayat. In an urban area, for opening a new secondary school, a minimum 10000 population is the criteria. A secondary school in any gram panchayat, managed by a private body, can be recognised provided it shall be managed and maintained solely at the cost to be met by its own resources without any claim for grant-in-aid from the State government. However, in case of an educationally backward district, these norms will be relaxed.

Assam— Norms for establishment and upgradation of Government and Aided Institutions

A Case Study

Before the advent of RTE Act, 2009, the system of granting permission and recognition to schools was as follows:

(i) Primary schools were directly provincialised without grant of prior permission or recognition to the schools concerned.

(ii) Middle Schools were accorded permission and recognition by the Director of Elementary Education on the basis of inspection reports submitted by DEEOs. A few years ago, reports of DEEOs were subjected to scrutiny by a committee, constituted by the government, for consideration of permission or recognition to middle schools. Middle schools were first accorded permission to open, followed by grant of recognition a year or so later, depending on the fulfilment of conditions of minimum enrolment, land for the school building, qualified teachers, etc. Only recognised schools are considered for provincialisation.

(iii) High schools are accorded prior permission to open by the government i.e. the Secretary of Education, following which the permission orders are issued by the Director of Secondary Education. In the case of high schools also, the actual opening of schools by the people concerned always precedes the permission granted by the government. The DSE also issues recognition to the high schools a year or more after permission is granted, when the schools concerned fulfil the required conditions, but such permission and recognition accorded by the government and the DSE are restricted to Clas VIII of high schools (or upto Class VIII in respect of certain high schools with Middle sections). Permission and recognition to Classes IX and X are under the purview of the Board of Secondary Education. The Board has laid down detailed rules for these purposes, and, on fulfilment of the conditions laid down in the rules, accords permission first to open Class IX and then Class X, after which provisional recognition is granted to the schools concerned. The process of permission and recognition to Classes IX and X in high schools generally takes three years (one year each for permission to Class IX and Class X and one more year for recognition to Classes IX and X), but in many cases, it takes several years owing to the inability of the schools to fulfil the required conditions. The consideration for permission and recognition by SEBA is based on inspection reports submitted by Inspectors of Schools through the DSE. As in the case of middle schools, high schools recognised by SEBA only are considered for provincialisation, depending on the availability of funds. Recognition to high schools by SEBA requires, among others, minimum percentages of pass in the HSLC Examination prescribed by the Board.

(iv) Higher secondary schools were also under the academic purview of SEBA upto 1984. After the establishment of the Assam Higher Secondary Education Council (AHSEC) in 1985, as per the Assam Higher Secondary Education Act, 1984, the powers of according permission and recognition to Classes XI and XII of higher secondary schools as well as junior colleges were vested in the Council.

Before according permission to the newly opened +2 classes in a higher secondary school or a junior college, the Council seeks prior permission from the government (the Secretary of Education) to that effect. No prior permission is, however, needed for according recognition to a higher secondary school or a junior college, which has already been permitted by the Council with the prior approval of the Government. Recognised higher secondary schools and junior colleges become eligible for provincialisation or deficit grants respectively, as per the present rules.

Permission and recognition to such institutions are based on the inspection reports furnished by Inspectors of Schools or officers of the Council or retired educationists engaged by the Council. Recognition by the Council requires minimum performance levels laid down for the purpose. Middle schools and high schools become eligible for recurring ad hoc grants and fee compensatory grants before their provincialisation, depending on the status of a school in terms of permission and recognition.

Conditions for Provincialisation of Schools

The conditions of eligibility for provincialisation of elementary schools, middle English schools and high schools have been laid down in the Assam Elementary Education (Provincialisation) Rules, 1977 and the Assam Secondary (Middle English Schools and High Schools) (Provincialisation) Rules, 1979. The conditions are as follows:

(1) Conditions for taking over Elementary Schools [Rule 5 of the Assam Elementary Education (Provincialisation) Rules, 1977]—

  (i) Every inhabited village shall have at least one elementary school. In a village where there are more than one school, the minimum distance from one to the other should be 1.1 km, provided that the population is more than 200, and, three (3) km in the case of lower primary schools and junior basic school and three (3) km in case of ME, MV and senior basic schools, provided that the population is more than 500.

  (ii) Enrolment in each school shall not be less than forty (40) in case of lower primary schools and junior basic schools and ninety (90) in the case of ME, MV and senior basic schools, provided that the enrolment may be relaxed by the Government in suitable cases.

  (iii) The teachers in Venture school may be retained at the time of taking over if they possess minimum qualification and age for recruitment; provided that such teachers have put in at least two years' continuous service immediately preceding the taking over of the school; and provided further that the prescribed ratio of students and teachers is maintained in the school.

(iv) A Venture school should possess at least two (2) bighas of land in rural areas and ½ bigha of land in urban areas. This condition may, however, be relaxed by Government in suitable cases. DEEO/D.I. shall take the advice of the Board in selecting the school, fulfilling the above conditions, for taking over and forward the list for approval of the DEE in suitable cases.

(2) Eligibility of middle english schools for Provincialisation – The minimum requirement, as on the fixed date of a middle english school to have the services of its employees provincialised, shall be as given below:

(i) One intermediate passed or matric-normal or normal passed teacher for every section of Classes V to VIII. There should be at least two (2) Intermediate passed teachers amongst them;

(ii) The minimum total enrolment is seventy (70), relaxable to fifty (50), at the discretion of the Director of Public Instruction or the Director of Elementary Education, as the case may be, in areas administered under Sixth Schedule of the Constitution of India and other more backward areas as defined by the Government from time to time;

(iii) Every such school must have –

(a) A headmaster who is a graduate, relaxable to intermediate, P.U. (two years) by the Government in exceptional cases;

(b) Assistant teachers who are either normal matric or intermediate passed;

(c) Minimum one teacher (including headmaster) for each section;

(d) One Hindi teacher having qualification in Hindi equivalent to intermediate examination;

Provided that the Government may relax any of the minimum requirements in public interest in the areas prescribed in the Sixth Schedule of the Constitution.

(3) Eligibility of the high schools for provincialisation – The minimum requirement, as on the fixed date, for a high school to have the services of its employees provincialised shall be as given below:

(i) Minimum enrolment shall be 120 in case of three (3) class high schools and 240 in case of six (6) class high school; provided that this minimum shall be 70 in case of secondary schools meant only for female students and 140 in case of any School in the areas administered under the provisions of the Sixth Schedule to the Constitution of India;

(ii) Every such school must have –

(a) A trained graduate teacher, with at least 5 years' teaching experience as headmaster;

(b) Where there are six (6) classes, an assistant headmaster who is a graduate with minimum three (3) years' teaching experience;

(c) Graduate teachers, excluding the headmaster and the assistant headmaster, equal to the number of sections in the upper three classes and at least one of them must be a graduate in Science. In case of a school where there is co-education, there should be at least one graduate lady teacher;

(d) One graduate, with classical subject in his degree course, or having a matric (HSLC) title for every classical subject;

(e) One Hindi teacher having qualification in Hindi equivalent to Bachelor's degree;

(f) One office assistant.

Provided that the Government may relax any of the minimum requirements in the public interest in the areas prescribed in the Sixth Schedule of the Constitution. At present, the Government Memorandum has issued Notification on 24th February, 2014 regarding the neighbourhood norms in compliance of RTE Act 2009.

Norms for Upgradation of EGS Centres to Government School

The Government of Assam was committed to upgrade the EGS centres into government regular schools after functioning for or completing a maximum of two years of its establishment. The Project Approval Board (PAB) of SSA approved 5054 EGS centres for upgradation. Accordingly, the government of Assam had upgraded all the existing 5014 centres to new government schools in a phased manner i.e. in 2009, 1519 schools and, in 2010, 3495 EGS centres were upgraded. Against these 5014 EGS centres upgraded to government schools, 10,028 of teachers have been engaged on contract basis. From amongst the erstwhile Siksha Mitras serving in these centres, 3282 have been appointed as teachers under contract, complying with the NCTE norms.

District Information in School Education (DISE) has been introduced in the year 2002-03 for identification of the existence of primary schools in the State, as per format of DISE prescribed by NIEPA, New Delhi.

Initially the DISE was introduced only for government/ provincialised schools. Since 2006-07, the other schools have also been included under DISE data. The DISE data is being updated every year. Prior to 2009-10, all the schools have been under consideration for provincialisation by the government in a phased manner. The schools, which have completed 10 years from the date of recognition and completed at least seven years after government permission, have been taken as the norm for consideration for provincialisation.

At present, through the provincialisation of the services of teaching and non-teaching staff of Venture Secondary Schools and Junior Colleges was a big task, it was carried out successfully by the Directorate of Secondary Education, Assam. After a school completes ten (10) years and a junior college completes seven (7) years from the date of recognition and government permission, they can be considered for provincialisation. After scrutinising the school records at directorate level if it is found that the school completes seven years then proposal of provincialisation of school is sent to the State Scrutiny Committee of the Government. During the year 2014-15, the following number of institutions, with teaching and non-teaching staff of the school and junior colleges, which completed 10 years and 7 years from the date of recognition and permission from Government w.e.f. 01-01-2013 and 01-08-2013 respectively, were provincialised.

Category of Institutions	*No. of Institutions Provincialised*
2 Class High School/ High Madrassa	1343
5 Class High School/ High Madrassa	127
Higher Secondary School	73
Junior College	12
Total	**1555**

Source: DISE, 2015

Process of Decision-making at the Institutional Level

A Case of Karnataka

Decision-making is among the important functions of an administrator. Compared to private institutions, government schools have to follow the instructions of the higher officers and also follow the norms, rules, regulations of the department. In private and aided schools, decisions are made by the management of the institution. According to the primary sources of information given by the heads of institutions, SDMC is the main stakeholder for decision-making in primary and secondary schools. In lower primary government schools, meetings are conducted with SDMC members to discuss necessary issues and decision taken accordingly. In upper primary and secondary government schools, the higher authorities are also consulted after discussions with SDMC members. In upper primary aided schools, management is the main decision-making authority. The school head consults with the management on decisions. Parents are also involved in certain cases, where necessary. In senior secondary schools, the decisions are taken as per Karnataka civil services rules and regulations. The heads of the institutions, either government or private, take immediate decisions to solve the challenges, issues, or problems in the spheres discussed hereunder, namely academic, administrative, co-curricular, development and community involvement.

Academic Decisions

On the basis of the norms of the department, the head of the institution takes certain decisions in relation to preparing time-table, annual action plan, work allotment to the staff, alternate arrangements in case of vacancy in any subject, conducting of examinations etc. In case of shortage of attendance of students, various curricular programmes, seminars, workshops in schools and programmes for improving the results are conducted.

Administrative

On the basis of the funds provided, either from community contribution, government grants or fees collected, the head of the institution takes necessary decision in preparing a plan and budget. He also takes decision in respect of spending funds for the required materials, infrastructure or teaching-learning materials, purchase of books, laboratory materials, sports equipments etc. as also those related to construction of rooms, repairing, maintenance and provision of facilities like toilets, drinking water and mid-day meals.

Co-curricular

Head of the institution takes decision with regard to conducting of various competitions, sports meets, farewell meets, talent day programmes, tours, excursions, picnics, various level sports meets, Prathibha Karanji, Science, Arts and exhibition programmes.

School Development

Head of the institution plays a very important role in taking decision pertaining to developmental activities. His /her ability as a head of the institution can be judged well at the time of preparing the School Development Plan. It is the head who makes best decision, with the suggestion and guidance of his staff, about the actual requirements of the institution, both physical and academic. Building, water facility, toilet facilities, furniture, teaching materials, sports materials, community support, professional development of the staff, which find a place in the school development plan is a good decision taken by the head while preparing and implementing the plan.

Community Involvement in Decision-making

All the school activities need the support of the community, which includes parents, SDMC members, NGOs and members of the local self-government. The head of the institution has to involve all the members of the community while taking decisions because their support is very essential for the development of the institution. In most cases, the head of the institution takes decisions with the help of other colleagues. In an era of democracy, collective responsibility is safer than individual risk.

Maintenance of Office Records

Office records of institutions are maintained by the Institution. At the primary stage, there is no provision for non-teaching staff in schools run by government/local body. The office records in these schools are maintained by the teaching staff which is limited in number. In private management schools, there is provision for appointment of non-teaching staff, based on number of students. In secondary or higher secondary schools, there is provision for appointment of clerical staff, depending on the number of students in the schools concerned. Presently efforts are on to bring complete automation in maintenance of records and office functioning by using computers and e-governance system.

Procedure and Mechanism of Maintaining Office Records

The procedure to maintain the record of school is followed by using the following registers which are kept in the school in primary, upper primary, secondary and senior secondary. Almost all the States more or less follow the same procedure.

A) Pertaining to pupils:

1) General register.
2) Attendance register for all students in the prescribed form.
3) School Leaving Certificates received from other schools..
4) Counter Foils of school leaving certificates issued to pupils.
5) Records of pupils' attainment and examination results.
6) Records of health and medical examination of pupils.
7) Answer books of annual examination of the preceding year.

B) Pertaining to staff:

1. Service books of school employee.
2. Register of attendance and leave to employee.
3. Discharge certificates received from teachers employed in the school.

4. Headmaster's logbook (observation, supervision notes, suggestions to teachers etc.)

C) Form of Confidential Reports of teachers pertaining to school.

- Daily Cash Book.
- Ledger showing receipts and expenditure, including separate account for form fees.
  1. Fees account book.
  2. Provident Fund account register.
  3. Vouchers.
  4. Register of dead-stock articles.
  5. Laboratory and library register.
  6. Inward register.
  7. School gradation book.

D) Records pertaining to Government Schemes and scholarships and orders of the department:

1) Scholarship register (separate register for various scholarships).
2) Mid-day meal register.
3) Book bank register.
4) The proceedings of co-ordination committee meetings, SMC, PTA, teachers' meeting etc.
5) School gradation note book.
6) Seniority list.
7) Institution recognition and certificate of registration under 1950 and 1860 provisions.
8) Routine letters, proposals and correspondence pertaining to students, school, teachers, training, physical facilities, committees, social participation, extracurricular activities etc.

Number of Days the School Functions

Almost all State governments started implementation of RTE Act 2009 from 1st April 2010. Accordingly, Rules and Regulations were framed in 2011. The minimum number of school working days, instruction hours in the academic year are-

(i) 200 working days for Classes I to V.
(ii) 220 days for Classes VI to VIII (i.e. upper primary).
(iii) 400 instructional hours during the academic year for Classes VI to VIII excluding weekly holiday on Sunday and another half-day, as given in the manual.

Total number of days for vacation shall not exceed 80 days per annum (excluding Sundays and half holidays) and shall include summer vacation, government holidays and other local holidays.

As specified in the RTE Act, 2009, the number of days that a primary school is expected to function is 219 days, in addition 14 days are utilised for conducting examinations and seven days for conducting other school functions, and hence a school functions for a total of 240 days. However, in the case of secondary and higher secondary schools, the scenario is different, as in Maharashtra, secondary and higher secondary schools function for a total of 244 days, of which teaching days are 219, while examinations are conducted over a period of 20 days and five days are utilised for other school functions.

In Andhra Pradesh, the Directorate of School Education provides the academic calendar every year to all the schools in the State. The calendar contains the details of working days, holidays, school timings, subject-wise and class-wise weightage in the allotment of classes, schedule of examinations and all relevant instructions for the improvement of the teaching-learning process. Normally, every school functions for 220 working days or 1200 hours every year. Out of 220 working days, 180 days are for classroom teaching and 40 days are for evaluation. Every school celebrates all national festivals, and other functions like Gandhi Jayanti, Teacher's Day, Children's Day, School Day, etc.

Issues and Suggestions

Cohesiveness amongst the teachers is a pressing problem in secondary schools. Lack of team work and cooperation often leads to poor school management. Hence, an effective HR system should be put in place wherein the teachers can be managed by way of channelising their energies to create a positive and healthy school environment. As the school principal is a key head and leader of his/her respective school, it is often observed that the principal is mostly engaged in administrative tasks of the school. Delegating the same to the staff leads to increased pressure on the staff members as it is in addition to their teaching duties.

Lack of teachers in school and delay in appointing teachers in a timely manner is one of the most common problems in the education system. This causes a lot of burden on the existing teaching staff. Hence, it is important that a waitlist of qualified teachers should be created and used to allot teachers wherever required. RTE Act 2009 covers children of 6-14 years age for their primary schooling, but below the age of six years, pre-schooling is silent. Hence, there should be emphasis to cover the children below the age of six years. Almost in all the States, this group is covered by Aanganwadi under ICDS programme, which requires upgraded policy.

School development work can be carried out through convergence with schemes like MGNREGA for which the norms of the scheme may be revisited. The headmaster of primary schools are facing problems in dealing with the punctuality of teachers, preparation of lesson plans and use of TLM in the classroom process. The teachers are unwilling to conduct CCE. They like to follow the unit test, half-yearly and annual examination system. Teachers are also assigined the tasks other than the teaching works, like census duty, various surveys, election duty, etc. Some teachers do not like to take part in non-scholastic work. Absence of Science teacher and functional Science laboratory is a problem for secondary schools. Non-filling up of existing vacant posts is a problem for high enrolling schools. It creates problems in conducting CCE where there is no teacher for a particular subject.

7

Changes in Administration of School Education in India during Last Two Decades

Traditional Educational Administration

India inherited the British model of educational administration in the early nineteenth century and, specifically, with the Wood's Despatch in 1854. It was a hierarchical control model, based on rules, regulations, codes and acts. The system continued to be from top to bottom viz., from centre to the block level, rigid and authoritarian, despite the recommendations of Education Commissions and Committees. The accountability of educational administrators follows the chain of command within the hierarchy. Maintenance and control being the twin responsibility of educational administrators, they were answerable to their immediate supervisors for the proper deployment of financial and physical resources and all the policies and directives. There was no audit of performance and little accountability for results produced. The education departments had no coordination with and convergence from other departments at State or district levels. Education policies in 1966, 1986 and 1992, several Commissions and Committees evaluated administrative structures and identified serious managerial dysfunctions, poor performance and systemic inefficiencies. Countrywide studies of NIEPA (1991 to 2001), on educational administration, indicated that in spite of diversifying management structures, we were still not able to take the administration out of the practices of routine bureaucratic administrative procedures, which were based on educational codes, acts, rules and regulations. The development of competent management capacity and sound delivery system continues to be one of the most critical challenges facing the mainstream educational administration.

The organisation and administration of school education in India had to be strengthened as the number of institutions, teachers and scholars increased by leaps and bounds during the post-Independence period

(Tyagi, 2001). The renewed thrust and priorities, as envisaged in the National Policies on Education, are continuously emphasising on universalisation of elementary education, vocationalisation of secondary education and raising the standard of education at all levels. Consequently, States and UTs, in order to focus on these programmes, strived to make concerted efforts and transformed their educational administrative set-up and functions so as to make them more responsive to the programme implementation mode, right from district to the secretariat levels. Schools are the ultimate delivery points in the overall education management structure. The various educational structures at State and sub-State levels are required to provide administrative support to the schools for efficient delivery of educational services to the target clientele. As the trend of reforms in educational administration indicates, while at the secretariat level, the unified command of the Education Department had been bifurcated or trifurcated into school education, higher education and language and sports, at the directorate level, separate directorates had come up for primary, elementary, secondary, adult and non-formal and higher education for making them effective for the programme implementation mode. Experience shows that this helped in focussing programme implementation and decentralising various functions of administration. This has, however, had its adverse effect, principally, in three main directions. It has led to the lack of coordination among the different sectors of education. There was no word between primary and secondary education sectors since in a majority of the States, both the sectors have separate set-up of administration, right from institutional level to secretariat level. And thirdly, increasing expenditure was incurred on maintaining separate offices and departments.

Studies have indicated that there was absence of clear guidelines for teacher recruitment and selection. Vacant posts of teachers and administrators and capacity-building programmes, lack of the system of performance appraisal, lack of accountability of teachers and schools and inadequate promotional avenues were some of the areas that needed immediate attention (Singhal, 2001). Furthermore, frequent transfer of teachers, along with problem of teacher absenteeism, had acquired a serious dimension in a majority of the States. There were unsatisfactory service conditions in terms of pension, gratuity, leave pay etc. The more surprising was the lack of administrative initiative to create a responsive grievance redressal system that would be responsible for judicious and timely solution of teachers' problems. Grievance redressal is a major problem with most of the States and UTs. Large number of court cases, pending in different courts in various States were clearly indicative of the dissatisfaction that prevails among the personnel regarding their individual service matters. Most of the cases generally relate to seniority, fixation of pay, pension, posting, transfers, disciplinary action etc. It takes energy, time and money of the teachers and administrators, and, consequently, adversely affects the studies of children. Senior officers, including even Director of Education, sometime face contempt of court proceedings. Some States have grievance redressal mechanism but the same is totally ineffective.

The Education Acts, Codes, Rules and Regulations do not make teachers accountable to the education system, children, parents and community, resulting in providing low quality education. Few States have legislation to stop the use of unfair means in public examinations but these cannot be enforced due to political interference and other compulsions. There are rigid provisions of rules related to grant-in-aid, recognition and affiliation of schools. In spite of the best efforts of the States for diversification of education sector-wise administrative structure, there was a lack of delegation of administrative and financial powers, particularly at the district level. The powers are delegated for a specific period to the District Level Education Officers and are withdrawn after the task is complete. The powers of transfers, service conditions and disciplinary action generally vest with the directorate. Even ordinary matters relating to teachers, which could have been easily disposed of at the regional/district-level offices, are referred to the directorate for final disposal.

Impact of Globalisation and Decentralisation

Studies have considered globalisation and decentralisation as a weakening of the State role in education since decisions are taken at the local level. It results from the abolition of borders for all kinds of economic, financial and cultural activities. It affects not only the economic and financial sphere but also national culture and services, including education (Caillods, 2003). Globalisation involves changes in the development paradigms from social welfare, equity, and nation-state philosophy to one that emphasises economic efficiency, market economy, a weak State and global economy (Tilak, 2003). Education sector is also affected by the global wave of globalisation, as the education policies in many countries of the world, including India, are engulfed by the series of educational reforms, involving drastic changes in the planning and management of education (Bhola, 2003).

Cheng (2003) advocated that globalisation is related to localisation. It includes decentralisation at the community or site level; development of indigenous culture; meeting community needs and expectations; local involvement, inter-institutional collaboration and community support. Globalisation has implications for localisation of educational reforms which maximises education's relevance to local development while bringing in community support and resources, local partnerships, and collaborations in learning, teaching and research (Grauwe, 2004). In decentralisation, schools are given greater educational decision-making autonomy, which devolves local control over curriculum and teaching methods to local communities and the teachers and principals of school themselves. If the local educational authorities see themselves as responsible for educational delivery, reformers reason that educational quality will improve (Carnoy, 1999). Decentralisation makes the planning process people-friendly and participatory, plans more local-specific and the educational institutions more efficient and effective (Varghese, 1996). Govinda (2003) highlighted that decentralisation policies are closely linked to the specific country context. At Jomtien (Thailand) in 1990, the international community committed themselves to renewed efforts to provide primary education for all children and massively reduce adult literacy by the end of the decade.

Impact of National Policy on Education and Jomtien Declaration

In the perspective of globalisation and decentralisation, the task of providing basic education for all with a concrete plan of action gained greater momentum after the National Policy on Education 1986, which was revised in 1992. The World Declaration on Education for All (EFA), adopted in Jomtien in 1990, gave further fillip to the national commitment for providing basic education for all. The Jomtien Declaration, together with several positive developments within the country, brought to the centre stage the need for viewing basic education as a fundamental right of every citizen. India is one of the countries where, during the stabilisation stage of structural adjustment, emphasis on basic education has been stepped up (MHRD, 2001). It was emphasised that to identify and bring to schools those children, who, at present, are not with the system, there was a need for local-specific strategies which necessitate decentralisation in decision-making.

Emergence of Development Programmes

In accordance with this concept, the Total Literacy Campaign (TLC), which was introduced in decentralised mode in the country and implemented through a participatory management approach, was a first significant step towards localising the educational decision-making process. Other development programmes, which were conducted for universalising elementary education, were the Bihar Education Project, the Lok Jumbish Project and Shiksha Karmi Project in Rajasthan and the Basic Education Project (Education for All Project) in Uttar Pradesh. These programmes very well argued for participatory management in the planning and decision-making process and provided the experiences for launching similar educational development programmes, like the District Primary Education Programme (DPEP), in some selected districts in the country. Subsequently, the Government of India launched the Sarva Shiksha Abhiyan (SSA) in 2001, where the focus of planning and decision-making was decentralised administration and management.

The emergence of educational development programmes, as discussed above, have brought the much needed shift in the delivery mechanism of educational services, increased investment in basic education, in expenditure pattern, specifically from staff-salary oriented budget to infrastructure development oriented budget, with financial aid from international agencies. There is also shift from supply-oriented paradigm to demand-oriented paradigm as far as the educational needs at the local level are concerned. As a result, planning and management of elementary education has become participatory at the local level with the help of Village Education Committees and School Management Committees (Govinda, 1997). This can be better understood as the impact of globalisation on localisation and decentralisation of planning and management strategies for achieving the goal of universal enrolment, retention and achievement. Management of Sarva Shiksha Abhiyan is a case in point. The trend of transformation of management strategies from development programmes for elementary education is explicitly clear from the fact that there has been a major shift in the downward swing in the command and control from Central and State level to district level, from district level to block level and from block level to village/habitation level. These changes are primarily directed to make the educational system, in general, and its administration, in particular, more responsive to the needs of the people at the grassroots.

As a result, the administration, in which the parallel management structure was created for project management, takes a holistic view of education, wherein education is seen as an instrument of social change. After implementation of SSA, even earlier development programmes like Lok Jumbish and Shiksha Karmi Programmes in Rajasthan, the Bihar Education Programme having imprints on SSA, were managed in the mission mode, that is, programmes are task-based and target-oriented, instead of management of educational programmes within the framework of rules and regulations, education codes and Acts, as was done earlier.

Accountability of administrators is now based on performance instead of seniority. In several States, SSA and other related programmes like MDM and adult literacy are now managed by regular educational administrators, i.e. DEOs at district level and BEOs at block level. Consequently, the capacity of educational administrators has been developed as they were provided training on planning and management of education in the mission mode. They are now well-versed, not only with the rules and regulations, but also with the mission-mode management, that is task-based and target-oriented. Implementation of the Right to Education Act, 2009, which was implemented from April, 2010 and implementation of the Rashtriya Madhyamik Shiksha Abhiyan provided much impetus in transforming traditional educational administration towards performance and target-based mission mode of management.

Increase in Accountability, Performance and Transparency

Since the beginning of the programme management of elementary education like SSA, implementation of RTE and RMSA, several changes have taken place in the functioning of educational administration. Participatory decision-making in these programmes, right from preparation of Annual Work Plan and Budget (AWP & B) to implementation, and appraisal and feedback for further development, involves accountability and target-based performance of all stakeholders, including officials of regular education department and parallel management functionaries at the district, block, cluster and school levels. All the functionaries at DEO and DPC office, BEO office and BRC, cluster and school level set targets to achieve in a year. They are now accountable for their performance in a given timespan. Consequently, not only the officials of parallel management structure or DPO office, but also officials of regular education department have developed their capacity in implementation of educational programmes. Since there is participatory decision-making by SMC, SDMC, PTAs, CRC, BRC, DEO and DPC in planning and management and implementation of educational programmes, this has resulted in clear transparency in the system while making the delivery of programmes more effective.

Sarva Shiksha Abhiyan as a Vehicle of RTE

Several recommendations were made for an appropriate governance structure for RTE (SSA Framework for Implementation, MHRD, 2011). The report says that the RTE Act confers a permanent right to free and compulsory education of equitable quality on the children of India—for all times to come. It requires the whole education department to work together in a unified manner, and necessitates a fundamental change in the governance structure. It is, therefore, necessary to put in place systems and mechanisms for a shift from the SSA project-based approach to RTE implemented by the mainstream education department.

Since then, the SSA has become the vehicle of RTE implementation. The entire funds of SSA have been diverted to the implementation of RTE in all the States. In some of the States, with regular departments managing SSA, district and block-level educational administration have, therefore, developed their capacity to implement the programme. The report further recommended that the administrative roles for the RTE authority should vest with the mainstream education department functionaries instead of a parallel system of management. All administrative structures in the States, till now separated into the project management and education department, would be merged into one cohesive and effective administrative structure.

E-governance in Educational Management

E-governance in educational management has become the main instrument in the working of administration. It has made administrative processes and procedures easier, and more effective, without any time gap in the information management for implementation of the educational programmes. Almost in all the States, administrative, academic and financial matters, including GOs, circulars, and other documents, are directly sent by the directorates at regional, district, block, cluster and school levels. For organisation of any kind of training programmes, meetings and seminars, the information is sent by e-mail, through websites, whats-app groups and SMS. This has also given impetus to making the delivery of educational programmes more effective. The use of computers and Internet has dramatically reduced repetitive work in many departments, especially the finance department. Use of PCs, E-mails, fax facilities, creation of official websites of all the departments and periodical upload of revised information has made the administration effective. In the Education Department, particularly, the use of software in several educational programmes, like online teacher recruitment and transfers, computerisation of teachers' service conditions, and making the facility available online facilitates users in accessing information from anywhere.

District as a Unit of Educational Governance

Studies have found (NIEPA Third Survey Studies, 2015) that the district has become a unit of educational governance. In some of the States like

U.P., Gujarat, Uttarakhand, Karnataka, Himachal Pradesh and Bihar, the district education officer, besides overseeing and monitoring the regular administration, is also the incharge of SSA, MDM, literacy and other educational programmes. In the States having a separate DEO for secondary education, s/he looks after RMSA and other educational programmes, while in some States, like Andhra Pradesh, having only one DEO, he/she looks after both SSA and RMSA. He/she is specifically responsible for managing RTE in the district. As SSA has become the vehicle of RTE, DEO also coordinates and converges with the other departments and also with the local bodies and NGOs for seeking their involvement and support in planning and management of elementary education and implementation of RTE. DEO ensures 25 per cent admission of children belonging to deprived sections of society into private schools and, alongwith the other aspects of school management, is responsible for age-appropriate admission of children in the neighbourhood school. Almost all the States in the country are following the 25 per cent admission criteria of children belonging to deprived sections of society into private schools.

Block Education Office as a Unit of Educational Management

In recent years, majority of the States have created Block Education Officer Cadre, where BEO is a leader and overall incharge of elementary education while managing SSA, RTE and literacy programme, besides regular administration, including service conditions of teachers and non-teaching staff. In majority of the States, BEO is also the incharge of Block Resource Centre, which is responsible for teacher-training and conducting other academic programmes for planning and management in the block. Earlier, there used to be Sub-deputy Inspectors or Education Inspectors for inspection and supervision of schools and, in some of the States, like Gujarat, they were answerable to the Block Development Officer of the Revenue department, and, as such, they had less time for educational work and more for non-education work. Block Education Officer has been made Class II gazetted officer answerable to the DEO. In some of the States like Karnataka, Uttarakhand, Odisha and Haryana, BEO also looks after secondary education as National Policy on Education, 1986, as revised in 1992, suggested that at the block level, school education from Classes I-XII should be one unit for better coordination, monitoring and supervision.

Cluster Resource Centre for Coordination of Educational Activities

A Cluster Resource Person (CRP) heads each CRC (a cluster of 10-15 primary and upper primary schools). CRP is under the control of block-level BRC Coordinator and is expected to carry out academic and administrative duties specified by BRC or BEO. CRP spends most of the time in monitoring the schools in the cluster, pertaining to academic issues. CRPs are the primary school head teachers or teachers, who are selected to work for a fixed period. The CRP visits all the schools in the cluster and facilitates the teachers in academics. Besides, s/he helps senior officials in performing academic supervision and school inspections in the cluster.

Decentralisation of Educational Planning and Management

Decentralisation of administration is advocated to make the delivery of educational programmes more effective by ensuring the complete and meaningful participation of students, parents and the larger community. Decentralisation mobilises and involves people to take the responsibility for identifying their own educational needs and participate in planning and management of education at different levels. This makes the planning process people-friendly and participatory, plans more local-specific and the educational institutions more efficient and effective. Planning has become demand-based instead of supply-based by conducting habitation-wise school-mapping and micro-planning and preparing Annual Work Plan and Budget (AWP & B) at district level on the basis of school, cluster and block level plans. Management has become participatory with local governance through involving community in VEC/SMC/PTA/SDMC at school, block and district level and by involving expert committees, constituted for different purposes like planning, management of different programmes, for training and capacity-building for quality improvement, for providing physical facilities and for the programmes of disadvantaged groups. Cluster resource centres are meant for the delivery of resource support to the teachers.

Strengthening of Educational Management Information Systems

Earlier, educational planning and management were based on the data collected and published by States and MHRD, Government of India. This process took several years and resulted in delays in implementation of programmes. DISE and, thereafter, U-DISE have now made the information management more effective while minimising the time-gap in the availability of data and made the governance of education at district, State and national levels more effective. School-level data is available through the school report card. Planning and implementation of educational programmes of elementary and secondary education (AWP & B) have become more effective.

Sustainable and Increased Investment in Basic Education

Before implementation of SSA, more than 90 per cent of State education expenditure had to be incurred on teachers' salaries and, as a result, lesser funds were available for infrastructure development. Since the SSA is based on the premise that financing of elementary education has to be sustainable, a long-term perspective on financial partnership between the Central and State governments has been adopted. On the basis of AWP & B of the district, through which the funds are provided for educational programmes, the problem of school infrastructural facilities in the States has almost been solved. Implementation of RMSA also provides additional funds for infrastructure development and professional development of teachers in secondary education.

Changes in the Delivery Mechanism

Due to decentralisation and participatory planning and management of elementary education, delivery of educational programmes has become more effective. Establishment of BRCs, CRCs for providing academic support to schools, recruitment of teachers at block and district level, thereby minimising time-gap, has given impetus to the educational programmes. Participatory decision-making by VEC/SMC/PTA/SDMC at school level has provided much support in making the delivery of educational programmes more effective. Each activity of the programme is planned on task-based and target-oriented approach. It has helped in making the delivery of programmes more effective.

Quality Improvement in Recruitment and Selection of Teachers

In all the States and Union Territories in the country, recruitment and selection of teachers is based on essential eligibility conditions, which include academic and professional qualifications and passing the Teacher Eligibility Test. This process has a positive impact on quality improvement of the teaching-learning process in schools. Several States have cent per cent trained teachers and new teachers are being recruited from the list of TET-passed teachers. Under SSA, RTE and RMSA, there is much emphasis on in-service teacher training which is provided by DIETs, SCERTs and NGOs.

Management of Disadvantaged Groups

There have been more focussed educational programmes for the children from disadvantaged groups, like SC, ST, CWSN, children in difficult circumstances, like street children and children living in difficult areas, since the implementation of development programmes like SSA. Apart from the regular educational management programmes by the directorates concerned, like Tribal Welfare, Social Welfare, SC, ST, and programmes like SCP and STP, SSA has given more intensive focussed programmes and identified the backward blocks where it has established KGBVs. Different types of incentive schemes and incentives have also been started.

Convergence of Resources

Management of development programmes is not possible in isolation. It has to converge and coordinate with different departments and agencies. The SSA is conceived as an "umbrella programme" which subsumes all the on-going projects, programmes and schemes aimed at developing basic education. A convergent approach helped overcome the problems of coordination between intra-sectoral and inter-sectoral programme initiatives and, at the same time, facilitated effective planning, implementation, monitoring and evaluation of the programme. Figure 7.1 points out the main agencies with which the education department converges at school, cluster, block, district and directorate levels.

These agencies include Health Department for school health programme; Women and Child Development Department for (ICDS) Anganwaris; Rural Development Department for total sanitation programme; Revenue Department for MDM; Department of Water Supply for drinking water facility; Department of Roads and Building for construction of school building. Among the other agencies are Social Welfare Department for scholarships, uniforms, bicycles, education for CWSN, SCPCR for child labour, juvenile justice, child protection migratory children and street children; Civil Societies (NGOs) for help in managing teaching-learning support, inclusive education for CWSN, migratory children, street children, teacher training, survey work, SMC & PRIs training; Youth Welfare Department for sports; Education Departments of Universities and institutions like SCERTs, DIETs for academic support; and IT Agencies and PRIs for programme management.

Fig. 7.1: Inter and Intra-Department Coordination, Linkages and Convergence

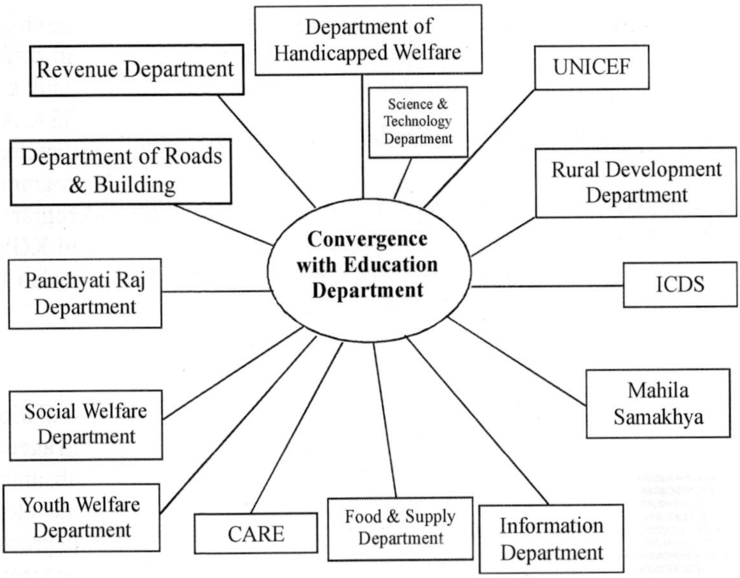

Disaster Management in Schools

Almost in all the States, awareness and sensitisation programmes regarding managing disasters and safe schools have been conducted at school level alongwith the distribution of printed materials and installation of equipments like fire-extinguishers in schools. In some States, safety drills in schools are conducted to deal with emergency situations. Precautions under emergency circumstances are displayed on notice boards in schools, and teachers and education officers are provided training by organising programmes at block and district levels.

School Development Plan

The practice of preparing school development plan in primary and upper schools and also in secondary schools, under RMSA, has been started in almost all the States, as preliminary findings of Third All India Survey of Educational Administration indicate. The SDP, which is prepared with the help of SMC in primary and upper primary schools and with the help of SDMC in secondary schools, provides opportunity for schools for target-setting of educational activities for development and growth.

Best Practices in Educational Administration

Educational Administration, over the years, has also witnessed some innovative practices along with the programme management. Few practices have been discussed below.

Library Movement for Quality Improvement in Ganjam District of Odisha

The main objective is to develop reading habits of children as this not only creates learning environment in school but also inculcates love for books in children and, in the process, helps in shaping and enriching their character. DEO, Ganjam constituted a team of BEOs, CRCs and SMC members, meetings were organised with them and programme of library movement was discussed. Available books of each grade, including story books and magazines, were labelled by the children with colours like green, pink, yellow and violet. A library corner was created in each classroom in elementary school and grade-wise books were displayed with the help of a rope. The children pick up the books of their choice in their free time and return them in their proper place after reading. They are encouraged to narrate the stories, read by them in these books, in the prayer class. The seventh period of every Wednesday is dedicated to reading books other than the textbooks in each and every school in the district. In the seventh period, when the school bell rings, everybody present in the school—students, teachers and non-teaching staff—leaves whatever they are doing at the time and starts reading the books, including story books/magazines/newspapers etc. Students are also encouraged to bring books from their homes and read them during this period. Headmasters are given the responsibility of adjusting the school time-table as per their local situations. This has created a movement that promotes a learning environment in schools, enabling children to engage in developing their creative skills and group activities by preparing wall magazines and class magazines. Involving teachers in all these activities has enhanced the teaching-learning process and resulted in quality improvement of education in schools.

Communitisation of Elementary Education in Nagaland

With the principal aim of improving the standard and quality of education and developing institutions of excellence, through the active participation of the community, teachers and parents, the Government of Nagaland has introduced the Communitisation initiative in the education sector, through the Nagaland Communitisation of Public Institutions and Services Act, 2002. Under this novel Act, certain responsibilities like management of financial resources and administrative powers of the communitised schools have been transferred to the village communities through the Village Education Committees (VECs). The objective of this policy is to help create a sense of ownership of public institutions and better management of resources. The Village Council is empowered to constitute the Village Education Committee (VEC), which acts as the local authority to manage the elementary education in the village. The VEC is empowered to control teachers in a variety of ways, including the powers to withhold salaries for irregular and absentee teachers and staff. This power to withhold the salaries for erring employees was made possible because the salary amount for the government employees in the schools is deposited in advance into the VEC account and the VEC is delegated with the power to disburse the salary. The community also receives funds for key purposes, such as purchase of textbooks, furniture, repair of school buildings etc. However, all these actions of monitoring and control are done with the supervision and support of the government. This achievement was recognised globally and the government of Nagaland was selected for the prestigious United Nations Public Service Awards for communitisation programme in recognition of its innovative use of rich social capital. The award was conferred to the State government on June 23, 2008 at New York, USA.

An Empowered Cluster Head in Maharashtra

In Maharashtra, the cluster head below the Block Education Officer is appointed on a regular scale. It is both an administrative and academic post. S/he looks after the functioning of about 10 schools, and monitors and supervises the activities of headmasters of elementary schools. S/he helps guide the teaching-learning process, curricular and co-curricular activities in schools, takes at least four demonstration lessons per week in the schools in his/her cluster, reports to extension officer regarding irregularities detected in the schools, arranges remedial teaching for the slow learners in schools, visits and monitors the activities in pre-primary schools, anganwadi, mahila prabodhan centre, rural libraries, ashram shalas etc. and meetings at school, block and district levels, as and when required.

Human Resource Development Bank at Block Level in Bageshwar District of Uttarakhand

DEEO Bageshwar has introduced the practice of preparing a list of human resources available at the block level. These resource persons will include anyone who can help the school or education office in training, teaching or preparing any good scheme for school development or provide any other resource, including finance. These resource persons will include retired persons from any department in the area, including education department, NGOs, or any interested person in the community. This practice has helped the schools very much, particularly when a teacher has retired or is transferred and studies of children suffer. A substitute teacher provides help in the continuation of studies of children in school.

8

Major Issues and Future Directions in Administration of School Education

Major Issues

Wither Governance of School Education

Educational governance, comprising four areas of educational policy, planning, administration and management, encompasses the spirit of comprehensiveness in looking after educational processes and activities for achieving educational goals. Educational management refers to individuals or groups of people who are given the authority to achieve the desired results. It encompasses processes, structures and arrangements that are designed to mobilise and transform the available physical, human and financial resources to achieve concrete outcomes. Governance systems set the parameters under which management and administrative systems operate. Governance is about how power is distributed and shared, how policies are formulated, priorities set and stakeholders made accountable. Governance mainly refers to structures and processes that are designed to ensure accountability, transparency, responsiveness, rule of law, stability, equity and inclusiveness, empowerment, and broad-based participation. Good governance in education systems promotes effective delivery of education services. It is expected to be participatory, transparent, accountable, effective and equitable and promote rule of law.

Education Secretary of the State acts as Chief Executive Officer and head of the Education Department and is mainly responsible for policy and programme formulation. He is also responsible for enforcement of rules and regulations for educational management. However, it has been found that the education secretaries of the states are frequently transferred for no reason. Sometimes, political pressure is also a factor in this regard. It has been found that transfers are necessary when political dispensation changes in the State. Newly-joined officers may not necessarily belong to the education department but are appointed from any of the development departments. Consequently, it takes time for the officer to understand about the educational programmes, policies and functioning of the department. If he/she is transferred in a short period of time, another officer will also take time to understand the functioning of the department. As a result, there is no focus on policy and planning of the programme in a frequently changing environment of educational programmes and developments in education. Accountability of the officers in a given time, which should be an essential condition for the achievement of tasks and the target in the State, is not fixed. It leaves the development of education in the State without any vision for policy and programme planning for the progress of education. This situation is also the same in the case of other senior officers at the directorate, regional and district levels. The State education department runs on the basis of Government Order or Circulars. There is no time to understand the legal base of education department by any of the educational administrators, and, as a result, educational programmes are delayed for years and sometimes end without achieving the goal. It seems to indicate that when there is no vision and no accountability to implement policy and programme planning, the governance of school education is found withering at all levels of educational administration, either at secretariat, directorate, district or at block level.

Lack of Accountability and Transparency

The development programmes of SSA and RMSA envisaged the provision of accountability and transparency by making these programmes task-based and target-oriented. It also created institutions like SMC, CRC, and BRC for making the delivery of programmes more effective, with participatory decision-making at the site level, and for continuous monitoring of programmes for their timely completion. Experiences have indicated that in SSA and RMSA, the targets for completion of the programmes, which had been fixed for one financial year, were not achieved in spite of having resources and manpower, and these programmes were carried over in the next financial year. As a result, the targets in SSA could not be achieved as fixed and the whole programme, since its inception, kept on being extended from time to time. SSA has become the vehicle of RTE but barring some of the educationally advanced States, wherein RTE has been implemented in letter and spirit, several other States like U.P., Bihar, Odisha and Bengal, the provisions of RTE have not been achieved even after seven years of implementation of RTE. There are non-enrolled children, high dropout rate, high Pupil-Teacher ratio and posts of teachers remain vacant for years. If non-enrolled children are admitted in school, there is no special training for age-appropriate children admitted in a particular class. While there are lakhs of vacancies of teachers in all the States, the posts are vacant for unjustified reasons. There are overcrowded classes which affect the quality of education. There are single-teacher schools. This scenario existed in the States since implementation of SSA in 2001. Despite RTE and the compulsory admission of all non-enrolled children in age-appropriate classes, the target has not been achieved in several States. If there are high enrolments, the retention of children is a problem being faced by the States. This has led to the question regarding lack of accountability and transparency on the part of teachers and educational administrators and the education system in the State as a whole.

Parallel Management Structures

The mission mode management for implementation of SSA was expected to influence and reform the mainstream education department to take up the challenge of universal elementary education. It was expected that it would build the capacity of mainstream education department in respect of educational planning and management. This has met with only limited success, and, over the last two decades, barring few States where SSA is the responsibility of mainstream education department, the education departments and SSA mission agency have tended to function as dual and parallel structures. The already existing structures at the mainstream education department have remained aloof of it, and have tended to hamper the functioning and deprive the programme of crucial support. Ideally, the Directorate of Elementary Education, SCERTs, DIETs, BRC/CRC, State Textbook Corporations etc., and SSA should have been functioning in tandem and pursuing a unified vision of universalisation of elementary education, but this has not happened, leading to a gap in the coordinated approach towards educational management.

Management of Education by other Departments

Many other departments are also conducting educational programmes in several States like the Department of Social Welfare, Department of Scheduled Castes, Department of Tribal Welfare and Department of Minorities. These departments provide scholarships, incentives and other related activities to the students of SC, ST, OBC, Minorities etc. However, they do not have any coordination with the education department. Some States also manage hostels for these students but the education department remains unaware of these programmes for the students and does not have any kind of convergence with these departments. However, some of the States, like Madhya Pradesh and Chhattisgarh, have included the educational programmes conducted by other departments in the education department so that education officers know about their overall responsibility for implementation of total programmes for disadvantaged groups in a well-coordinated manner.

Lack of Coordination and Convergence

As the trend of reforms in educational administration indicates that while at the secretariat level, the unified command of the education department has been bifurcated or trifurcated into school education, higher education and language and sports, at the directorate level, separate directorates have come up for primary, elementary, secondary, adult and non-formal and higher education in order to make them effective for the programme implementation mode. Experience shows that though this has helped in focussing on programme implementation and decentralising various functions of administration, it has, however, had its adverse effect principally in three main directions, resulting in lack of coordination among the different sectors of education. There is no coordination between primary and secondary education sectors since in majority of the States, both the sectors have separate set-ups for administration, right from institutional to secretariat levels. Further, there is increasing expenditure incurred on maintaining separate offices and departments. Besides, in majority of the States, as mentioned above, the problem of coordination is further compounded between SSA, RMSA, and other departments like SC, ST, Minority and the respective management structures of mainstream educational administration at directorate, district, block and cluster levels.

Implementation of SSA, RMSA, RTE requires convergence with several other departments and this appears quite inadequate, as indicated in third survey reports of different States. These programmes should have convergence and coordination with different department and agencies. The SSA has been conceived as an "umbrella programme" which subsumes all the on-going projects, programmes and schemes aimed at developing basic education. A convergent approach helped overcome the problems of coordination between intra-sectoral and inter-sectoral programme initiatives and, at the same time, facilitated effective planning, implementation, monitoring and evaluation of the programme. The agencies, with which education officers have to converge, are Health Department for school health programme; Women and Child Development Department for (ICDS) Anganwaris; Rural Development Department for total sanitation programme; and Department of Water Supply for drinking water facility; and other departments like Roads and Building for construction of school building.

Increased Workload of the Administrative Machinery

Barring a few States like Punjab, Haryana and Madhya Pradesh, there are no norms for fixing the size of the administrative machinery at any level. Even in these States, administrative machinery is not fixed as per norms. As a result of the all-out efforts for the universalisation of elementary education and, of late, secondary education, the size of the school education system, in terms of schools, enrolment and teachers, has increased tremendously and the pressure is continuing on the educational administrators. In the absence of proper planning, size of the administrative machinery has not increased and consequently, pressure of workload, particularly on district level education officers and block education officers, has been increasing. Due to the implementation of SSA, RMSA, RTE and other programmes the pressure of workload of educational administrators, specifically at district and block levels, has multiplied. Even though all the States have established their block-level set-up of educational administration for elementary education, for secondary education, in spite of recommendations by the National Policy on Education, 1986/1992 that school education should be as one unit, this has not been done. All these reasons have led to heavy workload on district education officers. As a result, they find little time to visit the school for monitoring, inspection and supervision.

Inadequate Linkages with Local Bodies

Local bodies in majority of the States are mostly functional at the village level. Their participation involves mostly keeping a check on teachers' vacancies, problems of administration arising in the school, maintenance of the school, keeping a check on students' achievements etc. These bodies also have committees at district and block levels for representing their participation in decision-making bodies in the education department. Local bodies, generally, participate in recruitment, selection, posting and transfer of teachers. There are three States where local bodies are given major responsibility of school education. These States are Madhya Pradesh, Maharashtra and Kerala. After 73rd Amendment Act, Madhya Pradesh became the first State to enact new Panchayat Raj system and form PRIs. After formation of PRIs, the State government assigned several powers and duties to PRIs, with education being one of such areas. Elementary education was transferred to the panchayats under such devolution of powers. As such, in rural areas, all schools, from pre-primary to higher secondary, are now managed and operated through panchayats. The main functions of panchayats are management and operation of schools, construction and extension of school buildings, making available teaching aids for school, exercising control over operation of non-formal education system, appointment of Shiksha Karmi and implementation of promotion schemes. In Maharashtra and Kerala, elementary education from Classes I-VIII is managed by local bodies.

The handing over of schools to Panchayat Raj Institutions have their own problems. Sometimes the members try to get such resolutions passed that do not come under the purview of the department and are also not State priorities. Due to lack of interest and awareness among PRIs, the decision taken by them is neither practical nor feasible. Although the PRIs have been given powers but their involvement is limited to engagement and transfer of teachers. They have yet to involve themselves in development activities of school management. It was expected in the rural areas that panchayats, in general, and Gram panchayats, in particular, would have critical roles to play in SSA. Panchayats do figure in the text of SSA documents, but they do not seem to have been assigned any crucial responsibility in respect of educational planning and management, monitoring and supervision of the school system. At the district level, the entire task is handled by the district SSA cell.

Insufficient School Inspection and Supervision

While SSA strengthened the academic support system of the schools, the administrative and academic supervision of the schools remained a neglected area. The BRCs are neither able to conduct academic supervision nor provide help and guidance to the teaching-learning process. BRPs provide training to teachers in different subjects or are involved in monitoring of different activities of SSA in schools. The mainstream departmental structures also remained weak, under-staffed and under-trained to do this job effectively. If education officers of the mainstream education department go for inspection and supervision, their work remains confined mainly with the head of school offices only. As such, they are not able to fully inspect some of the basic requirements of a functional school, such as punctuality and regularity of attendance of teachers, maintenance of records, effective liaison with parents and the community, follow-up action on training programmes etc. Academic supervision, wherein education authorities need to provide help and support to the teaching-learning process by assessing gaps between competencies and expected performance of teachers through classroom observation, is completely absent in a majority of States (NIEPA Survey Studies on educational administration—1973-81,1991-2001, 2014-16). They either do not visit schools as per norms, or if they do visit, they do not spend enough time there.

Inadequate Teacher Management

The fact is that despite recognising the central role of teachers in improving the quality of education, the progress in filling up teachers' vacancies has not been encouraging, particularly in States faced with greater shortage of teachers. Recruitment of teachers has not taken place, as per the need of the schools in the light of RTE norms, as a result of which various posts are still lying vacant. Besides, there has also been an inability to take effective stand with regard to service conditions of the teachers, those who were sanctioned under SSA. State after State recruited contract teachers with meagre salaries and poor service conditions. Despite equal work, different pay scales and nature of job (regular and contractual) imply a different status for contractual teachers. Therefore, different mechanism of performance evaluation exists. If recruitment is done, the posting of teachers delayed for unknown reasons. Frequent transfers of teachers and educational administrators lead to uncertainties, indecisions and instability. Furthermore, in most of the States, frequent transfer of teachers has acquired a serious dimension alongwith the problem of teacher absenteeism which leads to proxy teachers being assigned the work by the regular teacher, who himself remains absent from school. There are unsatisfactory service conditions in terms of pension, gratuity, leave pay etc.

There is no provision for promotion of contractual teachers. Till date, not all teachers have been receiving long-term training to be abreast with the latest techniques and methods of teaching-learning. There is no provision for exposure visit of the teachers for their professional development. Several States, like U.P., have lakhs of vacancies in primary, upper primary, secondary and senior secondary schools. Studies have indicated that vacant posts of teachers and administrators and shortage of capacity building programmes, lack of the system of performance appraisal, lack of accountability of teachers and schools and inadequate promotional avenues are some of the areas that need immediate attention. All the States expressed concern about the shortage of subject teachers, particularly for Science, Mathematics and English, in upper primary, secondary and senior secondary schools as it hampers the studies of children while affecting the quality of education.

In the context of transfers of teachers, it has been observed that teachers generally prefer transfer to urban areas. When teachers get any metropolitan town school, they are reluctant to vacate their places, with the result that those teachers serving in rural area schools are deprived of the opportunity of going to urban areas. Rationalisation of teachers is a major problem in the States. Teachers do not want to be posted in difficult terrains and far-flung rural areas, and consequently, in some States, there are zero-teacher schools or schools that have been closed down due to the unavailability of teachers. States do not have proper planning for teachers' recruitment, with the result that on the retirement of teachers, posts remain vacant and studies of children suffer.

Lack of Devolution of Powers

In spite of the best efforts of the States for diversification of education sector-wise administrative structure, there is a lack of delegation of administrative and financial powers, particularly at the district level. The powers are delegated for a specific period to the district-level education officers and are withdrawn after the task is complete. The powers of transfers, service conditions and disciplinary actions generally vest with the directorate and, in some States, at the ministry level. Even ordinary matters relating to teachers, that could easily have been disposed of at the regional/district level offices, are referred to the directorate for final disposal.

Litigation Cases

Studies have indicated that district education officers and heads of institutions do not have adequate knowledge of various provisions of the Educational Rules, Regulations, Codes and Acts. As a result, there are a large number of litigation cases of teachers and non-teaching staff pending in the District Courts, High Courts and even the Supreme Court. These court cases are related to postings, transfers, promotion, pension, gratuity, and disputes over management of private-aided institutions. States do not have a grievance-redressal mechanism at any level of administration. And if some States do have a mechanism in the form of tribunals at the State level, it is not functional. It indicates an increasing dissatisfaction over service conditions among the teachers and non-teaching staff. With educational litigation on the increase, a large amount of money and other resources are being spent on them, both by individual teachers and district and State education authorities. A large share of time of district education officers is consumed by the court cases. It is not only the district education officers, who face contempt of court cases, but the directors of education too face such situations. What is more surprising is the lack of administrative initiative to create a responsive grievance redressal system that could be responsible for judicious and timely solution of teachers' problems. Grievance redressal is a major problem with most of the States and UTs. A large number of cases, pending in different courts in various States, is clearly indicative of the dissatisfaction that prevails among the personnel in respect of their service matters.

Inadequate Academic Management

Academic support institutions like the SCERTs have no doubt played an important role in educational development, particularly in dealing with what might be termed as the main concern, viz. the quality of education. The contribution of support institutions has been significant in conducting research and surveys, development of curricula, design of syllabi, preparation of print and non-print teaching and learning materials and training of educational personnel. Their role performance suffers from a number of handicaps: lack of adequate resources (staff strength and expertise, infrastructure, financial constraints), lack of coordination with other institutions, which would allow much sharing of expertise and resources and in designing an integrated and comprehensive strategy for educational development. They have yet to assume the think-tank functions. They seldom critically evaluate the value and impact of their activities and modalities for implementing them.

Future Directions

Effective Governance of School Education

In spite of changes in the education administration—from maintenance-based to programme management mode—the functioning of education administration is still based on traditional lines which is adversely affecting the governance of school education in India. It is necessary that steps should be taken to make the governance of school education more effective. While following the top to bottom approach, the first and foremost step would be that there should be a longer stay of Education secretaries at their posts. It should not be less than three years since it would take time for the new secretary to get acquainted with the situation at the ground level, prepare realistic plans and monitor the outcome of the adopted education policies and programmes. The time period of stay should be linked with the assigned tasks and the target to be achieved so as to reflect the accountability of the education officer when s/he achieves the task in a given span of time. Performance of the education officer would be manifest in the evaluation of the programmes in this period. There must be some reward for those who worked excellently in the department to achieve the target in the assigned job. This practice should also percolate down to the director of education and the regional, district and block education officers. Education officer should not be transferred during this period. Education secretaries should also go in for a one week induction programme before joining as head of the education department.

Indian Education Service

In order to make educational governance effective, there is a need to build a cadre of key decision-makers, with necessary professional competencies and who are deployed to positions with sufficiently long tenures. In this context, it is worthwhile to consider seriously the institution of an Indian Education Service, as recommended by the Education Commission, 1964-66, which had observed that one cannot be a good educational administrator unless one is also a good teacher. An educational administrator should have a blend of teaching, research and administrative capabilities. The Commission further conceptualised that there should always be a possibility of shifting the educational administrator from administration to teaching and research jobs and vice versa. The National Policy on Education, 1986 had stated that: —a proper management structure in education will entail the establishment of the Indian Education Service. It will bring a national perspective to this vital sector. The basic principles, functions and procedures of recruitment to this service will be decided in consultation with the State Governments.

Reforms in Mainstream Educational Administration

The organisation and administration of school education in India has been transformed into the programme implementation mode right from school to secretariat level, specifically since 2001, with the implementation of SSA. Since schools are the ultimate delivery points in the overall education management structure, there is a need for reforms in structure and functions to be more effective for delivery of educational programmes. The various educational structures at State and sub-State levels are required to provide administrative support to the schools for efficient delivery of educational services to the target clientele. In view of the major issues discussed in this chapter, the following are the proposed suggestions to make the educational management of school education more responsive and effective.

Coordinated and Unified Approach in Management: Administration of school education would require a complete overhaul of the structures, processes and systems. Much emphasis has been laid so far to the bifurcation of educational administration into different sectors for focusing on sector-wise programmes and decentralisation of functions. As the National Policy on Education advocated good governance of school education, its implementation would need coordinated efforts of all sectors of educational administration along with decentralisation of authority and participatory approach of management. As earlier discussed in this chapter, education policies and various committees had recommended making school education as one functional unit, right from block to secretariat level, in order to make educational administrative functions more coordinated and effective, barring few States like Uttarakhand, Bihar and, to some extent, Karnataka, other States were unable to make school education as one unit.

At Secretariat and Directorate Level: As suggested by the National Policy on Education, 1986/1992 and also by the report of 12th Plan, Sub-Group, 2011, MHRD, Government of India, there is a need to make a coordinated and unified approach in respect of management of elementary education. At the secretariat level, there should be a principal secretary of school education coordinating both elementary and secondary education in the States where elementary and secondary education secretaries are separate. Since SSA has become a vehicle of RTE, it should be managed by the mainstream education department, viz. Directorate of Elementary Education. As such, all administrative structures in the States, hitherto separated into the project management and education department, would be merged into one cohesive and effective administrative structure. Similarly, RMSA should come under Directorate of Secondary Education. In case of single directorate of school education, both programmes should be managed by the Directorate of School Education. The present system of autonomy of the State authority, including the powers for engagement of Consultants on contractual basis, should continue. In the event that both the directorates and other directorates are separate, there should be a Director General of School Education for coordinating the total school education.

At District Level: There is need to have a Chief Education Officer if there are two district education officers in the State for elementary and secondary education to ensure better coordination and monitoring. The DEOs should also manage SSA-RTE and RMSA respectively. Principal, DIET and CEO of PRI/municipal corporation should be linked with the District Elementary Education Officer for effective support and management of education. Chief Education Officer/DEO should have full powers of administration, management and financial management instead of the present arrangement wherein District Collector is the Mission Director of SSA at district level. Studies found that the work of the DEOs is hampered as the District Collector calls DEOs for even non-education work related meetings. The State government should also set up Grievance Redressal Cells at the district, block, municipal body and panchayat levels, with designated officers, assisted by adequate manpower and resources. This is necessary since the daily working time of DEOs is wasted in attending court cases of teachers and non-teaching staff. Court cases in the State are increasing. For instance, there are 37000 pending court cases in Uttar Pradesh. To deal with this situation, there is a need to constitute a legal cell at district level to deal with court cases. It would allow the district education officer to invest his time in the implementation and monitoring of educational programmes.

Focus on Block Education Office: As discussed earlier, States are in the process of empowering block education officers, as suggested by national policies on education, instead of appointing sub-deputy inspectors of schools (at block level) who were unable to perform their role of inspection and supervision. This was because they (the SDIs) had to work under the block development officer of the revenue department at block level and, as such, were always busy in completing the work of the revenue department rather than that of school supervision. The States are now in the process of creating a full-fledged post of class-II gazetted officer as block education officer under the district education officer. It would be imperative to empower block education officers to make the delivery of educational programmes more effective, with monitoring and implementation of programmes of elementary education, and to provide supervisory support to teaching-learning process in schools for quality improvement. Thus, the block education officer needs to be considered as a leader for managing elementary education, SSA-RTE, literacy, MDM and other flagship programmes at the block level. Each block education officer should have a contingent of additional BEOs, who would help him/her in dealing with the administrative issues, and Extension Officers, who would be expected to undertake visits to school. The BRC should be merged with the establishment of BEO which has academic staff of five resource persons and a number of CRCs. States would need to look into the adequacy of the supervisory staff and consider strengthening of the block education office. There is also a need to devise and frame effective cadre management rules for the block-level functionaries and organise orientation and training programmes for them.

Procedural Reforms in Teacher Management

The issue of reforms in teacher management needs urgent attention by the State governments. As far as recruitment of teachers is concerned, since the implementation of RTE, there are fixed eligibility conditions at primary, upper primary and secondary level. S/he is required to meet the stipulated academic qualifications along with professional qualifications and also pass the State Teacher Eligibility Test. Besides these specified conditions, some States select teacher only after conducting a written test. On the basis of merit, the qualified candidates are selected and posted as teachers. After the selection of teachers, they are kept on a consolidated salary on contract basis and not fitted in a regular scale. Their services are not regularised for years. The whole process of keeping a teacher on a consolidated salary, on contract basis, is demotivating. This has created different types of teachers for the same work at the same level of education. The extension of the contract of teachers is based on their yearly evaluation. Their services are not continued if their performance does not come up to the mark. It is suggested that these teachers should be kept n a regular pay scale, like the regular teachers.

Postings and transfers, particularly of teachers, are issues that require urgent attention. The States need to formulate their transfer policies with the provision of rationalisation and justification. A roster of teachers should be maintained to regulate the posting and transfer of teachers on the basis of the information fed into the computer. In principle, a teacher should be posted near his or her home village. Though the Programme of Action, 1992 also recommends that we should move towards a policy of zero transfers unless it is expedient to do so, there should, therefore, be a system of minimum transfers, since there will always be grounds for transfer on compassionate grounds (location of spouse, ill/aged parents, etc.). Transfers may be restricted to wider geographic levels – more liberal at cluster/block levels and stricter across blocks and districts.

It has been found that a State like Madhya Pradesh has given the management of school education to Panchayati Raj Institutions. It has been found that PRI functioneries are involved in teacher recruitment, selection, postings and transfers only and there is more political pressure in all activities of teacher management. Barring this, they are not involved in any of the academic activities. Teachers in PRIs have been given lower scales, which is even one-third that of the regular teachers. This is because of the argument that PRIs do not have enough financial resources. It has been noticed that when any regular teacher retires from service, his or her post is kept in dying cadre and, in place of the teacher, vacant post recruitment is done by PRIs. No other State has such a process of teacher recruitment. It is suggested that the process of teachers' management may be transferred to the education department since it is affecting the quality of education in a big way.

School-based Supervision in Schools

Education authorities are not able to give feedback to heads either on improvement in teaching-learning processes or on teachers. In such a situation, the question that arises is what should be the mechanism of academic support and supervision to be given to schools? If given the required freedom and support, the heads would certainly strive to improve teaching-learning process and give professional support to teachers. School-based instructional supervision has its emphasis on improving the teaching-learning process as well as on heads giving effective professional support to teachers. It explores the idea that the supervision process needs to be decentralised at the school-level to heads in government and private-aided senior secondary schools. While school-based instructional supervision by heads of institutions will emphasise on support to teaching-learning process and professional development of teachers, external supervision by education authorities will continue to observe policy guidelines of education and audit of several other aspects of school management.

Adequate Capacity Building of Education Officers

NIEPA studies on educational administration indicate that after selection of persons to the post of DEO or BEO, no pre-induction training is provided to them during or before their probation. DEOs or BEOs, who are selected to the posts on promotion from the lower cadre, do not possess managerial skills and those who come through direct selection neither possess management skills nor educational administrative experience. It is suggested that at least three months' induction training be provided to BEOs and DEOs before they are given charge of their respective positions.

Strengthening Regulatory Mechanism

There is need to strengthen the regulatory mechanism. Legal basis of education in each State includes Codes, Acts, Rules and Regulations. There are provisions that are unrealistic and obsolete. For example, for opening of schools, while there are general norms regarding playgrounds, libraries and other facilities, the norms are silent on how a playground will be provided in a school that is set up in an overcrowded area. Rules and regulations should not be a burden on the system but it should facilitate efficiency and effectiveness of planning and implementation of educational programmes. There should be provisions for reward and punishment. They should lead to timely promotion and career development of the teaching and non-teaching staff. Rules related to pension, gratuity, leave, recruitment, selection, posting and transfers should be very clear. There is a need to have rules to minimise litigation, and grievance-redressal cells should be established at the school, cluster, block, district, region, directorate and secretariat levels where minimum time should be taken to redress grievances.

Institutional Management

Institutional planning and management is an important activity in the education system. The first and foremost is the management of teachers. The posts of teachers need to be filled up in time. Secondly, it is essential to tackle teacher-absenteeism. Studies on educational administration have revealed that teacher-absenteeism is a major problem in most of the States. Absentee teacher appoints a proxy teacher in his or her place with the consent of the school. To deal with this problem, teacher as well as school appraisal should be made compulsory and accountability must be fixed, in terms of effectiveness of teaching and achievement level of the students. This would also make the head of the institution perform better and be accountable to students, community, parents and the education authority. The code of conduct of teachers is enforced in some of the States in private-aided schools to make the teachers accountable. The provisions of this code must be extended to government schools as well to make the teachers of these schools more accountable.

Training in required competencies in management should be provided at school complex/cluster level. Ironically, educational institutions in India have little autonomy although the quality of education depends substantially on how they plan and perform various tasks. Detailed syllabi and their completion within the prescribed timeframe and the requirement of preparing students for public examinations leave little scope for institutional innovation. Institutions need to be provided with freedom and authority to plan and execute educational tasks.

References

Bhola, H.S. (2003). "Practical Policy Analysis for Education Policy Making Under Globalization", in the book *Education, Society and Development: National and International Perspective* (Edited by J. B. G. Tilak), New Delhi: National University of Educational Planning and Administration, pp. 50.

Caillods, Francoise (2003). *The Changing Role of the State, New Competencies for Planners*, Newsletter, Vol. XXI (April-June), Paris (France): International Institute for Educational Planning.

Carnoy, Martin (1999). *Globalization and Educational Reforms: What Planners Need to Know,* Paris: UNESCO-IIEP.

Cheng, Yin Cheong (2003). Local Knowledge and Human Development in Globalization of Education in the Book *Education, Society and Development: National and International Perspective* (Edited by J.B.G. Tilak), New Delhi: National Institute of Educational Planning and Administration, p. 28.

Dhar, T.N. (2001). "Role of Local Bodies, Private Effort and Community Participation in Education", in Marmar Mukhopadhyay and R.S. Tyagi (Eds.) *Governance of School Education in India,* New Delhi: NIEPA, pp. 89-106.

Government of India (2009). *Right of Children to Free and Compulsory Education Act,* No. 35 of 2009, Legislative Department, Ministry of Law and Justice.

Government of India (2011). *Sub-Group Report for the 12th Plan, Elementary Education*, Department of School Education and Literacy, Ministry of Human Resource Development, New Delhi.

Govinda, R. (2003). *Decentralized Education: Trends and Issues,* Newsletter, Vol. XXI, No. 2, (April-June), Paris (France): International Institute for Educational Planning, Paris.

Grauwe, Anton de (2004). *Decentralization: Can it Improve Schools?* Newsletter, Vol. XXII, No. 4 (October-December), International Institute for Educational Planning, Paris.

MHRD (1986). *National Policy on Education,* Government of India, Ministry of Human Resource Development, New Delhi.

—— (1992) *National Policy on Education and Programme of Action,* Government of India, Ministry of Human Resource Development, New Delhi.

National University of Educational Planning and Administration (2017). *Studies on "Educational Administration: Structures, Processes and Systems" in Different States and UTs 2014-2016 (Third All India Survey of Educational Administration),* NIEPA, New Delhi.

Sapre, Padmakar. M. (1998). "Management Education: Promise and Performance", in the book *Education India: The Next Millennium* (Edited byMarmar Mukhopadhyay and others), NIEPA, New Delhi.

Singhal, R.P. (2001). "Revamping Personnel Management Policies and Practices in Education", in Marmar Mukhopadhyay and R.S. Tyagi (Eds.) *Governance of School Education in India*, NIEPA, pp. 131-147, New Delhi.

Tilak, J.B.G. (2003). "Introduction to Education, Society and Development: National and International Perspective", in the book *Introduction to Education, Society and Development: National and International Perspective* (edit.), National Institute of Educational Planning and Administration, New Delhi.

Tyagi, R.S. (2001). "Organization and Administration", in Marmar Mukhopadhyay and R. S. Tyagi (Eds.) *Governance of School Education in India*, NIEPA, pp. 61-87, New Delhi.

Varghese, N.V. (1996). *Decentralisation of Educational Planning and the District Primary Education Programme*, Occasional Papers, NIEPA, New Delhi.

Index